MAD AS HELL

MAD AS HELL

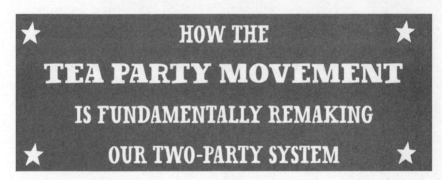

★ HOW THE ★
TEA PARTY MOVEMENT
IS FUNDAMENTALLY REMAKING
★ OUR TWO-PARTY SYSTEM ★

SCOTT RASMUSSEN

AND

DOUG SCHOEN

HARPER

An Imprint of HarperCollinsPublishers
www.harpercollins.com

Library of Congress Cataloging-in-Publication Data
Rasmussen, Scott W.
   Mad as hell: how the Tea Party movement is fundamentally remaking our two-party system / Scott Rasmussen and Doug Schoen. — 1st ed.
      p. cm.
   Summary: "Today's raucous revolt against Washington and Wall Street is a classic populist uprising. Two political pollsters show us what it means for the future of American politics"—Provided by publisher.
   ISBN 978-0-06-199523-1 (hardback)
   1. Tea Party movement.   2. United States—Politics and government—2009–
   I. Schoen, Douglas E., 1953–   II. Title.
JK2391.T43R37 2010
322.4'4—dc22   2010018200

10 11 12 13 14 DIX/RRD 10 9 8 7 6 5 4 3

CONTENTS

MAD AS HELL

ONE NATION UNDER REVOLT

I'm not a Republican, I'm not a Democrat, I'm *American*. I'm here because I believe we need to do something about what is happening in our country. And I notice that millions of people across the country want this too. Every time I come out to a rally, I ask people, "Have you ever been to a political rally before? Have you ever come out to stand up for your family and your country and say: I need to be heard!" and every time, about 90 percent say no.

We aren't racists or bigots, we aren't Astroturf puppets, and we aren't fringe right-wing zealots. We are just ordinary hardworking Americans who love our country but are mad as hell!

**—Neil, 56-year-old small business owner,
Tea Party Express rally, Fresno, California**

The Tea Party movement has become one of the most powerful and extraordinary movements in recent American political history.

It is as popular as both the Democratic and Republican Parties. It is potentially strong enough to elect senators, governors, and congressmen. It may even be strong enough to elect the next president of the United States—time will tell.

But the Tea Party movement has been one of the most derided and minimized and, frankly, most disrespected movements in American history. Yet, despite being systematically ignored, belittled, marginalized, and ostracized by political, academic, and media elites, the Tea Party movement has grown stronger and stronger.

The extraordinary turnout on April 15, 2010, at rallies across the country speaks volumes to the strength, power, and influence of the

Tea Party movement. with over 750 protests held across the country, demonstrating a level of activism and enthusiasm that is both unprecedented and arguably unique in recent American political history.

Survey data collected at about this time bears out the same point. In mid-April 2010, a Rasmussen Reports survey in which nearly one quarter (24 percent) of the electorate self-identified as being members in the Tea Party movement—up from 16 percent a month earlier. And a mid-April 2010 CNN/Opinion Research Corp. survey showed that 10 percent of Americans say they have actively supported the Tea Party movement: gone to a rally, contributed money, or taken specific steps to support the movement.

Even a *New York Times/CBS News* poll showed that close to one in five Americans call themselves supporters of the Tea Party movement.

This book will explore why this has happened, how it happened, and what the implications are for American politics—now and in the future.

On April 15, 2009, in honor of Tax Day, seemingly spontaneous tax protests sprung up across the country. At the time, no one in the media or in the political elite thought that these protests were important. In fact, many said they were irrelevant. Some, ignoring the obvious, said they did not exist at all.

In an April 15, 2009, interview, Speaker Nancy Pelosi said, "This initiative is funded by the high end—we call it Astroturf, it's not really a grassroots movement. It's Astroturf by some of the wealthiest people in America to keep the focus on tax cuts for the rich instead of for the great middle class."[1]

"[They are] evil-mongers" spreading "lies, innuendo, and rumor," stated Senate majority leader Harry Reid.

When the elite looked, their first reaction was to say: *Well if it was real (which we really don't believe it was), it is a one-time occurrence, it is no big deal, and it is worth neither our time nor attention.*

This was evidenced in the findings of an April 2010 study conducted by the Media Research Center, which found that ABC, CBS, and NBC aired 61 stories or segments on the anti-spending movement over a 12-month period, and most of that coverage is recent. "The networks virtually refused to recognize the tea party in 2009 (19 stories), with the level of coverage increasing only after Scott Brown's election in Massachusetts" in January, the report said, referring to the Republican's win of the Senate seat long held by Edward M. Kennedy.[2]

The first reaction from political and media elites was that these were insignificant gatherings, just small numbers of people inflated by the media.

"It's incredibly stupid," said former *Atlantic Monthly* writer Matthew Yglesias on the early Tea Party movement.

"It can be expected from the margins, but it's troubling to see it [The Tea Party movement] embraced and validated by more mainstream entities," said writer Stuart Whatley in a post on *The Huffington Post*, April 14, 2009.

Next, they said that these protests were by no means spontaneous, that the Tea Party movement was not a legitimate grassroots movement. Rather, it was being fed and fueled by conservative talk radio and cable television.

"Our number two story tonight, the sad reality behind the corporate sponsored Tea Parties, visual proof that this is not about spending, deficits, or taxes, but about some Americans getting riled up by the people who caused these things, and finally about some Americans who just hate the president of the United States. According to both the conservative organs, the *New York Post* and the *Washington Times*, see there was another double entendre coming, the protests only drew tens of thousands nationwide, despite relentless 24-7 promotion on Fox News, including live telecasts from several locations," said Keith Olbermann, MSNBC Host.

"Much will depend on just how cynical those encouraging the mob frenzy are, while denying responsibility. What shall we call them?

Mobsters?" asked former CNN correspondent, Bob Franken, on conservative leaders allegedly orchestrating the Tea Party movement.

Some charged conservative media icons, such as talk radio host Rush Limbaugh and Fox News, of manufacturing, enabling, or facilitating it—together or simultaneously.

"As has always happened when progressive change is in the air, the backlash gets fierce, ugly and anti-American. . . . Let's be clear who we are talking about. Call them attack dogs, call them Teabaggers, call them Glenn Beck," said Andy Stern, President of the SEIU.

"That's right. Despite repeatedly claiming its coverage is 'fair and balanced,' despite its attacks on anyone who dares claim or imply the cable outlet tilts to the right, despite encouraging viewers to say 'no' to biased media, Fox News has frequently aired segments imploring its audience to get involved with tea-party protests across the country. Protests the 'news' network has described as mainly a response to President Obama's economic policies. Organizers of these tea-party protests have no bigger cheerleader (or crowd-builder, for that matter) than Fox News, which has provided attendance and organizing information for the events on air and online dozens of times. You name it; they've likely done it. Fox has offered viewers and readers such vital organizing information as protest dates, locations, and addresses of websites where people can learn more. It has even posted information and publicity material for the events on its own website. Tea-party planners are now using the planned attendance of Fox News hosts to promote their protests and listing Fox News contributors as 'Tea Party Sponsor[s]' on their website," said Karl Frisch, Senior Fellow at Media Matters for America, on April 10, 2009.

Others insisted that elements of the Republican Party—in a sinister and underhanded way—had maneuvered it.

All of the above is patently false.

In this book, we will set the record straight.

Mad As Hell will provide the first comprehensive explanation of what we are experiencing in America today, its origins, and its impact on the future of our country.

In the chapters that follow, we will make the case that:

1. The Tea Party movement is a genuine grassroots phenomenon
2. It has been systematically misunderstood by political and media elites
3. It is not only America's most vibrant political force "at the moment,"[3] to quote *The Economist*, but a movement that has unprecedented broad-based support, and the power to influence the 2010 and 2012 elections and, indeed, the future of American politics in ways that have been fundamentally misunderstood and not appreciated.

Using our polling research and on-the-scenes accounts, we will clearly, comprehensively, and definitively define what the Tea Party movement means, and what it represents as a spontaneous outpouring of anger. We will document how in the span of one year the Tea Party movement became the most potent force in American politics, with the potential to change America.

Our analysis of the genesis and evolution of the Tea Party movement sheds light on a heretofore underecognized power in social media, blogs, activist right who largely used online communications vehicles to organize the very first spontaneous Tea Party gatherings, which came to be called meet-ups, and then to mobilize a grassroots movement that has become the most energetic and powerful political force of its time.

This process has not been documented nor understood to date.

The hidden story of the development of the Tea Party movement is the story of blogs, online, social media, and communications that has heretofore not been fully described nor explained. To be sure, it was facilitated largely by Fox News and talk radio. However, it was by no means the brainchild of cable news, or any figures in talk radio. Rather, it has been a ground-up movement, spread virally, blog by blog, website to website beneath the surface in a way that few, if any, have understood until now.

And when the Tea Party movement was recognized to be a viable and real organization, the media said a number of things about it as a means of discrediting it.

First, they said it was just an adjunct of the Republican Party, despite polls such as the mid-April *New York Times/CBS News* poll, released on Tax Day 2010, which showed that half the Tea Party supporters are non-Republicans.

Others said it is being run and manipulated by elites in Washington and across the country, despite the fact that it has produced an extraordinary and spontaneous level of support that goes well beyond those elites. Indeed, in interviews, a number of those organizers said that they were stunned by the level of visibility that the Tea Party movement was able to produce, having gone well beyond their own efforts to facilitate it.

Some said that the Tea Party movement could not influence elections, or that it would somehow destroy the Republican Party.

And others, despite ample evidence that suggests Tea Party members are part of the American mainstream, have insisted that it represents a bunch of right-wing extremists or racists.

In fact, every one of these claims is obviously false. We are on the eve of the 2010 midterm Congressional elections, and it is our position that the Tea Party's energy is such that it has the power to dictate the ideology that is driving the Republican Party, and to influence if not control Republican nominations and primary outcomes.

Moreover, the broad-based enthusiasm and energy for the Tea Party's agenda of limited government, balanced budget, returning to core principles, could very well bring a massive change in the American political landscape, potentially resulting in a Republican takeover of the House and Senate this November.

We will prove this claim with original reporting and poll data that show that for the first time, both parties have net negative ratings, and there is an unprecedented and growing desire for change in the electorate. We will show that the Tea Party movement has recorded its highest levels of support in early: with 28 percent in an April 2010 Gallup poll calling themselves supporters of the movement,[4] and with an April 2010 Rasmussen Reports poll showing that on major issues, more Americans (48 percent) agree with the Tea Party movement on major issues than with the President of the United States.

Think about it. More people said in April 2010 that they felt closer to a movement that did not exist slightly more than a year before, than they did to the President of the United States, whose election was historic, of both national and international significance. Think about the implications of that for our politics and our country.

And the rallies that we saw on Tax Day 2010 show that in the span of a year the Tea Party movement has only gotten stronger, more vigorous, more vibrant, and potentially more powerful and influential as well.

Moreover, we will make the case that if the various activists, members, and supporters of the Tea Party movement are able to stay united behind a simple set of principles—advocating limited government, limitations on the recently passed healthcare reform bill, and deficit reduction, and a return to Constitutional principles—and use this platform to recruit members and mobilize supporters to turn out in November, they will develop a movement that is certainly strong enough to influence and potentially elect the next President of the United States.

Put another way, and to be crystal clear, the dissatisfaction in the American electorate with the established political order—particularly toward the Congress and toward the president, both having majority negative ratings—has led the Tea Party movement to become as potent a force as any political party in the United States.

As of the end of June, in states like Utah, Nevada, Kentucky, and Florida, Mike Lee, Sharron Angle, Rand Paul, and Marco Rubio—four candidates who just less than a year ago would have had little to no chance of being successful, but for the Tea Party movement—now have a very good chance of being elected to the United States Senate come November.

At the time of this writing, we have already seen the Tea Party movement influence the whole direction of the country, transforming a virtually unknown state representative into a populist hero, and facilitating his election to the U.S. Senate in the state of Massachusetts—one of the most liberal states in the country.

The Scott Brown election is a ratification of the argument of this book, that there is a force and a spirit in the American electorate that animates a degree of anger that is unprecedented, largely undocumented, and, until now, not understood.

Both parties will have to integrate the Tea Party philosophy and indeed its advocacy into their core or they will run the risk of further marginalization and disaffection from the American electorate.

The Tea Party movement, to quote the editor of the *Wall Street Journal*'s online editorial page, James Taranto: "A remarkably broad-based and nonideological movement—one that has gained strength as the Democrats who currently run Washington have proved themselves to be narrow and ideological. Had President Obama governed from the center—above all, had he heeded public opinion and abandoned his grandiose plans to transform America, he might well have held the allegiance of many of the people who now sympathize with the tea party."[5]

Taranto is undeniably right. The Tea Party movement is avowedly nonpartisan. And there is no reason why the Democrats in Washington could not have made as much of an appeal to its supporters as the Republicans. In fact, the Tea Party members were initially animated by frustration with the Bush administration's taxing and spending policies. And close to one-third were once supporters of Barack Obama, and many held out great hopes for him at the beginning of his Presidency, hopes that they believe have not been at all realized.

But the fact is that they didn't. They failed to appreciate the movement's significance to their detriment, as will most likely become evident in November's midterm Congressional elections, and potentially in the 2012 presidential election.

And while there was a short-term boost in the polls for Democrats after the passage of health care, every recent poll has shown a much higher level of enthusiasm among Republicans with regard to the upcoming congressional elections and in opposition to the passage of healthcare reform. This is in part due to widespread backlash against perceived overreaching of the Obama administration in terms of the size and scope of its governance, but it is also a reaction to the mobilization of the Tea Party movement.

"When Hamas does it or Hezbollah does it, it is called terrorism. Why should Republican lawmakers and Astroturf groups organizing on behalf of the healthcare industry be viewed differently?" said MSNBC's Keith Olbermann.

The mainstream media's bias toward the Tea Party movement has been undeniable. On MSNBC, it is rare for hosts such as Rachel Maddow or Keith Olbermann to discuss the movement without the use of unfounded accusations and slurs such as "teabagging" and the "Tea Klux Klan." FNC's Bernard Goldberg addressed this bias, noting that "Every fringe event at a Tea Party rally, real or imagined—real or imagined—is covered by the 'lamestream media,' but flag burning at an antiwar rally isn't covered. And, you know, I've been thinking about, well, why is this? Well, because these fringe events at Tea Party rallies . . . this fits into the narrative of most mainstream news reporters, that the Tea Party people are not too smart, they're bigots."

"This is racism straight up. That is nothing but a bunch of teabagging rednecks. And there is no way around that. And you know, you can tell these type[s] of right wingers anything and they'll believe it, except the truth. You tell them the truth and they become . . . it's like showing Frankenstein's monster fire. They become confused, and angry and highly volatile," added Jeannette Gafalo.

"It [the 9/12 March] was a Klan rally minus the bedsheets and torches," said William Rivers Pitt, former spokesman for Democratic congressman Dennis Kucinich.

According to an April 2010 report by the Media Research Center: Overall, 44 percent of the networks' reports on the Tea Party suggested the movement reflected a fringe movement or a dangerous quality. "Signs and images at last weekend's big tea party march in Washington and at other recent events have featured racial and other violent themes," NBC anchor Brian Williams said in a September report.[6]

And while many in the media accused the Tea Party movement of racial and ethnic stereotyping, the available data shows that their energy and enthusiasm against the bill has continued to build the Tea Party's power and influence with the electorate.

Recent polls now show that despite the unfounded claims by media and political elites below, the Tea Party movement is racially, ethnically, and culturally diverse, and, as evidenced in an April 5 Gallup poll, remarkably similar to the country as a whole demographically.

While traveling on board one of the Tea Party Express RVs through Southern California in late October 2009, we met a diverse group of Tea Party organizers, members, and supporters including Lloyd Marcus, a black man who wrote the Tea Party Anthem and sings/entertains on board the tours, and William Owens, a prominent black conservative and author of *Obama: Why Black America Should Have Doubts*, who was traveling with the Tea Party Express along with his wife Selena.

Indeed, the June Primary results from South Carolina—where two people of color, an Indian-American and an African-American, received the GOP nomination for Governor and Congress—offer a decisive and unambiguous rebuttal to the notion that the Tea Party movement is either racist or race based.

What this shows is that despite attempts by liberal political and media elites to portray the movement as being driven by racism, bigotry, and white supremacy, it is the Tea Party agenda of fiscal responsibility, limited government, and deficit reduction that unites its supporters.

And ignoring the fundamental concerns of a majority of the electorate is a prescription for disaster.

Moreover, others have attempted to denounce the movement as being nothing more than an offshoot of the Republican Party.

Nothing could be further from the truth. As we will show, the Tea Party movement is made up of three distinct groups:

1. The first group is comprised of newcomers to politics. People who have never been involved, may not have voted, but have shown a spontaneous and significant degree of outrage that mobilized them to participate.

2. The second group consists of political Independents who feel betrayed by both the Democratic and Republican Parties for out-of-control spending, big government, and a ballooning deficit and debt in which they feel neither of the established major Parties have paid any attention.

3. And the third group is made up of core Republican conservatives who feel like they do not have a home. But it would be a profound mistake to see this movement as more narrow or limited than it really is. The polling we will review shows that it is comprised of a broad cross section of the American people. Somewhere between one-quarter and one-third of Tea Party members voted for Barack Obama in 2008, 40 to 50 percent are non-Republicans, including one-third of self-identified Democrats, and about one-third are moderates or liberals.

Put simply, the Tea Party movement is a broad-based national movement whose scope, breadth, and depth of support have been unappreciated and fundamentally misunderstood.

In the late '90s, the Democratic Party under Bill Clinton understood the critical importance of the Perot movement and public support for the conservative fiscal, and limited government policies he stood for in the 1992 election and beyond. By revamping their policies to reach out to these voters, and by supporting a balanced budget in 1995, the Democrats were able to resurrect the Party after its cataclysmic defeat in 1994, retain the Presidency, and build record levels of support for the Clinton administration, notwithstanding a gut-wrenching scandal that nearly toppled Clinton's presidency.

For the Republican Party, the Tea Party movement has been more of a blessing than a curse, but it has been deeply problematic as well.

On the one hand, it has energized conservatives and created a positive counterforce on the right for the Republicans. On the other hand, the strength of the Tea Party movement demonstrates the absence of any real ideas or philosophy in the Republican Party.

As *New York Times* columnist Frank Rich put it: "The old G.O.P. guard has no discernible national constituency beyond the scattered, often impotent remnants of aging country club Republicanism. The passion on the right has migrated almost entirely to the Tea Party's counterconservatism."

We will discuss in great detail the Tea Party's influence in individual elections and overall in the upcoming chapters, but it is safe to say that in the absence of clear leadership within the Republican Party, the Tea Party movement—in terms of ideology and impulse—are driving the direction and the agenda of the Republican Party.

There does not appear to be strong impetus within the Tea Party movement to form a third political party. And it is more likely that its members will overwhelmingly support Republican candidates in the November elections. Of course this could change, but for now, they appear to be much more inclined to bolster enthusiasm and support for the Republican Party than to go in an independent direction or to offer any support for the Democrats.

That being said, Tea Party activists have tried to infiltrate the Republican Party to perhaps take it over, perhaps influence its direction, tensions between the Republican Party establishment and activist Tea Party members have become clear and evident.

There have been contentious primaries, the possibility of third-party candidates always looms on the horizon, and a level of division and suspicion has made cooperation that much more difficult.

That said, it is entirely clear that in the upcoming November election, the vast majority of Tea Party support will go to the Republican Party, in large part, because the Obama administration has been either unwilling or unable to reach out to them personally or substantively on issues.

Indeed, even President Obama, in a March 2010 interview with the *Today* show's Matt Lauer, acknowledged that the Tea Party protesters have serious, legitimate concerns, stating, "I think that there's a broader circle . . . of people who are legitimately concerned about the deficit, who are legitimately concerned that the federal government may be taking on too much."

Obama is probably the first Democrat to recognize that in any serious way. At the same time, he still felt compelled to talk about the extreme elements of the Tea Party movement, such as the "birther" movement, which he quite legitimately suggested are pursuing outrageous allegations against him, telling Lauer: "There's still going to be a group at their core that question my legitimacy. . . . There's some folks who just weren't sure whether I was born in the United States, whether I was a socialist."

Where President Obama and the rest of the Democrats are wrong is underestimating, and underestimating fundamentally, the power of the ideas that animate the Tea Party movement.

"The media, as a whole, isn't covering us at all, with a few exceptions. Washington? They're not listening. If they were listening, why would they try to ram this [health care] reconciliation through? They're not listening. The polls are all going down. Look at any poll you want to see. There's something near 60 percent against healthcare reform. Yet they're going to ram it through? They're not listening. They work for US; we don't work for THEM. We're not their little serfs. This isn't their kingdom," said one interviewee from Arlington Heights, Illinois, on a Chicago March on the Media outside ABC news studios, back in October 2009.

The reason why the public doesn't know how broad-based the Tea Party movement actually is has to do with the media's inherent partisanship, class and regional prejudice, and a myopic insistence on shoving the legitimate populist outrage of Tea Party members—40 percent of whom are non-Republicans—into a preconceived, narrow, right-wing extremist box.

And on Kathy Barkulis' Smart Girl Politics blog: "You know, the Lyndon LaRouche people come at every single tea party protest I've been at. They have signs that show Obama as Hitler. They are not tea party people. And then the mainstream media puts a camera on them and tries to make off that they are tea party people."

The media has systematically treated it as an extremist movement because of the alleged behavior of some of its more visible and apparently more expressive members, particularly following the alleged incidents of abuse during the healthcare debate. The media has focused its attention on the alleged death threats and vituperation against Democratic lawmakers and their families, and alleged racial and anti-gay slurs directed at African American and gay lawmakers who supported the health overhaul.

Reports about extremists in the movement, about right-wing manipulation, about inauthenticity continue to drive mainstream and liberal cable media coverage.

And while some of these obvious abuses and excesses have occurred, no evidence has come forward to point the finger at specific individuals, and it seems that the vast bulk of the charges are unsubstantiated or, at the very least, significantly exaggerated. There is, as we will show demonstratively and definitively in this book, a significant amount of evidence that the Tea Party movement is genuine, ongoing, and growing every day.

In doing so, writes the *Wall Street Journal*'s James Taranto: "They [the media] have been trying to demoralize America's . . . majority by presenting them with an ugly choice: accept the fate the Democrats have imposed upon us, or side with (as the *Christian Science Monitor* puts it) 'neo-Klansmen and knuckle-dragging hillbillies.'"

The national breakdown of the Tea Party composition is 57 percent Republican, 28 percent Independent and 13 percent Democratic, according to three national polls by the Winston Group, a Republican-leaning firm that conducted the surveys on behalf of an education advocacy group. Two-thirds of the group call themselves conservative, 26 are moderate, and 8 percent say they are liberal.[7]

And recent polling suggests that not only has the Tea Party movement not been hurt by this media attack, it has grown stronger, and is now comprised of a broad cross section of the American people. Thus, 40 percent of Tea Party supporters are Democrats and Independents, and one-third are moderates or liberals.

In fact, the recent Gallup poll that came out on April 1, 2010, shows that neither the Democrats nor the Republicans have benefitted by the passage of healthcare reform. The only one to benefit has been the Tea Party, whose favorability rating has grown to a record 37 percent, while favorability for the two major Parties has plummeted—each having net negative ratings.

What this shows is that the real issue driving the movement is not partisan rage on the right but a profound crisis of governmental legitimacy that should deeply concern us all.

And, finally, in the weeks leading up to the one-year anniversary of the Tax Day Tea Parties, there is some recognition in the mainstream media that the Tea Parties represent a broader phenomenon than just right-wing anger.

In an April 8 post on his *Congressional Quarterly* blog, Craig Crawford noted that while Tea Party protesters have been systematically written off as "irrational" and "loonies," "Their argument is more mainstream . . . if you sift through to the core of their claim it is not the fringe craziness so often portrayed. Growth of government, whether led by Republicans or Democrats, is on a march like nothing in our recent history."[8]

And one producer, CNN Political Producer Shannon Travis put it, while covering a March 31 rally in Grand Junction, Colorado:

> They are not typical Tea Party activists: A woman who voted for President Obama and believes he's a "phenomenal speaker." Another who said she was a "knee-jerk, bleeding heart liberal."
>
> These two women are not alone.
>
> Some Americans who say they have been sympathetic to Democratic causes in the past—some even voted for Democratic candidates—are angry with President Obama and his party. They say they are now supporting the Tea Party, a movement that champions less government, lower taxes, and the defeat of Democrats even though it's not formally aligned with the Republican Party.
>
> Ann Ducket attended the Tea Party rally in Grand Junction, Colorado, on Wednesday.
>
> A lawyer and lifelong Democrat, Ducket made her political leanings clear: She said she was a campus community organizer for Democratic Sen. George McGovern's 1972 presidential campaign, voted for Jimmy Carter and Al Gore, and previously ran for elective office in Colorado as a Democrat.
>
> Roxanne Lewis expressed a similar point of view. A small business owner in Grand Junction, Lewis described herself as a lifelong Democrat and called the president a "phenomenal speaker." She voted for him because she "believed in what he was saying: change."
>
> But, Lewis added, "I should've listened a lot closer when he talked about 'spreading the wealth.'"

Asked how she feels about having voted for the president, Lewis said, "I feel lied to, cheated and raped."

Lewis criticized the taxpayer-funded bailouts of financial institutions, which began under former President George W. Bush, and the bailout of General Motors and Chrysler.

"These are not the Democrats that I have been brought up with," Lewis said. However, she said she would continue to be a Democrat.

"We hear from folks, probably at every rally, who say, 'I was a Democrat,'" Levi Russell, communications director for the Tea Party express tour, said.

"Having more Democrats join the movement shows that it is more representative of the American people than the antics of the Obama, [House Speaker Nancy] Pelosi, Reid leadership," Russell said.[9]

But most of the recognition by the mainstream media has been tentative at best.

And to be sure—even if one points to the defeats that Tea Party candidates have faced, the fact that many are self-funded, the lack of leadership—as this is written, the strongest movement both ideologically and practically is, without a doubt, the Tea Party movement.

At a Tea Party Express rally in Los Angeles, CA, we met first-time Tea Partiers, Mark Derek, 38, and his boyfriend. These athletic, fashionable, and educated men were a far cry from the colonial costume-wearing, gun-toting, hate-criming stereotypes of the average Tea Party protestor.

Derek, had in fact, learned about the Tea Party movement on the news, and while as a gay man he was initially turned off by the racist undertones that media and political elites used to define Tea Party movement, he is also a staunch capitalist and economic conservative and, as he learned more about the movement, he realized that the Tea Party movement is really about small government/anti-union/anti-spending, a platform that he supports wholeheartedly: "I think that I'm a moderate. I think that what I'm saying is reasonable. The Obama taglines during the election versus where he is as a leader, he basically tricked the centrist people, and since he took office, the government in Washington and in Sacramento has been driving us real hard down the wrong path.

"The current leadership and the country is driving our country far away from free markets and capitalism, away from the kind of things that provide incentive for people to create value.

"When we say that we want to save and create jobs, we don't mean that we want more government, and safety nets for unionized government jobs.

"Think about the most important government workers we have, the people who MUST be successful, the military. Our soldiers aren't unionized. Why? Because it would make them ineffective. They'd say: 'I'd love to jump in that foxhole, Colonel, but I have to talk to my union first.'

"My problem is these people who are union members and work for these government agencies and don't have to be held accountable. They don't have to make a profit, they're never going to get laid off."

The dissatisfaction in the American electorate with the established political order—particularly with regard to the Congressional leadership and the president—has led the Tea Party movement to become as potent a force as any political party in the United States. And contrary to many inside-the-beltway analyses, it shows no signs of going away. In fact, it only gets stronger and stronger.

1

THE **TWO STRANDS** OF **POPULISM**

> At its core, populism in the United States remains what it has always
> been: a protest by ordinary people who want the system to live up to
> its stated ideals—fair and honest treatment in the marketplace and a
> government tilted in favor of the unwealthy masses.
>
> **—Michael Kazin**[1]

American voters across the decades have been guided by certain quintessential values. A broad strand through American political history
of a strong sense of urgency held by ordinary people for the system
to respond to their needs and interests first, rather than being most
responsive to governmental or political elites. When these values have
been challenged, they have provoked an unmistakable reaction from
the American people. Sometimes this reaction has manifested itself as a right-wing anti-systemic populist movement; sometimes left
wing.

Today, our country is in the midst of a massive, unprecedented,
underreported, underappreciated, new populist revolt that has emerged
overwhelmingly from the right, manifesting itself as Tea Party
movement—initially described in the Introduction, and the primary
focus of this book—as well as a smaller, and probably less significant
reaction on the left.

The means of expression for these two strands varies, as does the
ideology that underlies the sentiments they cacophonously voice. Yet,
together they comprise the new populist revolt.

For the first time in recent history, the majority of Americans qualify as populists. And make no mistake: their anger is real. We have seen it.

At the time of this writing, failed leadership in Washington, obscene greed and abuse on Wall Street, and continued economic suffering on Main Street have provoked widespread anger, resentment, and frustration. There is a deep distrust of the elite in government and in business, and a pervasive sense, which is wholly justified by outrageous current events, that the powerful are conspiring against ordinary Americans. There is an overriding sense of loss of control, fear about the direction in which the country is heading, and despair that the pursuit of the American Dream is no longer possible. Confidence across the public and private sectors is at a historic low, and public anger is near stratospheric.

This is a very difference picture of America than what most of us foresaw during the prideful moment on November 4, 2008, when an inspiring new leader promised a new era of change. After the historic 2008 elections, many Americans felt that we were on the brink of a new era of racial and political harmony. The inauguration of a dynamic new president, who campaigned on economic, political, and social change, suggested the dawn of a new American morning.

It is nearly impossible to comprehend from this vantage point. A president with near universal approval, who inspired hope across the political spectrum. An election that inspired a flush of confidence in the body politic. A public that was hopeful for meaningful progress on pressing issues of domestic and foreign policy. A country that was largely united by its faith in the future. This was America at the end of 2008: weathering the worst of the Great Recession, but hopeful for the change that Barack Obama promised.

America has indeed changed. But not in the way President Obama and his advisers foresaw. A new political era is at hand in the United States, but not the gilded age of bipartisan cooperation that the Obama administration hoped to bring about. Since 2008, politics as usual have reined, our leaders have terribly botched the economic recovery, and

Americans continue to suffer as a result. Adding insult to injury, the very financial institutions whose actions led to a staggering loss of jobs, homes, and wealth raked in record profits as the unemployment rate climbed to double digits.

Instead of a new era of hope, there is a new populist revolt afoot that is real, that is here to stay, and that represents a fundamental and generational transformation of American politics. Even worse, the significance of the new populist revolt has been all but ignored by politicians in Washington, and entirely maligned by journalists and pundits in New York.

There are two strands of populism today: one on the left and one on the right. All populists, regardless of ideology, agree that government is unresponsive and controlled by special interests. As American industries dry up, and jobs are sent overseas at their expense, they have come to share a common belief that the country's economic arrangements work against their interests.

However, not all populists think alike.

We will discuss the points of agreement between these two groups, which are quite substantial, but we will also outline the more significant divergence on policy that has led to a growing divide in our society between those on the left and those on the right, making cooperation and conciliation extremely different if not impossible.

The fundamental difference between the two strands is that right-wing populists believe that government is the problem, not the solution.

Put simply, right-wing populists want government to get out of ordinary people's lives. This group emerged in reaction to big government and special interest politics—the K Street politics of the Bush administration, as well as the Obama administration's systematic expansion of government interest and influence. They believe that the Obama administration has been overrun by left-leaning ideologues, controlled by the labor unions, and informed by statist policies being advocated and implemented by the populist left. In addition, global economic strains continue to impact communities in Middle America, contributing to right-wing populism. Populists on the right are aghast at big government spending. They see a deficit that is out of control, social programs that don't seem to work, and a level of taxation that appears to be confiscatory. Put another way, the populist right view the government as an alien force that takes but does not give.

These right-wing populist principles influence much of the political dialogue, as the Tea Party movement has become the most vibrant and powerful political force. This is the principal focus of this book.

There is a smaller group of left-wing populists, who believe that the only cure that can fix our broken system is greater state involvement in the economy and the day-to-day life of ordinary people.

In fact, left-wing populists seek more government intervention, regulation, ownership, and control. Put simply, left-wing populists want to alter traditional capitalist arrangements in America and give the government unprecedented influence and control over the financial markets and private sector industries in ways that were virtually unimaginable years ago.

In Chapter 8, we will discuss how a populist movement, albeit smaller in size and importance than their right-wing counterparts, has emerged on the left as well. We will document how left-wing populists have effectively taken over large parts of the Democratic Party in response to the economic downturn. They have advocated, and in some cases successfully implemented, many policies that fundamentally alter traditional arrangements in capitalist society and have succeeded in securing an unprecedented level of state involvement in the financial system, the regulatory system, and the healthcare system.

We will also examine the groups that comprise the populist left. Labor unions are a major component of the populist left. They are driving the Obama administration's agenda. When the White House released its visitor log in October 2009, the most frequent visitor was SEIU leader Andy Stern, not to mention SEIU's extensive contributions to Obama's presidential campaign. It is instructive that in March

2010 the unions' reaction to lagging economic recovery was to take on the banks directly by launching a two-week long national protest movement "Good Jobs Now, Make Wall Street Pay."

The populist left is also comprised of liberal activist groups, including MoveOn.org, a nonprofit, progressive advocacy group and political action committee that was launched in response to the Clinton impeachment trial in 1998 and now functions as a left-wing pressure group; Daily Kos, a liberal/progressive discussion forum and blog seeking to influence and empower the Democratic Party; and a variety of issue-based activist groups, such as the Sierra Club and the Chicago Single Payer Action Network.

These groups are coming together in a coordinated effort to achieve their mutual goals.

And while left-wing populism is certainly smaller in size and scope, the left-wing populist agenda has largely emerged as the dominant ideology inside the Democratic Party and, indeed, the Obama administration.

It is tempting to read the anger and disillusionment of the American electorate as simply a response to the epic failures and economic hardships of recent years. In fact, the economic crisis fully exposed a fundamental change that has been under way for the past generation.

Today, we are reeling not only from an economic collapse. The social fabric of the nation has been stretched by the loss of jobs to foreign competition, by the flattening of wages, the shrinking or failure of big businesses, such as steel mills, car companies, and so on, that used to anchor whole communities. Frustrations have mounted due to the deficiencies of American primary education, which hamper American workers vis-à-vis global technological competition, as well as the increasing cost of higher education and health care. In general, the pervasive sense among the middle class is that upward mobility is stalled and downward mobility looms.

Over the last decade and more, globalization has transformed the lives of everyday Americans. Millions of jobs and entire industries have been sent overseas and whole communities, towns, and even cities have been eviscerated. Sweeping demographic transformation has ignited the flashpoint of illegal immigration, exacerbating the anger and frustration of job losses during the downturn. In the midst of this turbulence, just when we need government to protect the interests of the public and the nation more than ever, our leaders have failed us. Washington has become increasingly unresponsive, our politics increasing repulsive, and our system increasingly broken.

Financial institutions that were "too big to fail" received unheard of rescue packages, proceeded to rake in record profits, and subsequently disbursed billions in bonuses to the wealthiest Americans. All the while, middle-class families have been forced out of their homes by the very banks propped up by the federal government.

Put simply, there is a political crisis and an economic crisis in America. This is American in 2010. And the impact of this pervasive anger among the electorate has had a tangible and immediate impact on our politics.

The first is governmental. Today, a solid majority of the American people have come to believe that their government in Washington is neither responsive to, nor interested in their concerns. Rather, they view government as being solely responsive to organized special interests or to financial elites. There is an all-pervasive sense within the American electorate that government is unresponsive, ineffectual, out-of-touch, wasteful, and, frankly, just plain corrupt—rarely serving the interests of the people who elected it and pay the taxes. An Ipsos/McClatchy poll conducted in late February 2010 found that across the board, 80 percent of the electorate now believes that "nothing can be accomplished" in Washington. What is most significant is that the percentage is just as high among Democrats as it is among Republicans and Independents.

Voters are frustrated with the ongoing partisan battling, wrangling, and gridlock that skyrocketed in recent years, as well as the systemic failure to address the serious problems that Americans face.

But it is more than a loss of faith in government that drives the new populist revolt. The second component is a catastrophic economic crisis that exacerbated the populist backlash against political, economic, and social institutions. Over one year following the crash of 2008, ordinary Americans are finding themselves increasingly unable to make ends meet. Many are experiencing downward mobility for the first time as they find themselves unable to provide their families with the lifestyle they had once taken as a given. In fact, Scott Rasmussen conducted a poll in early March 2010 finding that only 48 percent now say it's possible for anyone to work their way out of poverty.

And preliminary economic recovery has not minimized or reduced the populist fervor and the levels of anger and mistrust that exist.

To be sure, the economic crisis and the political crisis are intertwined. People face economic pressures that government has proven incompetent at addressing. And government's failure to resolve the economic crisis has only deepened their frustration with their personal circumstances.

Since the onset of the Great Recession, and in the wake of the historic 2008 election, we have witnessed an unprecedented degree of anger and division within the American electorate, and with good reason. The economic collapse put our leaders to the test, and the political establishment failed that test cataclysmically.

While the primary sources of ordinary Americans' sense of dislocation and frustration is related to economic malaise due to the downturn in the housing and financial markets, it would be wrong to assume that cultural and lifestyle issues have no role.

Many critics have tried to dismiss the new populism, particularly the Tea Party movement, as simply a manifestation of anger, rage, and even racism. This is profoundly wrong. Certainly within the broad umbrella of contemporary right-wing populism are groups such as the birthers, the Patriot movement militias, anti-immigration zealots, and extreme libertarians calling for the abolition of the IRS and the Federal Reserve, as well as a fair share of cultural conservatives; these are not representative of the force that is driving the movement.

They see communities being uprooted, they see traditional values being undermined, and they believe that their way of life is being threatened on many fronts. Indeed, the most public manifestation of this was the surprise votes against gay marriage in the states of Maine and California. In 2008 and 2009, ordinary citizens in two relatively tolerant states demonstrated their unwillingness to embrace what has come to be generally accepted among political elites as a necessary and appropriate alteration of social arrangements based on a sense of equity and fairness. For populists on the right, gay marriage represents a fundamental alteration of social arrangements they are just not prepared to embrace.

The resulting sense among the American electorate is all too clear: We are no longer living in the country we once knew. A country where everyone has the opportunity to thrive and succeed. Where hard work equals opportunity. Where the powerful submit to the people. Where democracy reigns. Where those who play by the rules are rewarded with a better life for themselves and their families.

That America is gone.

Today, the majority of Americans feel a deep sense of rage and hopelessness because of the occasionally perceived and oftentimes real injustices of life after the Great Recession. To a growing group of populists on the right and the left, there is a sense that the American Dream has been perverted, if not lost. Those who cheat are the ones who win. Those who steal are the ones who profit. The corporations that fail on every imaginable level are the ones who attain unimaginable earnings. Individual investors lose their lifelong savings, while profiteers on Wall Street make short-term fortunes. The least responsive governments have become entrenched bastions of corruption, collusion, and unbridled power. This is the view of many, and this perception—right or wrong—is the driving force of a new movement.

As we mentioned above, driving the new populist revolt on the left and the right is broad-based anger with government, business, and other institutions, which a large segment of the American electorate sense are fundamentally working *against* their interests.

Two years after the uplifting 2008 elections, the cynicism most Americans feel toward politics is back, and gridlock has returned to Washington. In truth, the worst aspects of our politics never really went away—a subject that Doug has written on extensively in his book, *The Political Fix*. The institutional dysfunction was merely obscured for a brief moment by the genuine joy and accomplishment Americans felt in electing not only the nation's first African American president, but a politician who seemed to promise transcendence, a man who, we hoped, would lift the nation above and beyond old divisions of race, class, and politics.

In 2008, the president ran from the center, but in 2010, his administration governs from the left. The government bought controlling stakes in financial institutions such as AIG and in manufacturers such as GM. The administration advocated taking over the student-loan market, proposed a sweeping new bureaucracy to oversee the financial and consumer credit markets, and intervened massively in the housing market. Indeed, the level of influence that unions and their political allies have is so great that it is no surprise that the most frequent visitor to the White House during the first six months of Obama's presidency was none other than SEIU president, Andy Stern.

As a result, the Independent voters that largely elected Barack Obama feel betrayed and forlorn. They believe in fiscal freedom and the recognition and acknowledgment of the importance of the ordinary person making decisions in American political life. And they are enraged by the special interests, aloof politicians, faceless corporations, and the disinterested elite that, in their view, have literally trampled our sacred social compacts.

They are furious about the stimulus bill that has further plunged the nation into debt, yet hasn't resulted in meaningful improvement in their personal economic situations. In other words, they have been asked to mort-

gage their children's future for benefits they have yet to experience in their own lives. About this, they are seriously and rightfully angry.

And they are now flocking to the Tea Party movement. To be sure, the Tea Party movement is avowedly conservative, but anyone who says they are an adjunct of the Republican Party is just plain wrong. In fact, a significant number of their supporters—20 to 30 percent, depending on the poll—did vote for Obama, and they are as hostile to the Republican Party as they are to the Democratic Party.

While the mainstream media dismissed the Tea Party movement as being a Republican party orchestrated, radical-fringe Astroturf movement, we find that this is far from the case. Take, for example, the case made by Mary Ann Franzese at a Fourth of July tea party in Morristown, New Jersey: "There is a lot of anger and resentment over the way this country is being run. And it's nonpartisan. Some of our members were big Obama fans who don't see the changes and transparency he promised. So we have Democrats and Republicans here, and independents. These are people who do not like the direction the country is going in."

Meanwhile, the far left feels slighted by an Obama administration that they feel has ignored many of its core priorities. Many of their dearest held positions have been cast aside by the very man they worked so hard to elect, and in whose administration they put limitless faith.

We witnessed this movement firsthand, up close and personal. Since June 2009, we have been on the scene at left- and right-wing populist protests, rallies, marches, and events throughout the country, conducting interviews with populist activists, organizers, and supporters from all points along the ideological spectrum. We met with Tea Party protesters. We talked with left-leaning community organizers. We interacted with town hall participants. From this firsthand experience, we gained unprecedented insight into the size, shape, composition, and future of the new populist revolt. In addition, we carefully compiled our own proprietary public opinion research to supplement our in-person observations and reporting.

The qualitative and quantitative data we gathered is deeply fascinating, highly troubling, and politically portentous. What we uncovered is not only shocking; it is literally groundbreaking. From our firsthand experience—and our deep delve into the numbers—we reached the unambiguous conclusion that the American political landscape itself has irreversibly shifted.

As a result, new players have suddenly emerged in this incredible national drama. New voices in the public debate are demanding to be heard. It is our view that the myopic mainstream media has badly distorted these voices.

Indeed, the political elites in Washington and affluent communities across American have been entirely dismissive of the populist movement burgeoning across the nation. To a large degree, the political elites mistake the anger of populists for ignorance. And the reason is simple. They are living in a different world. Not only have they been isolated from the hardship of the Great Recession; many of them have in fact grown richer. They continue to be upwardly mobile, to send their children to expensive and exclusive schools, and to believe that the country is heading in generally the right direction. This confidence stems from their personal involvement and close association with K Street and Wall Street. They trust government and financial elites to solve America's problems, because they themselves belong to this exclusive social subset.

In addition, there is no question that the populists have been maligned as mere caricatures by the facile punditry of talking heads on cable television. But these are real people and what they have to say needs to be heard. The political elite has misunderstood and underestimated them, but, in truth, they are a force to be reckoned. Their perspectives are important, their arguments are sensible, their outlook is astute, and their emotions are real.

We have met the men and women on both the right and the left who are raising their voices to protest the unacceptable direction in which they see America heading. Largely—and in direct opposition to the way they are characterized in the press—the populists defy easy categorization.

Elisa, a single working mother from New Jersey, works as a supervisor of medical technicians. She grew up in a household of immigrant Czechoslovakian parents with strong conservative values. She is divorced and has one son. She is extremely conservative and has routinely voted Republican; however, she now considers herself an Independent as she is fed up with the inaction of the Republican Party. While she has never been active in politics per se, she votes consistently, and is well versed on the issues. However, the economic and political crisis has caused her to become a vocal critic of political elites, Democrat and Republican alike.

"Well, as a working mother whose probably never even going to be able to *hit* retirement, because I'm probably going to work until the day I drop, trying to put my kids through school so that they have a better future. . . . I'm fighting right now to give them that chance. You know, our country is going so deep into debt. Will they have it worse? I always thought, if they get a good education . . . But there's a lot of people that graduate college and can't even get a job these days, and that's a sin. Imagine somebody like me who just graduated high school? Where are they going to work, McDonald's? I fear for my children, and my future grandchildren, I just don't know where it's going to go for them. And I worry that when I get to a ripe old age that I'm going to have to use my savings to take care of myself. And I'll get nothing back that I worked fifty years for. And there'll be nothing there to give me because our country will be in so much debt."

Elisa feels an acute apprehension about the future, an intense hopelessness that is characteristically un-American, and a loss of control that is palpable. Despite her moderate political leanings, these are sentiments she shares with conservative activists that we have met and spoken with across the country.

Matthew, 25, is a single worker from urban Pennsylvania. He is socially and fiscally conservative. But more than anything else, he identifies not with a political party, but with the same sentiments that Elisa expressed to us.

"I think that what you're seeing from center-right folks and the far right is a *fear* that the Obama administration and the current Congress truly believe that government is the only solution to all of our problems. And because of the super-majority that they have, we basically have no say in the matter . . . and that's scary. That's scary in the sense that the future of our country—economically. The ambivalence and incompetence of our government when it comes to the amount of debt and taxes that might be levied on the middle class and businesses in this country. It's scary. Right now the country is on autopilot toward growth of our government and spending. And I think that is scaring a lot of people. At some point, the buck has to stop, literally. We have to find a way to pay for it. I mean taxes? Cutting money from one and moving it to another, taking from Peter to pay Paul. I mean, this is turning into one giant Ponzi scheme!"

Matthew and Elisa come from two very different walks of life. They have different political leanings. But they share the same misgivings about life in America today. Their strong, common emotions caused them both to get organized and get involved. Moreover, their outlook, their arguments, and their actions are representative of an emerging political force that we will introduce you to in the following pages.

Two things are clear from these voices and the millions like them across the country today. First, in a very real sense, entire worlds have been turned upside down by the economic collapse. Industries that were once mighty are on the verge of extinction. Business that had existed for generations vanished overnight. Millions of homes that held the wealth and life savings of countless families have been seized in foreclosure. Second, and only to make matters worse, the institutions meant to safeguard the interests of ordinary Americans have literally been turned against them.

The sum total of this economic and institutional wreckage has begun to manifest itself in a number of ways that Elisa, Matthew, and countless other populists expressed to us in dozens upon dozens of in-depth interviews: pervasive fear, anger at the system, a breakdown in trust across society, the dissipation of hope, and the notion that things are beyond our control. It is clear that these strong emotions need an outlet. And they have found a vent in two distinct and virulent strands of populism—left and right—that are powered, at their core, by the powerful events and sentiments described above.

These groups and the emergence of the new populist revolt are both complicated and completely misunderstood. It requires sophisticated analysis, but, in the press, it has only been treated to simplistic think-ing and superficial scrutiny. Furthermore, despite being pervasive and sustained, this movement has attracted little to no attention from the academic community.

Indeed, this book is an attempt to fill an enormous void, and to explain what we firmly believe to be an incredibly complex and never-before-seen phenomenon in American politics. We hope to describe how the new populism has taken shape and operates, and to provide a clear, unbiased explanation of how the new populists—particularly those on the right—are reshaping American politics.

We will also describe how the common ground—the great Ameri-can center—has begun to crack under the pressure of hardcore, aggres-sive populism from both the political left and the political right. While Americans remain united in their generally pessimistic view of their leaders and the state of national affairs, consensus and common ground have utterly frayed under the strain of the new American scarcity. The result is an entirely new, unprecedented, and as-of-yet unexplained American political environment.

Many people want and hope to dismiss the new political environ-ment that is emerging thanks to the proliferation of the new populist revolt. They think things will somehow return to normal. They believe that we are in the middle of a clearly reversible cycle. There is a word for these people—political elites—and they are fundamentally misunderstanding the exigencies of today's America. What they don't realize is that *normal* no longer exists.

It's easy to explain away the populists as just another ephemeral moment in the long, winding road of American politics. It's a much more difficult task—and one that hasn't yet been attempted—to put the political changes we are experiencing into context.

That is our charge.

Who are these groups? What do they have in common? What traits do they share, and why? How are they changing our politics? How are they changing out government? Why does the political elite so easily dismiss them? How should the parties respond?

We are highly interested in the answers to these questions. Our personal experience, along with reams of new data, allows us to offer a perspective and analysis that the mainstream media fail to deliver. After all, as we will show, they're part of the problem.

The media and the political elite have tried to force the America public to view the new populist revolt through the tired political prism used to make sense of previous political realignments. The powers in Washington and New York are bent on seeing this as an issue of Democrats versus Republicans in the eternal battle for political majorities. In reality, what is happening in America today is bigger than either political party. Much bigger.

The new populist revolt isn't about partisan identification. It's about a loss of identification. Americans no longer know whom to trust. They no longer know who is on their side. They no longer identify with the political establishment, because the political establishment no longer understands them.

The underlying dynamic driving the populist renaissance isn't Democratic versus Republican. It's about the insiders in Washington versus the outsiders in Middle America. It's about the elites who think they know what's best for the American people, versus the American people who believe more ardently than ever in their own self-determination.

It's about the CEOs who think they are entitled to government bailouts and tremendous windfalls, versus the everyday Americans whose lives have been shattered by corporate greed and ineptitude.

If the political elites continue to ignore and fail to address the valid concerns of everyday Americans, they're courting disaster. This is no exaggeration. We've seen the anger on the faces of people whose homes, careers, and families have been upended. We've seen the voracity of the emerging populism in our recent polling. And we are convinced that what is on the horizon is nothing short of a seismic change in the balance of power in America. What lurks around the bend, in other words, is a potential political collapse.

America can't afford a constitutional crisis on top of the economic crisis we already endure. And that's why we were compelled to write this book. We hope this work will help to avert the disastrous course we are on, by explicating the realities of the current political situation.

First, we will describe the emergence of populism, a wholly new and underappreciated occurrence in American politics. We will briefly describe the history of previous populist movements, explain the recent collapse of centrism that has long defined the political parties, and show how the rise of new populist revolt is completely unprecedented in the history of our democracy.

Second, we will define, for the first time, the actors in this incredible drama. We will show that the emerging left and right populism share several fundamental aspects. They are anti-systemic, anti-institution, and anti-Washington. They distrust business, feel a loss of control, believe in protectionism, disdain the political class, and are driven by fear and anxiety about the loss of the American Dream. However, they diverge on the critical issue of the role of government in American life: spending, ownership, regulation, and taxation. They also feed off one another. Right-wing populism has mobilized, in a certain sense, in reaction to the impact left-wing populists have had on the Democratic Party generally, and on the Obama administration specifically.

Third, we will describe the nemesis of the populists: the political elite. These are the entrenched special interests, the unresponsive partisan leadership in Washington, and the myopic and self-centered celebrity journalists who have underestimated and underreported the new populist revolt. Additionally, as we will argue going forward, it is our belief that the reaction of the political elite has only *exacerbated* the political transformation we are undergoing.

Finally, we will offer our unique perspective—from our experience on the ground, to our careful analysis of the numbers—on the implications of the populist revolt. And we will answer the pressing question at the heart of this incredibly consequential historical moment: *How will this populist schism impact the future of American politics, government, and society?*

2

THE POPULIST STRAIN

We already suggested in the Introduction that the Tea Party movement, a movement that did not exist at the time that President Obama took office, is now the strongest political force in America.

The obvious question is: Where did this movement come from?

In fact, the roots of the Tea Party can be traced back to the social and economic conservative movements, beginning with Barry Goldwater and spanning the latter half of the 20th century.

And there are even some historical antecedents with earlier populist movements such as Father Coughlin during the Great Depression, and 1950s McCarthyism.

Populism in America is nothing new. The populist strain in our politics is as old as the Republic itself. A number of issues and themes connect the populist resurgence of the 21st century with the many populist movements that have preceded it. From Pat Buchanan and Ross Perot during the 1990s, to Huey Long in the 1930s, to William Jennings Bryant in the 1890s, populism in America is certainly as old as politics in America.

Most analysts see the new populist revolt as simply another chapter in that long history. They don't distinguish between what we are seeing on the streets today, and earlier populist movements in the 19th century or the 1930s. They survey the current political scene and see populism as simply a new incarnation of an old ideology that's been around for as long as anyone can remember. And in all fairness, there's a good deal of truth to that observation.

Previous populist movements for the past two hundred years have been remarkably consistent and similar. They have been defined by their hostility toward elites, their distrust of government and business, their anger toward the system and how it works against the interests of the average, working-class American family. Populists for the past two hundred years have been an anti-systemic bunch, motivated by economic or social crisis to shake up the political class. Generally, these movements have had a brief impact on our politics, and then faded from the scene.

Populists in the 19th and 20th centuries were motivated by economic hardships, inequities in the social structure, the centralization of economic and political power in the hands of the elite, and political stagnation that suggested the government was disinterested or unable in coming to the aid of the average American. This is certainly the case today. Similar issues and grievances drive the 21st-century populists on the right and the left.

However, what we will argue here and in the following chapter—and what we believe is incontrovertible based on our in-person reporting and our recent polling—is that the new populist revolt is fundamentally different than what has come before it in size, scope, influence, and future impact. And the factors that give rise to this essential difference is precisely the reason why the new populism has arisen at this particular moment in history, and why it is so virulent.

A confluence of events has brought about an unprecedented change: globalization, economic crisis, technological revolution, and government dysfunction have resulted in the plummeting public faith in business, government, and the American Dream. These dramatic changes have been under way since the turn of the millennium and the first day of the presidency of George W. Bush. This series of unprecedented events that we will fully describe in the next chapter—economic, social, political, and cultural—have resulted in its explosion of the new populist revolt on to the political scene.

As a result, an irreversible transformation of the political landscape has occurred.

In this chapter, we will put both centrism and the new populism in historical context, but not for any esoteric reason. Populism isn't a mere curiosity in the fascinating annals of American political and social history. Historians aren't the only ones who should know or care about the transformation that has and continues to occur.

To the contrary, this new movement has serious implications for the next generation of American politics. A once-in-a-century realignment has occurred, yet no one today seems to know it. And it is impossible to understand the ramifications of this realignment without a firm grasp of its roots.

That is our goal in this chapter.

Above, we argued that two major shifts have taken place in American society: an economic shift, which has upended the lives of millions of Americans, and a related political shift, which has caused independents to become increasingly conservative over the course of 2009.

Together, these shifts represent the foundation of the Tea Party movement. But they also represent something new in the history of the conservative political tradition in American politics.

AMERICAN POPULISM DEFINED

Populism is a simple idea with an endless number of variants, as one moves across the American political spectrum. As Steve Sark penned for the *Atlantic* some fourteen years ago:

"Populism can be loosely defined . . . as a struggle between ordinary people and a self-serving, undemocratic elite."[1]

That definition hasn't changed much since the 1990s, or since the 1790s for that matter.

In a large sense, American populist movements across the centuries share a sense of moral decay, a suspicion of the conniving elite, an unshakable faith in the essential goodness of ordinary people, a disgust with a presumed business-government conspiracy, and a belief that the ordinary American has undergone a systemic betrayal by power-monopolizing institutions.

According to Michael P. Federici in his book, *The Challenge of Populism*, there are thirteen characteristics commonly attributed to populist movements. Among them, populists are generally suspicious of elites, especially business figures, bankers, bureaucrats, intellectuals, and scientists, as well as monopolies. They have faith in the common sense and virtue of the ordinary people. They believe in siding with property holders over corporations. And they are more often than not drawn to religion and sectarianism.[2]

As we will demonstrate below, these characteristics are certainly applicable to previous populist movements and that of the modern variety. Indeed, there are three traits of American populism from past to present worth highlighting in particular for our purposes.

First, populism isn't the domain of either party.

Throughout American history, there have been populist movements on both the political right and left. According to *New York Times* columnist David Brooks, the "populist tendency [has] continued through the centuries. Sometimes it took right-wing forms, sometimes left-wing ones. Sometimes it was agrarian. Sometimes it was more union-oriented. Often it was extreme, conspiratorial and rude."[3]

What's important to note—and what we will demonstrate in this book—is that populism is easily adopted by both conservative and liberal ideologies.

Second, American populism is perhaps defined above all else as a mass movement against the elite. In his book, *Populism*, Paul Taggart makes the case that populism can take a number of forms—to our above point. But the common thread, he argues, is populist disgust with the ruling class in government and business: "Populist figures such as William Jennings Bryan, Huey Long, Joe McCarthy, George Wallace, Ross Perot, and Pat Buchanan can not be categorized easily. They all, however, invoked the virtues of the common folk and the corruption of the elites."[4]

Populists were often united against economic elites, but political and intellectual elites have also been the target of their ire. It is easy to see this anti-elitism in populist movements throughout American history. In the early 19th century, Andrew Jackson led a populist movement against the economic elites who controlled the Second Bank of the United States—the "Monster Bank"—that had close ties to the political class. The Free Silver populists of the late 19th century, which we discuss below, were largely agrarian workers rising up against East Coast bankers. The followers of George Wallace, however, were less driven by economic populism than by their rejection of "pointy-headed intellectuals" and "limousine liberal" elites.

Third, populism in America (and elsewhere) is crisis-driven. In *Populism*, Taggart writes that every populist movement throughout American history—from the 19th century to the 21st century, from the right wing to the left—has had, at its core, a significant historical, economic, political or social rift: "The importance to US populism of a sense of crisis has not changed. The particular crisis may well have changed, but the populist response has been remarkably consistent."[5]

In other words, a crisis is what draws the attention of the nation to the actions of its government, and when those actions are subject to unusual public scrutiny.

These are the crucial building blocks of any populist movement. As we will demonstrate below, these three essential characteristics of American populism held true in the 19th century, and they still hold true today. They are the factors that unite the Tea Party movement of late 2000s to the Free Silver movement of late 1800s.

TEA PARTY ROOTS IN OUR DEMOCRATIC DNA

The Tea Party movement embodies many of the above traits in the long strain of populism that has run throughout American history, from the nation's founding to the present. Indeed, many of its core arguments have been part of our national DNA, thanks to our Founding Fathers. Although the term "populism" didn't exist in the late 18th century, the anti-systemic, anti-government, individualist principles of the nation's Founders influenced many of the core principles of modern day populism on both the left and the right.

Thomas Jefferson, whom we have to thank for the Declaration of Independence and key republican elements of our Constitution, was a staunch believer in the people over the powerful. For instance, in a letter to John Taylor in 1816, Jefferson voiced concern that the newly established federal and state governments were too centralized and did not provide citizens with an adequate degree of individual autonomy and control: "It must be agreed that our governments have much less of republicanism than ought to have been expected; in other words, that the people have less regular control over their agents, than their rights and their interests require."[6]

Thankfully, a Bill of Rights was shortly thereafter appended to the Constitution, much to Jefferson's approval. But Jefferson still believed in the supremacy of ordinary citizens over the governing elite. Indeed, he argued that ordinary Americans had a right, if not a duty, to rebel if government overstepped its boundaries and impeded upon the popular will.

In the late 1780s, Captain Daniel Shays led a small rebellion to stop the Massachusetts Supreme Court from taking action against economically distressed farmers. After federal forces clashed with and ultimately defeated Shays' insurrection, Jefferson wrote to James Madison: "The late rebellion in Massachusetts has given more alarm than I think it should have done. Calculate that one rebellion in 13 states in the course of 11 years, is but one for each state in a century and a half. No country should be so long without one."[7]

19TH-CENTURY POPULISM

This populist strain was extended and cultivated in the 19th century, in large part thanks to Andrew Jackson, the father of the modern Democratic Party and the nation's seventh president. Jackson had a distinctly populist appeal that brought him tremendous success in both politics and governing. As the *Weekly Standard*'s Matthew Continetti astutely noted: "More than any other politician of his era, [Jackson] aligned himself with the common man against self-dealing elites. Lacking formal education, he nonetheless understood that incumbents, whether in the market or in politics, raise barriers to entry in order to protect their positions. And because he sought to unsettle those entrenched interests, Jackson was at the vanguard of a spirited popular upheaval."[8]

This anti-elitist undercurrent may explain why left-wing populist movements that seek to expand the role of government in order to protect the hardworking masses through redistributive fiscal policies and increases in government spending, intervention, and ownership (which we will discuss at length in Chapter 8) have failed. This populist resistance to big government policies is ingrained in American history, dating back to Andrew Jackson. As Michael Barone noted in the *Wall Street Journal*: "Jackson was not a 'spread the wealth' populist. On the contrary, he opposed the American System of John Quincy Adams and Henry Clay to have the government build roads and canals and other public works. He killed the central bank and paid off the national debt.

"Jackson argued that government interference in the economy would inevitably favor the well-entrenched and well-connected. It would take money away from the little people and give it to the elites. . . . Why has the politics of economic redistribution had such limited success in America? One reason is that Americans, unlike Western Europeans, tend to believe that there is a connection between effort and reward and that people can work their way up economically. If people do something to earn their benefits, like paying Social Security taxes, that's fine. But giving money to those who have not in some way earned it is a no-no. Moreover, like Andrew Jackson, most Americans suspect that some of the income that is redistributed will end up in the hands not of the worthy but of the well-connected."[9]

The "spirited popular upheaval" of the Jacksonian age has never really left American politics. Populism has flared up with amazing regularity, consistency, and one could argue predictability throughout the course of the 19th and 20th centuries. And while it has always had a role to play in our politics, it never came to dominate them.

That is, until now.

DEPRESSION-ERA POPULISM

The 1930s were in many ways the golden age of left-wing American populism. As we noted above, populism is driven by anti-elitism and crisis, and is easily adopted by conservative and liberal ideologies. During the Great Depression, the elites in business and government had plundered the American economy. The resulting Great Depression, coupled with looming war in Europe, created the perfect political storm. And out of this storm would emerge a political consensus that held for much of the 20th century and right up through the presidency of George W. Bush.

While we will hold off our discussion of left-wing populist hero Huey Long and President FDR until Chapter 8, let us not forget Father Coughlin's social conservative right-wing populism.

Father Charles E. Coughlin was a prominent Roman Catholic priest and activist, and in many ways the pioneering Rush Limbaugh of his day. He used his widely popular radio program as a platform to criticize the excesses of capitalism, the dangers of communism, and the Roosevelt administration for his New Deal policies, which struck Coughlin as veering the nation on a destructive, socialist course. In

1934, Coughlin founded the National Union for Social Justice, an organization with a strong following among nativists and opponents of the banking elite, especially in the Midwest.

And while Coughlin was certainly the leading voice of pious right-wing populism, his rhetoric over time became increasingly anti-Jewish, pro-fascist, and downright ugly. Ultimately, his association with a violent Nazi group called the Christian Front led to a tarnished reputation and his eventual withdrawal from public life, though he never disassociated himself from his fascist and anti-Semitic friends.

POSTWAR POPULISM

In the 1950s, U.S. Senator Joseph McCarthy from Wisconsin, an anti-communist crusader, shook up the political establishment with his House Un-American Activity Committee hearings and accusations of a vast, left-wing, communist conspiracy. And while his heated right-wing populist rhetoric and outrageous claims captured the nation's attention, it did little to change the postwar consensus of the moderate majority. As David Oshinsky put it in the *New York Times*: "McCarthy didn't last long at the top. The rhetoric of populism is that of crisis, and his wild charges were muted by the election of President Dwight Eisenhower in 1952, the death of Stalin in 1953 and the subsequent armistice in Korea."[10]

Fast forward to the 1960s, where Barry Goldwater led a new (and much more sensible) populist uprising on the right, George McGovern championed the antiwar, social-democratic sentiment of the populist left, and George Wallace spoke for segregationist, disaffected, and economically dislocated whites in the South. All of these populist figures were popular, powerful, and important to the politics of the 1960s. At the end of the day, however, centrism ruled, and the postwar consensus held.

In 1964, Goldwater was defeated by Lyndon Johnson in one of the most lopsided presidential elections in U.S. history. Today, Goldwater's platform looks sensible, but, at the time, it was demonized. McGovern was bested by the Democratic machine, which nominated Hubert Humphrey for president in 1968, even though he didn't compete in a single primary. George Wallace failed miserably in every presidential effort he ever mounted, and he and his followers were rebuffed by the historic passage of the Civil Rights Act of 1964. (Not to mention the assassination attempt in 1972 that left him crippled, or his late-in-life rebuke of his radical and racist ideology.)

During the 1960s, right-wing populism was driven not so much by economic factors as social issues associated with the Civil Rights movement. Cultural populism on the left—which eventually spawned the women's movement, the environmental movement, and the gay-rights movement—helped spark counter-movements on the right.

During the late sixties and early seventies, right-wing populists were part of Richard Nixon's "Silent Majority." The anger and resistance many fundamentalist Christians felt toward the aggressive cultural changes ushered in during the 1960s triggered what became the Religious Right. The Christian Coalition became a core constituency of the Republican Party, which relied on the social conservative vote as part of its "base." In the 1980s, this base helped usher in the era of Ronald Reagan and the moral majority.

During the 1970s and 1980s, the populist strains on both the left and the right ends of the spectrum were largely internalized by the major parties. On the right, Ronald Reagan appealed to centrists and right-leaning populists alike. On the left, Walter Mondale and Michael Dukakis held sway over the left-leaning populists. Fringe populism during this period was successfully contained—co-opted one could say—by the national Democratic and Republican machines.

Look no further than Reagan's landslide victory in 1984, which we alluded to earlier, the last victory of its kind in more than a quarter century. Reagan's approach appealed to a populist refrain in a centrist package. His policies during his first term emphasized transparency and accountability. Indeed, he changed the rules of the game in Washington by introducing the indexation of income tax brackets. Prior to Reagan, revenue grew faster than the economy and politicians could vote for tax "cuts" every election cycle while still enjoying the benefits of added revenue. Reagan ended that game, to the enormous satisfaction of the great American center.

Moreover, during the 1980s, centrism had real champions in a number of congressional leaders of both parties, from Robert Byrd to George Mitchell to Bob Dole. These men were the Knights Templar of the postwar consensus, so to speak, who, despite heated partisan battles, kept American politics on a bipartisan, moderate trajectory.

This trajectory continued straight through the end of the 1980s. But the election of 1992 changed everything; it was the precursor to the populist wars playing out in the nation today.

At first glance, the populism that flared up in 1992 looked similar to previous populist spikes in American politics. Pat Buchanan became the Father Coughlin of the 1990s, railing against illegal immigrants and warning of communist infiltrators. Ralph Nader played the role of Huey Long, ginning up far-left liberals with redistributionist and populist rhetoric. Even Ross Perot, the best-known and most successful populist insurgent of the 20th century, was a moderate running as an outsider.

Perot's brand of populism was distinctly centrist and very much in line with the policies and rhetoric of the postwar period. Indeed, the essential planks of Perot's message were familiar populist mantras: disgust with elite; anger at politicians' fear of making hard choices and speaking to Americans honestly; concern about the reckless fiscal and financial policies of Washington, and how it would end up costing ordinary Americans; scorn for government's lack of understanding of how small businesses work, products are created, employees are developed and retained, and how families struggle to make ends meet; and an overarching concern that a terrible crisis was brewing.

Moreover, in 1992, a time of similar economic dislocation to what we are facing now, the desire for limited government and a balanced budget, as well as the libertarian virtues of a less intrusive state, manifested themselves in the Perot movement. Perot advocated conservative economic policies, but, more important, he espoused the libertarian virtues of small government, and of reducing the involvement of government in the private lives of citizens.

It's easy to see, then, how Perot won 19 percent of the vote in 1992, the best third-party presidential showing since Teddy Roosevelt in 1912. He got his name on the ballot in all 50 states, and for a time in late spring and early summer, he held a polling lead over both President George H. W. Bush and the Democratic nominee, Bill Clinton. If not for his volatility, unpredictability, and incredible stubbornness as a candidate, Perot surely would have done better than that.

The important takeaway here is that unlike previous populist movements, Perot-era populism—sparked by President George H. W. Bush's broken promise of "no new taxes"—has never really left our politics.

The resurgence of populism we are experiencing today is a continuation of the populist uprising of 1992 in the same way that World War II was a continuation of World War I, with a period in between that appeared quieter than it really was. Also, just like the World Wars, the second act of the Perot-era is likely to provoke far more turbulence and far bigger changes on the political battlefields of 21st-century America.

The Perot movement manifested itself in 1994 with the Republican takeover of Congress, which built on it to develop a Contract With America that offered a number of principles well beyond what Ross Perot himself supported two years earlier.

Six weeks before the 1994 midterm Congressional elections, the Republican Party released the Contract With America to "restore the bonds of trust between the people and their elected representatives." The contract was written by Larry Hunter, Newt Gingrich, Robert Walker, Dick Armey, Bill Paxon, Tom DeLay, John Boehner, and Jim

Nussle. Signed by all but two Republican members of the House of Representatives and every candidate running on the Republican ticket, the Contract detailed the values, principles, and goals that the Republican Party would uphold in the case that they became the majority party in the House of Representatives following the election.

With the Contract, the Republican caucus pledged their commitment to government accountability, fiscal responsibility, U.S. sovereignty in national security issues, common-sense legal reform, personal responsibility and welfare reform, strengthening families, middle-class tax relief, job creation, and greater efficiency in government. In retrospect, then, it is hard to see how the Contract was anything but a continuation of the populism that exploded on the scene in 1992.

As Jeffrey B. Gayner wrote in an October 12, 1995, article for the Heritage Foundation: "The ideas espoused in the Contract With America represented the culmination of 30 years of creative conservative thinking dealing with the basic social and economic problems of modern America. The ideas provided the background for the widest range of legislative initiatives, certainly since the 1930s, and possibly at any time in American political history. The fundamental principle involves re-examining the role of the government in society." [11]

In much the same way that the Contract stemmed from Perot's candidacy, the Tea Party movement shares many of the values, principles, and goals of the Contract of America. Moreover, many key Tea Party organizers and advocates are Contract With America writers such as Dick Armey and Newt Gingrich, now operating not as elected politicians but through their respective PACs: FreedomWorks and American Solutions for a Winning Future.

Yet, two fundamental differences exist between the 1994 Republican Revolution and the Tea Party movement. One pertaining to structure and organization, the other to ideology.

First, the Contract With America was an elite orchestrated, top-down movement designed to appeal to the mainstream. In 1994, Republican candidates and Representatives who aligned themselves with the Contract With America platform were successfully able to tap into the anger and frustration of a large segment of the population yearning for a government that would defend social and economic conservative values. The result was the Republican Revolution, with the Republican Party holding a congressional majority for the first time in four decades.

As Gingrich said at the time, "There is no comparable congressional document in our two-hundred-year history."[12]

In that sense, the right-wing populism exhibited in 1994 was a top-down movement, organized by Republican Party leaders with the goal of mobilizing like-minded, ordinary Americans to support Contract With America candidates on election day, and help the GOP take control of both houses of Congress for the first time since 1954.

The Tea Party movement, as we will discuss at length in Chapter 6, is a true bottom-up movement. While the Contract With America was penned by the most powerful Republicans of its time included a series of promises for what Republican lawmakers would do for "the people," the Tea Party's Contract *From* America is a grassroots collective effort, a manifesto of what "the people" want their government to do, compiled Wiki-style by Internet contributors.[13] Second, whereas the Contract With America pledged to establish a Congress that, "respects the values and shares the faith of the American family," the pillars of social conservatism, "God, life and family get little if any mention in statements or manifestos. The motto of the Tea Party Patriots, a large coalition of groups, is 'fiscal responsibility, limited government, and free markets.'"[14] And the Contract *From* America "mentions little in the way of social issues, beyond a declaration that parents should be given choice in how to educate their children."[15]

The *Christian Science Monitor's* Patrik Jonsson compared the social conservative driven Contract With America, with the fiscally conservative driven Contract From America in a March column, writing:

"The 1994 Contract With America specifically pointed out that it 'respects the values and shares the faith of the American family.' Today, the wiki-based Contract From America being compiled by the group Tea Party Patriots focuses primarily on issues around the national debt, the role of the Federal Reserve, states' rights, and the 10th Amendment, which they say limits the reach and scope of federal government.

"'At the end of day, [the Contract From America] will offer the biggest tent possible by setting forth 10 to 12 ideas that will really be about fiscal responsibility, limited government and good governance reform, which we think will enable a number of Democrats to sign onto it,' says Ryan Hecker, a Houston-based lawyer who is organizing the Contract From America by soliciting input from Americans over the Web." [16]

In the sixteen years since the Republican takeover, social conservatives have dominated the party. Throughout the 2000s in particular, Republican candidates have played to this critical Christian constituency, emphasizing moral issues such as abortion, gay rights, and the role of religion in public education and public life. A number of evangelical leaders emerged to become major players in national Republican politics, from Pat Robertson and the Christian Coalition to James Dobson's Focus on the Family.

More to the point, the small government and economic conservative strands of the conservative movement played only bit parts during the years of Bush, Lott, and Hastert. Economic conservatives were only given lip service, as the Bush administration dramatically expanded federal spending. Small-government libertarians were pushed to the fringe, as Republicans expanded the scope and size of the federal government.

Simply put, during the 2000s, despite the dominance of the Republican Party, the three strands of conservatism were fractured. Indeed, for fifty years prior, the strands have never been unified into a national movement.

Until now.

THE NEW POPULISM

Perot is remembered today as merely a fascinating historical curiosity. Buchanan holds court now and again on the extreme right, and Nader is largely seen as pompous, egotistical, and totally irrelevant. But none of these populist leaders or movements was particularly long-lived.

Therein lies the crux of this history lesson. Populism certainly played an interesting and important role in our politics through the end of the 20th century. In addition, the anti-elitist, political stagnation, and the economic crisis certainly link the new populist revolt to previous populist movements.

However, 19th- and 20th-century populism is nothing like what we are witnessing today for a number of important reasons that we alluded to above, and that we will describe at length in the next chapter.

The right-wing populism we are experiencing today is significant because it represents the conjoining of three separate, distinct, and not easily reconcilable strands of conservatism: economic conservatism, small-government libertarians, and social conservatism.

Historically, these strands have not worked in concert. And occasionally they have even been at odds. But in 2009, they seemed to converge under the broad umbrella of the Tea Party movement.

NEW POPULISM in CONTEXT

Do you know what really bothers me? Our Constitution hasn't been paid attention to in about 50 years. And it's absolutely a sin, because it's our document. This country was founded on people to create their own wealth not to live off of the redistributed wealth of others. We're all equal in one way and one way only, and that's to have the opportunity to achieve our best God-given abilities. Not to have the government share everybody's wealth equally. That's Russia. That's communism. I thought we beat 'em, and now we elected them.

—Ralph Sproveer

I just think that things are going to keep getting worse and worse. My opinion of what we've seen in the past year—the economy is not getting any better. The only thing that has gotten better is a stock market rally, which was fueled by government spending and a devaluing of the U.S. dollar which is making our assets more attractive. And that's really what you've seen. If you go and look at the jobless rate. The employment rate has not improved at all, which we know is a lagging indicator, but that being said—you talk to small businesses, they're not doing any better. The only people that are doing better are the bigger companies that are flourishing because of dramatic cost cutting and layoff. They haven't created any jobs, maybe they saved one or two.

—Freddie Roth, Wealth Manager & Private Banker, New Jersey

A decade into the 21st century, we have entered a new era in American politics. The postwar centrist consensus described in Chapter 2 has dissolved, and something new and not before seen has taken its place. American populism is no longer episodic, waxing and waning with the issues of the day. It is virulent, it is distinct, and it could very well be here to stay.

The new populist revolt is different in scale, tone, and impact from populist movements of the past. Because of the circumstances driving the new populist revolt, it is far more intense, and it is exerting itself to a much higher degree than previous movements. The new populists completely reject the political, economic, and social systems and institutions that have failed the public to a shocking degree, and simultaneously to boot. Like previous populist movements, populism in the 21st century is anti-systemic, anti-elite, and crisis-driven. But unlike movements of the past, it is pervasive and here to stay.

We are convinced of the long-term impact of the new populist revolt because of what we have seen firsthand, and because of the data that shows an unprecedented degree of anger across a wide spectrum of demographics. From distrust in government, to despair about the future of the nation, the public polling numbers are off the charts. And these numbers are a product of the remarkable forces at work that have caused the new populism to materialize and metastasize at an unforeseen rate.

This new brand of populism is characterized by a complete rejection of the prevailing economic and social systems, and an absolute sense that we need to find clear alternatives to the existing arrangements for the country to rebound. Five key factors are driving this sentiment, and they have made this new populism the dominant philosophy among Americans situated across the political spectrum:

1. The perceived upending of the world as we know it;
2. The failure of both governmental and private institutions;
3. The decline of American hegemony;
4. The decline of the position of the ordinary person; and
5. The increasing gap between the political elite and the political mainstream.

The sum of these factors is that we are in the midst of an *unprecedented crisis in confidence*. The world has fundamentally changed for most

Americans thanks to the rise of globalization, the near-collapse of our political system, and the Great Recession. People have lost jobs, homes, and cars. Wages have stagnated and income inequality has grown much more substantial. Lives have been turned upside down, and so has the worldview of the average American.

For many Americans, the world as they know it today is one of extreme economic dislocation, record-breaking levels of income inequality, devastating unemployment, and a growing crisis in underemployment.

This collective shift in outlook calls into question some of the most entrenched values of American society. A recent survey conducted by Doug and Mike Berland for *Parade* magazine showed that scarcely more than half of the country (52 percent) believes that if you "work hard and play by the rules," a "solid middle class life" can be attained. Meanwhile, 87 percent are worried about the future of the nation, 61 percent feel that they "did everything right and still lost," and 65 percent "can't believe that this happened to us today in America."[1] Beliefs that were once thought to be untouchable now seem exposed, vulnerable, and perhaps even puerile. Such is the state of the country's common consciousness.

Today, a majority of the electorate believes that the economic system works only for the elite, and against the average worker. American workers are furious that the government stood by while millions of jobs were sent overseas. "Americans have lost faith in their institutions," observed op-ed columnist David Brooks of the *New York Times*. "During the great moments of social reform, at least 60% of Americans trusted government to do the right thing most of the time. Now, only a quarter have that kind of trust."[2] The economic crisis of 2008 merely provided the spark of crisis that lit the populist fire now burning out of control.

The electorate is similarly incensed by the influence of special interests and economic elites over Congress and the White House, which has made government unresponsive to the needs of ordinary Americans. Partisanship has become more pronounced as people perceive that their leaders—left and right—put politics ahead of principle and doing what is right to effect positive change. As Frank Newport of the Gallup organization noted at the end of 2009, "Americans have less faith in their elected representative than ever before."

This decline is a direct consequence of the historic chasm between the political elite and the political mainstream. Indeed, this is the subject of the following chapter. As the political elite becomes increasingly detached from the nation at large, they give a strong tailwind to the other populist forces at work. As Scott noted elsewhere, "the gap Americans who want to govern themselves and the politicians who want to rule over them may be as big today as the gap between the colonies and England during the 18th century." Hence, the Tea Party movement, as well as the impetus behind this work.

The result of this incredible convergence of forces has been a rapid and unprecedented decline in public trust in our civic and business institutions, widespread anger among Americans of all political stripes, and uncharacteristic despair about the future of life in America. People no longer expect that their children will have a chance at a better life than they did. Brooks noted, "61% of Americans believe this country is in decline" while a mere "27% feel confident that their children's generation will be better off than they are."[3]

The very notion of the American dream, it appears, has been called into question. And the result of this crisis in confidence is the new American populism.

As we have noted, many believe that the new populist revolt is not very different from the many populist movements that we detailed in the previous chapter. The longstanding strain of left- and right-wing populism certainly played an important role in our politics during the 20th century, from the New Deal straight through the 1992 presidential election. And it is only natural, then, that the new populist revolt has been seen through this same historical lens.

We, however, believe this to be a faulty and dangerous reading of current events.

A HISTORIC CONVERGENCE

The new populist revolt is unprecedented because it has emerged from unprecedented crisis. Never before has there been a crisis in confidence driven by a fundamental, cross-systemic, broad-based breakdown of our economic, political, and social systems. Never before have so many American lives changed so quickly, so drastically, and so irreparably.

As we demonstrated in the last chapter, past populist movements have been typically driven by a contained economic, political, or cultural crisis. Rarely have previous populist movements resulted from the convergence of more than one of these crises.

The Populist Party of the 19th century arose out of an economic crisis. The Panic of 1893, dropping farm prices, rising debt, and restrictions on silver coinage were the issues of the day. And these economic issues were the rallying cry of the Free Silver populists. Similarly, McCarthyism in the 1950s had at its core a singular crisis: fear of the communist threat. Goldwater and Wallace became populist leaders as a result of a domestic social crisis.

The new populist revolt is different. It is a populist movement driven by multiple, simultaneous crises. The rise of globalization led to the outsourcing of millions of jobs. The economic crisis of 2008 and the Great Recession resulted in record unemployment. The failure of government to respond effectively to these crises has led to a widespread crisis in confidence.

Even worse, government and big business were equally implicated in the meltdown, often working hand in hand. Those who brought the financial system to the brink of collapse ran to Washington for more financing, as did the powerful union officials and corporate chieftains of Detroit, who flew to the nation's capital on private jets to drum up more funding. And they got it. Meanwhile, Americans were losing their homes. The collapse of the housing market and the unprecedented levels of public money given to prop-up financial institutions, such as AIG and Citibank, and automakers like GM and Chrysler, helped spark intense public disgust with leaders in business and politics alike.

And because of the way the bailouts worked—big banks yes, ordinary people no—both the left and the right asked a question: *Why them? Why not us? What does "too big to fail" mean except that they are rich and powerful and we are not?*

This disgust with government and big business is being articulated across the board. As *New York Times* columnist Frank Rich wrote: "The rage engendered by this status quo is across the political map. As unlikely as it sounds, Ron Paul and Jim DeMint, political heroes of the tea party right, and Bernie Sanders and Alan Grayson, similarly revered on the left, have found a common cause in vilifying the Federal Reserve Bank and its chairman, Ben Bernanke. The Fed is hardly the root of all evil, but you can see why it is a handy scapegoat. Like the institutions it failed to police during the boom, it wields its power from on high with little transparency to those below."[4]

The result of this convergence of crises and the resulting crisis in confidence has been twofold. First, it has eroded the postwar centrist consensus that has characterized our politics for the past half century. Second, it has given rise to a populist revolt that is categorically different from anything we have seen before.

Past populist movements typically attracted a following from a specific geographical, ideological, political, cultural, or religious base. However, the new American populism has a broad-based following that spans the entirety of the political spectrum, from far left to far right. In fact, the majority of Americans can be classified as populist today.

There is no doubt that 21st-century populism has its roots in the anti-elite and crisis-driven movements that have always been an important part of the American political landscape. But the new populist revolt doesn't fit into the same old mold. It is categorically different from populist movements of the past. A historic convergence of events has degraded the postwar consensus to the point that it no longer exists. Forces acting on every level of society have literally pulled it apart. We're not the first by any stretch to indentify these forces. They are well known and intuitive to all. But their impact on our politics has not yet been fully explained.

Below, we will describe the forces that have brought about the new populist revolt, as well as notable consequence of these circumstances: the collapse of postwar centrism, and the sharp polarization of left- and right-wing populists in the electorate.

Income Inequality

Income inequality, on the rise for over a decade, reached its highest level since 1917. University of California, Berkeley, Professor Emmanuel Saez accounts for this trend, reporting that as of 2007, the top 10 percent of American earners accounted for virtually half (49.7 percent) of annual wages, "higher than any other year since 1917 and even surpasses 1928, the peak of stock market bubble in the 'roaring' 1920s." According to Saez's calculations, in 2007 "the top .01 percent of American earners took home 6 percent of total U.S. wages, a figure that has nearly doubled since 2000."[5]

Frank Levy of the Massachusetts Institute of Technology, a leading scholar of income trends, has noted that median family income, in constant 2005 dollars, rose from about $22,000 to $50,000 during the period from the end of World War II through 1980. Since then, except for a slight increase during the boom of the late 1990s, median family income has been relatively flat. In fact, Census Bureau statistics show it actually fell from 2000 to 2007. Meanwhile, within the top 1 percent of American households, median income increased by about $250,000 between 1986 and 2005. Blue-collar wages have been almost stagnant since the days of Jimmy Carter, while the bottom-fifth of families have seen a 2.5 percent income drop since the late nineties.

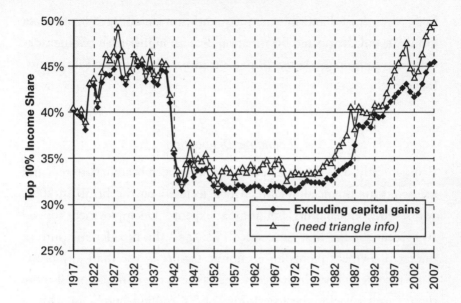

As MIT's Thomas Kochan notes, "Median worker wages have been stalled since 1980, when the post-war social contract began breaking down. As unions steadily declined in coverage and power, ordinary workers got less and less of the productivity gains they helped produce. Since the 1990s the top one percent of the population captured approximately 50 percent of the income gains from economic and productivity growth, thereby generating levels of inequality not seen since before the Great Depression."[6]

According to an April 2008 report issued by the Center on Budget and Policy Priorities, "Wage inequality is growing for several reasons, including long periods of high unemployment, globalization, the shrinkage of manufacturing jobs and the expansion of low-wage service jobs, and immigration, as well as the lower real value of the minimum wage and fewer and weaker unions. As a result, wages have eroded for workers with less than a college education, who make up approximately the lowest-earning 70 percent of the workforce."[7]

Wallace Peterson, a Keynesian macroeconomist at the University of Nebraska, argues that while economic growth and productivity increased in the eighties and nineties, American workers' standard of living deteriorated and income inequality worsened. By 2002, median family income, corrected for inflation, was no higher than two decades earlier, even though almost 20 percent more families now rely on two incomes.

Economic Dislocation

Economically, over the past decade, we have been beaten, battered, and bruised. Our financial system, which teetered on the brink in 2008, was saved from calamity, but at great expense. Unemployment topped 10 percent for the first time since 1983, and the broader measure of underemployment paints an economic picture worse than any previously recorded. The Great Recession has seen the elimination of more than 7 million jobs, the foreclosure of 2.8 million homes in 2009, a 21 percent rise over 2008 and 120 percent over 2007, the disintegration of some X trillion dollars in wealth, and the financial destruction of countless lives.[8] To top it all off, the federal deficit is now 10.64 percent of GDP[9]—a level not seen since Sherman tanks rolled across occupied France. And while federal spending continues to balloon—a subject that was ubiquitous in 2009, with the passage of a $787 billion stimulus package, and debate over a trillion dollar health care overhaul—many Americans struggled to pay their electric bills and buy groceries.

That's the picture on the surface. And it gets worse the deeper you dig into the numbers.

At the time of writing, while the unemployment rate is deeply troubling, far more disturbing is the underemployment rate—a broader measure of economic health that quantifies the percent of the workforce that is jobless, has given up on looking for work, or is working part time because they can't find a full-time gig. At the end of 2009, the underemployment rate hit a historically high watermark of 17.5 percent. In other words, roughly one out of every six American workers is in a desperate economic situation, resulting in what economists estimate to be the worst job market since the Great Depression.

Our country is suffering from a *jobs deficit*. And the implications are alarming. As Thomas Kochan of MIT's Sloan School explains in a March piece for the *Huffington Post*: "The Congressional Budget Office tells us that the economic recovery alone will not replace the 8.4 million jobs lost since the beginning of the current recession, much less generate the additional 2 million needed to keep up with population growth. Instead, unemployment will remain above 9% through 2011 and likely remain above 7% through 2012, leaving about a 4.5 million jobs deficit at the end of 2012. It could be even worse if the 'jobless recovery' trend of the last two recessions prevails."[10]

The jobs deficit, Kochan argues, has taken a significant psychological toll on American workers, which has resulted in deteriorating attitudes and a loss of trust. He writes: "The Conference Board recently reported that for the first time since it began collecting national survey data, overall job satisfaction fell below 50% (45% in 2009 compared to 61% in 1987). Not surprisingly, young workers (under 25) express the lowest levels of job satisfaction, declining from 56% in 1987 to 35% in 2009. In airlines where one quarter of the jobs have disappeared and wages and benefits of survivors have been cut by 30 to 40 percent, surveys report less than 20% trust management's ability to lead the industry out of its crisis."[11]

To complicate matters, unlike in previous times of economic unease, most people who lose their jobs today can't simply pick up and move to find work, an issue compounded by the housing and foreclosure crisis. Such an unprecedented lack of mobility will make the downturn longer and deeper, many economists say. According to Moody's Economy.com chief economist Mark Zandi: "There's really nowhere to hide in this economy. . . . If you lose your job, it's not clear where you should move to find one or even what training or education you need to retool yourself. . . . The hallmark of the current downturn is that it is so broad-based across industries, occupations and regions of this economy."[12]

The above notwithstanding, it's arguable that the impact of the economic crisis on white-collar workers has been equally devastating. While every American knows well the story of Lehman's collapse, the fire sale of Bear Sterns, the crumbling of Washington Mutual's house of cards, it's important to consider the real world effects of these calamities on the thousands upon thousands of middle-class and upper-middle-class American families. In the end, the lives they built for themselves proved to be no more durable than a housing bubble floating along on subprime mortgages.

There is no longer such a thing as job security in white-collar America, any more than there is in blue-collar America. Members of the Baby Boomer generation may have spent decades building their careers, but, at the same time, they bought homes priced at two or three times their incomes. Now, white-collar professionals in their fifties and sixties, people who have spent the past two decades getting in way over their heads with excessive borrowing, are losing jobs by the thousands. It's inconceivable at their age that they will be able to rebound to their former status.

It's the same story in industry after industry. High finance was the first domino to fall in a sequence that has toppled a number of white-collar sectors. A popular T-shirt that one sees from time to time in the United States quotes Shakespeare's *Henry VI*, Part 2: "The first thing we do, let's kill all the lawyers." What the play's Dick the Butcher couldn't accomplish, the economic downturn may achieve, at least figuratively. The credit and banking crisis has wrought havoc on prosperous, old-line corporate law firms like Proskauer Rose, Dewey LeBoeuf, and Clifford Chance, devastating these firms' profitable practices in areas like structured finance, mergers and acquisitions, and private equity. A firm dating back to before the Civil War, Thacher, Proffitt & Wood, shut its doors in 2009. And at century-old White & Case, described as "the quintessential gentleman's firm" in a *New York Times* story, over 270 attorneys have been laid off.[13] What makes it so much more disturbing is, unlike less severe recessions in which the junior associates are sent packing and most of the damage is contained, this downturn is putting senior partners out on the street. White & Case chairman Hugh Verrier had to break the bad news of layoffs to two hundred of his fellow attorneys in March 2009. As the *Times* reported, that number included not just associates but "some million-dollar-a-year ones" with "twin mortgages, kids in private school and no Plan B."[14]

If Americans hold one value in common, it's that hard work pays off in the real world. Years of experience lead to an upward trajectory of increased compensation and greater success. But as millions are learning in today's economic climate, a proven track record might be a deal-breaker for employers who fear the financial expectations of experienced candidates.

"There's nothing to apply for at my level!" a 49-year-old former corporate vice president, Lenora Kaplan, told the *Wall Street Journal*.[15] She frankly admitted to lying about her job history in an attempt to get hired. But instead of the common tactic of résumé inflation, people like Kaplan are now in the practice of deflating their resumes. Her retooled CV provides little evidence of her dirty little secret: that she has twenty-six years of experience in the marketing field and has held an executive position at her previous job. In looking for work, Kaplan has discovered a changed job market with an entirely transformed set of rules and priorities. Her extensive, impressive job experience puts her at a salary level that companies simply find unpalatable in the current climate. It's shocking, but true: In the wake of the Great Recession, experience is a liability.

And as MIT's Thomas Kochan points out: "These average unemployment rates mask even more serious problems facing specific groups. Nearly 30% of teenagers are either unemployed or out of the labor force and 50% of recent college graduates are working jobs that do not require a college education. Forty percent of those unemployed have been out of work more than half a year and are again at risk of losing unemployment benefits."[16]

The college graduating class of 2009 is feeling how harsh those trends can be. Graduates went out into the most fiercely adverse job market in at least twenty-five years, and perhaps several generations. Many, if not most, of them entered saddled with the burden of college loans. According to American Student Assistance, the average college graduate is $20,000 in debt. Most nonwealthy parents take out loans to afford to send their children to the best colleges. Until recently, this seemed sensible, with the expectation that earning a bachelor's degree from a respected college is an investment in one's future. Upon graduation, these students would be hired to the job of their choice. The loans were nothing more than a down payment on a lifetime of prosperity.

This is no longer the case. *The employment rate for college graduates has dropped by 22 percent since 2008.* What's more, many of the students who are finding themselves jobless and drowning in debt, with no prospects on the horizon, just graduated from Ivy League schools—the most revered and most expensive academic institutions in the United States. What has become obvious is that a college degree no longer ensures employment. This is a harsh realization for members of the class of 2009, the largest class of college graduates in ten years.

"Even those who land jobs will likely suffer lower wages for a decade or more compared to those lucky enough to graduate in better times," wrote Sara Murray in a *Wall Street Journal* analysis of the class of 2009's plight. Murray pointed to a study from the National Association of Colleges and Employers showing that the average starting salary for graduates dropped to $48,515 this spring, down 2.2 percent from the same time last year.[17]

Lisa Kahn, a Yale School of Management economist, cites data showing that white men who graduated college during and after the early 1980s recession suffered in terms of their starting salaries to the tune of 7 to 8 percent less pay for *each percentage point increase in the unemployment rate.* She said that the trend persisted for up to two decades of working life.[18]

Globalization

Globalization has literally emasculated blue-collar America. Manufacturing, construction, and the building trades have been devastated not only by the economic crisis of 2008 and 2009, but also by the steady outsourcing of jobs to India, China, and elsewhere over the past fifteen years.

The downturn, of course, only exacerbated this trend, particularly in the manufacturing sector. For all the attention Wall Street gets, the current recession is hurting blue-collar Americans much worse than bankers. Blue-collar positions have accounted for about 70 percent of the 6 million jobs that have been shed since late 2007. It's notable that men held most of these jobs. The unemployment rate in construction, for example, is nearly 20 percent. While the U.S. manufacturing sector has been contracting for decades, it has been devastated by the economic crisis far beyond the normal course of downsizings and globalization. In this decade alone, in fact, America has lost nearly 5 million manufacturing jobs. The contraction has accelerated considerably since September 2008. A February 2009 CNN report, "The New Jobless," portrayed some of the Americans displaced from what had once seemed like nearly permanent blue-collar jobs. In Jay, Maine, Cory Clapsaddle, 37, had always envisioned staying in the industry—paper mills—that had employed his father. In Clapsaddle's words: "If it was good for my father, it was good for me." The century-old mill, owned by Wisconsin-based Wausau Paper, was a mainstay in the community and employed 235 workers. Clapsaddle thought it "seemed like a mill that could never die." But he became one of 150 workers laid off—nearly 65 percent of the workforce—shortly before Labor Day 2008 due to "difficult market conditions." Now, Clapsaddle, like millions of blue-collar Americans, has seen his dreams turned upside down and finds it difficult to sleep at night. "It's always on my mind," he says. "Looking for a new job, losing a job, bills. The whole picture."[19]

In the once mighty Midwest, the plight of the auto industry and rapid decline in the manufacturing sector has literally transformed once vibrant small towns into modern-day Hoovervilles. For instance, in early 2008, unemployment in Elkhart County stood at 4.7 percent. A year later, Elkhart had the highest unemployment rate in the nation at 15.3 percent, fueled largely by the rapid decline in its recreational vehicle business. Elkhart's RV industry was built by residents like the Bontrager family, who started an RV enterprise in 1968 that went on to thrive for four decades. But starting in fall 2008, the Bontrager's company began laying off employees—over one thousand of them, including many personal friends. The industry that had powered Elkhart ran aground of high fuel prices, the credit crunch, and the foreclosure crisis. Derald Bontrager and his family had weathered ups and downs, such as the energy crisis of the 1970s, but during the Great Recession he sensed that the problems were "beyond our control." Elkhart residents are today receiving help from churches and food banks. The town's entire identity and way of life has been upended.[20]

Elkhart is just one of hundreds if not thousands of smaller towns and communities that have been brought to the brink. "We're doing anything and everything to stay afloat," says Nawab Manjee of nearby Granger, Indiana. When tickets for President Obama's February visit to Elkhart became available, Manjee promptly bought four, putting two on Craigslist for $1,000 apiece. He planned to use the money to help make payroll for his struggling commercial real-estate company.

We cannot overemphasize the political ramifications of this economic transformation among the blue-collar workforce. Their worlds have been flipped upside down. The government has failed to protect their jobs, and when the economy tanked, so did any lingering savings or retirement security. This, on its own, would be enough to spark a populist outcry. But combined with other forces at work, as we will describe below, the cumulative effect is sufficient to transform American politics forever.

All of this adds up to the pervasive sense, supported by hard numbers and anecdote, that what we've experienced is much worse than the end of another prosperous economic cycle. It feels much more like *the end of the game*.

For millions of Americans in places like Elkhart, for white-collar professionals in the law firms in Manhattan, for graduating college students in every region of the country, the tectonic plates of American prosperity have shifted. It's not a matter of simple economic recovery. The economy *will* recover eventually, in some fashion. But what was lost, this time, is not coming back, and Americans seem to know it.

Like globalization, this dramatic and historic period of economic dislocation is contributing to a political dislocation that is just as profound. When you experience a dramatic change in your personal economic situation, it's a simple fact that you look at the world differently. When you see your family, friends, coworkers, and neighbors experiencing economic hardships for perhaps the first time in their lives, it's impossible to think about politics, government, or society in the same way.

That is what is happening in America today. There is the pervasive sense that everything has changed: our employment, our outlook, our quality of life, and our prospects for future prosperity. And this sense is the result of frightening and dramatic changes in the lives of real people. It's naïve to think that such profound change would not impact our politics in an equally profound way.

Indeed, it has.

Government Meltdown

Our government has failed the average American. It's that simple. Our duly elected representatives are supposed to protect the interests of their constituents, not just their campaign contributors. They didn't. Our watchdog agencies like the SEC are supposed to prevent the Bernie Madoff's of the world from robbing us blind and leaving us for broke. They were asleep at the switch.

We have a broken government. And our troubles are well documented. Indeed, Doug's recent book, *The Political Fix*, is an entire treatise on the subject. But let us quickly provide the Cliff's Notes here, to summarize the dysfunction of politics and government in America today.

America's system of campaigns and elections is fundamentally broken. The average American has been shut out of the political process. Money has overrun the system, and attempts at reform have all failed—a fact underscored by the Supreme Court's January 2010 decision in the Citizens' United case, which gutted the McCain-Feingold campaign finance law. There are a number of culprits. The national political parties exert increasing influence over local politics, thanks to their large coffers and the need of local candidates for large sums to run successfully for office. Our gerrymandered congressional districts have resulted in incumbents that have no incentive or need to reach out across the aisle; in fact, the more extreme they are in their partisanship, the safer their seats. Massive loopholes allow members of Congress to collude with lobbyists, special interests, and political action committees that preserve the status quo. The result has been that most Americans don't want to or simply can't participate in the political process. More often than not, government no longer works for the American people, but against them.

The deep flaws and failures of our political process have resulted in gridlock in Washington. Even with a comfortable majority in the House and a supermajority in the Senate, Democrats have been stymied at every turn by rampant partisanship that President Obama has failed to stem. Of course, the partisan gridlock didn't start with Obama. In many ways, it poisoned both the Clinton and Bush presidencies. And it has prevented action on the pressing problems that have gone unresolved for decades, from the looming entitlement crisis to healthcare reform.

Washington is not only out to lunch, it's out of touch. Look no further than the deeply unpopular bank bailout that started under George W. Bush, and continued under Barack Obama.

Our mass media is no longer serving the public interest. Of course, one could argue that the mass media has *never* served the public interest. It is poetic that the subprime mortgage crisis coincided with the death throes of the fourth estate. It is well documented that our newspapers are dying, and what is replacing them is a far cry from journalism. The proliferation of cable news, the bankruptcy of traditional newspapers (we mean financial, though many would argue that nearly all of the news is America is no longer fit to print), the induction of a 24-hour news cycle—these and other phenomena are fundamentally transforming journalism in America, and mostly for the worse. The result is that television pundits have exacerbated the partisanship described above and the anger of ordinary Americans at their dysfunctional government.

And in Scott's recent book *In Search of Self-Governance*, he uses comprehensive polling data to make the compelling case that Americans are just angry. Rather, years of mounting tensions between the political class and mainstream brought about by an "unholy alliance" between government and big business has culminated in a fundamental rejection of our nation's governing bodies. Americans don't want to be governed from the left, the right, or the center. They want to govern themselves. Scott argues that self-governance is about far more than politics and government. It requires a lot of the American people, and it has nothing to do with the petty partisan games played by Republicans and Democrats.

In short, Americans have found themselves in the peculiar position of desperately needing competent governance precisely at the moment when our civic institutions are performing at an all time low. A confluence of tragic structural failures that has directly contributed to the emergence of the new populist revolt.

This is no small point. Americans might be critical of individual politicians, and of a system that seems often to work slower and provide fewer results than we like. But we are, generally speaking, fiercely proud of our democracy. For all its flaws, it's still the best. Or so we thought.

In the wake of continuing scandal, economic devastation, and government waste, abuse, and mismanagement—all of which contributed to and prolonged the economic collapse—many Americans have been shaken out of their characteristically moderate political views. The failure of government, combined with economic dislocation and the perils of globalization for American workers, have radicalized the electorate in many ways, which has contributed directly to the rise of the populists.

It's easy to see that the fundamental problems with our malfunctioning government aren't going anywhere anytime soon. Consequently, neither are the populists.

Technological Revolution

Doug has written extensively about the ways in which the technological revolution of the 1990s and the proliferation of the Internet have transformed every aspect of our politics. These changes have been both positive and negative.

On the one hand, increased access to the Web has allowed more Americans to connect with and interact with their communities and government at all levels. Indeed, some governments have used Web-based technology to make government more open, transparent, and accessible to the average citizen. This is a trend that is, we are glad to say, on the rise. In addition, the Internet has forever altered political fund-raising. Average citizens are now able to give millions of small dollar donations that, in aggregate, can counteract massive special interest spending.

On the other hand, Web-based communication has given rise to some tremendously troubling developments that have exacerbated the worst aspects of our politics. For instance, the proliferation of Internet news, in addition to cable television, has created the 24-hour news cycle described above. The rise of the blogosphere, while potentially beneficial in the long run, has created new outlets for rancid partisanship.

Together, these phenomena have made our politics less civil, and our government less effective.

Both the positive and negative aspects of this technological transformation have implications for the rise of populism. As we noted above, political organizing is much easier and much more effective in the Internet age. And partisanship has flourished as well. Taken together, technology is an accelerant that amplifies the forces at work driving the new populist revolution. From globalization to economic dislocation to government dysfunction, technological revolution has made these problems much more real, and much more emphatic.

In our digital world, in other words, populism is more powerful, more viral, and more unstoppable than ever.

Psychological Damage

What is most transformative about the economic crisis of 2008, and the ongoing political and governance crisis, is the underlying sense among Americans that the nation's trajectory is, for the first time, downward.

This is a stunning development, and a stark reversal of our characteristically upbeat national outlook, and it has serious implications for the emergence of the new populist revolt.

America has been, since its founding, a place of possibility, where prosperity is always within reach. We determine our own future. We chart our own course. These concepts are ingrained in our collective psyche, and, over the years, this national myth has informed nearly every aspect of our history from Manifest Destiny in the 19th century, to preemptive war in the 21st century.

In the wake of the Great Recession, however, this defining national characteristic is on the verge of extinction. The perceived upending of the American Dream is apparent across data that we have collected on a range of subjects, which is worth briefly detailing here.

Happiness: Since 1979, Gallup has taken a broad measure of American's satisfaction—not only in their personal lives, but also with life in the United States in general. In early October 2008, satisfaction with life in the U.S. plummeted to a record low of 7 percent. Some 91 percent of Americans identified themselves as being dissatisfied with the direction of life in the United States. No doubt, this is understandable in the midst of a devastating downturn. But Americans have been through recessions before, and this time something is different. While satisfaction levels have fluctuated substantially over the past thirty years, they've never hit such a low ebb.[21]

Trust: The General Social Survey has polled Americans on confidence in public institutions since 1972. Over the last decade in particular, the survey shows a significant drop in those saying that they had a "great deal of confidence" in nearly every public institution. Consider that between 2000 and 2008, trust in big business fell from 30 percent to 16 percent, trust in banks fell from 30 percent to 19 percent, trust in organized religion fell from 29 percent to 20 percent, and trust in the press fell from 24 percent to 11 percent. It's notable here that even at the height of public outrage over the bailout of AIG, public trust in business still far exceeded trust in government.[22]

Columbia law professor and editor of *Public Opinion and Constitutional Controversy*, Nathaniel Persily, said, "The Tea Party movement is interesting in that there is a combination of localism, nativism and populism that we've seen at various points in America. . . . It's coalescing at a time when the government is growing to an unprecedented size."[23]

In a *USA Today*/Gallup Poll conducted in late March 2009, 55 percent of respondents identified "big government" as the main threat to the country, compared with only 32 percent who identified "big business." In fact, most Americans today view big government to be more pernicious than Islamic fundamentalism.[24]

Respondents to the Harris Poll indicating a "great deal of confidence" in Congress dropped from 22 percent in 2002 to 13 percent in February 2004, to 10 percent in February 2006, and ultimately to the single digits—*just 8 percent*—in February 2008.[25] Similarly, Gallup reported its lowest-ever approval rating for Congress in July 2008, at a higher but still dismal 14 percent. Even more remarkable is that in the thirty-four years that Gallup has measured congressional approval ratings, this figure has fallen below 20 percent only six times, three of them between 2007 and 2008.[26]

Belief in the future: The hallmark of American life has always been our steadfast belief in the future, and our confidence in the continuation of American supremacy, both as a global superpower and a global brand. Our national creed has held for generations that the United States as we know it—the idea, the dream, the stalwart of freedom—will exist in perpetuity. Our children will inherit this great country, in which they can achieve even more than we have. The world will continue to benefit from a strong America that protects and promotes the supremacy of democratic governance and the market economy. And therein lies the most disturbing change in public opinion since the onset of the Great Recession. For the first time, Americans no longer express their trademark confidence in the future of the American way of life. A Rasmussen telephone survey in June 2009 showed that just 31 percent of U.S. voters believed that the United States would be the most powerful nation in the world at the end of the 21st century. Thirty-five percent disagreed, and 34 percent weren't sure. In other words, as a nation, we are utterly confounded by the change swirling around us. Moreover, these views hit home on a personal level as well. Scott has found majorities indicating that they don't believe their children will be better off than they are, a stark reversal of the traditional American expectation of betterment. Most also express less confidence that the future will offer better jobs or economic stability, and few expect that the housing market will turn around anytime soon. A CBS poll showed that an overwhelming 91 percent of Americans worried that the nation's enormous budget deficits would create hardships for the next generation.

This recent polling on the attitudes and outlooks of Americans is genuinely shocking. We've simply never seen numbers like this before. Just as the economic downturn has meant not only lost jobs but also lost careers, the data on our national outlook suggest something deeper than just cyclical social and economic distress. Today, the American people have experienced a loss of identity, both for themselves and for their country. Not only is our economic future in doubt. There is a fundamental question weighing on the collective conscience of the nation: *Is American centrality a thing of the past?*

The impact of this profound doubt on our politics has not been previously understood. These indicators are the equivalent of a seismograph going off the charts, portending a devastating earthquake or tsunami. For whatever reason, most pundits and other pollsters have been too quick to dismiss these warning signs. But we are convinced that combined with the above tectonic forces, these indicators foretell an ominous change under way in American politics.

THE CENTRIST COLLAPSE AND THE RISE OF NEW POPULISM

Columnist Gerald F. Seib said in the *Wall Street Journal*:

> Many Americans, seething at a Congress that seems ever less able to resolve big issues, ask why lawmakers aren't more willing to come together in compromise.
>
> Here's part of the answer: Robert Bennett, John McCain, Blanche Lincoln, Lindsey Graham and Lynn Woolsey.
>
> That isn't a list of people standing in the way of compromise. Rather, it's a list of lawmakers from both parties under attack from within their own camps precisely because they have dared to reach toward the middle—often just barely—in the hopes of getting an agreement on something important.
>
> Their experiences show why, particularly in an election year such as this, the safest tactic in Washington today is to retreat to your respective partisan foxhole and stay crouched

down there along with the other foot soldiers from your army. Those who stick their heads out of the foxhole, or actually wander out onto the battlefield in search of a truce with the other side, are the ones who get shot.[27]

One of the most striking results of the populist resurgence has been the collapse of centrism. The implications of the centrist collapse has become increasingly clear in the months leading up to the November 2010 midterm Congressional elections. As North Dakota Senator Kent Conrad explained during a March 2, 2010, interview on *Countdown with Keith Olbermann*: "We see this happening on the right and the left. Republicans are afraid they're going to get challenged on the right. That's their only meaningful competition. Democrats in certain states afraid they're going to get challenged on the left . . . what it means is the ability to actually get things done is being reduced, because what's happening is you've got a push to the extremes. The left and the right. The result is it's much more difficult to have people who are centrist still survive and play a role in actually getting results."

Such was not always the case. In fact, for the past several generations, from Eisenhower in the 1950s through Clinton in the 1990s, American politics was largely dominated by centrism, thanks to a postwar political alignment that resulted in a concentration of power in the hands of moderates from both sides of the aisle. The extreme wings have been a constant presence and source of tension. Particularly since 1972, when the primary system was recalibrated to give voters and not delegates a central role, the wings of the parties have grown in prominence. In 1960, for instance, President Kennedy captured the White House by competing in only five primaries, because to win he needed the backing not of primary voters but of party delegates.

"Of course, there's nothing new about intraparty fights, and elections are supposed to be about resolving ideological disagreements," added Gerald Seib.[28] However, both major parties have tended over time to hew to the center, and been punished electorally when they have temporarily knuckled under to their outlier bases. "The difference today is that both parties are more determined to seek uniformity and internal discipline than they were when, say, Republican senators cast the crucial votes for Democratic President Lyndon Johnson's civil-rights bill, or House Democrats cast the deciding votes for Republican President Ronald Reagan's tax-cutting budget blueprint."[29]

Over the past several years, a convergence of the forces, episodes, and systemic problems described above have caused an unmistakable centrist collapse.

Centrism, which has been gradually withering, is officially dead— the first victim of the new populist revolt.

In the fall of 2009, *Washington Post* columnist Eugene Robinson perfectly captured the dramatic change underway in American politics: "The rule among politicians in Washington used to be that when the provincials become restless, as they are now, the safest thing to do is run to the center. But as this sour and unsettled summer ends, the political center looks like the white line running down the middle of a busy street—a foolish place to stand and an excellent place to get run over."[30]

This sentiment, well put by Robinson, represents a profound change in the American political landscape. There has always been a strong centrist impulse in American politics. But today, the system simply doesn't allow for it anymore.

Everywhere you looked just a few years ago, the conditions seemed ripe for a centrist surge. In spring 2006, Princeton Survey Research Associates released a poll showing that an astonishing 53 percent of Americans supported a third major party. An even more remarkable 73 percent agreed with the statement that "it would be a good idea for this country to have more choices in the 2008 election than just Republican and Democratic candidates," and 85 percent agreed that the United States had "become so polarized between Democrats and Republicans that Washington can't seem to make progress solving the nation's problems."

Doug Schoen has seen plenty of evidence for these sentiments in earlier polling work. In early 2007, he conducted a series of polls for the Aspen Institute that examined the American public's opinion of the current two-party system. The results were shocking. Sixty percent said that our country was headed in the wrong direction, and 80 percent said that U.S. relations with the world had worsened over the past five years. While over half the voters thought bipartisanship was very important, 70 percent believed that the two major parties disagreed on most issues and hardly ever worked together, and were largely dysfunctional and indifferent.

At the same time, Americans expressed strong desire to see bipartisanship and consensus to solve the nation's problems; policies that unified the country and brought people together; and moderate, even conservative policy prescriptions in most areas. Eighty-four percent of my respondents agreed with the statement "America is more divided than united," but 90 percent agreed, "Working together America can remain united and can address all the problems we face."

We now know why this centrist trend failed to take hold. The forces described above created a snowball effect that has changed the course of American politics.

For moderate lawmakers, one profound difference between elections in post-centrist collapse American politics and the way things were, is that those who stray from party orthodoxy today know that they risk not just a fight back home, but a fight in which national political organizations, wielding national money, will go after them.[31]

And the implications for traditionally centrist lawmakers, seeking re-election in November 2010 have been profound.

In Utah, moderate Republican Senator Robert Bennett has been taken on by conservatives both in and outside the Republican Party. Conservative organizations, such as Club for Growth, have launched an aggressive media campaign against Bennett, running television ads and launching a website called stopbennett.com to portray Bennett as a

Republican in Name Only (RINO), a traitor to conservative values who pals around with liberals.

"His principal transgressions, according to the ads and Web site, are that he voted for the rescue plan for Wall Street—that would be the bipartisan rescue originally proposed by Republican President George W. Bush and subsequently endorsed by the Obama administration—and that he 'even joined with liberals supporting big government health care.'"[32]

That Bennett actually voted against the healthcare reform bill when it was brought to the floor of the Senate is of little matter. "Instead, his sin was to sponsor an alternative, more centrist approach with Democratic Sen. Ron Wyden that is less sweeping and costly—and that leaves many liberals cold."[33]

Meanwhile, in California, Democratic Representative Lynn Woolsey is under siege from the groups that comprise the populist left because of recent comments that she would be willing to vote for the Senate healthcare reform bill that does not include a public option.

"The broader problem lies in the signal sent to everybody else in Congress that breaking ranks brings headaches from those you thought were on your side. Thus, the Republican Party's standard-bearer in 2008, Sen. John McCain, now finds himself challenged from the right by a former Republican congressman, J.D. Hayworth, in no small measure because Mr. McCain has a history of seeking bipartisan compromise on the explosive immigration issue. The challenge already seems to have caused Mr. McCain to pull back on his bipartisan stands."[34]

Together, these forces make the new populist revolt we are experiencing today fundamentally different from populist movements of the past. The best illustration of this collapse is the campaign and early presidency of Barack Obama.

And with moderates and conservatives convinced that Obama's policies will fundamentally alter our capitalist system, there has been an explosion of right-wing reactions against Obama, which we will discuss at length in Chapters 5 through 7.

POPULISM: THE NEW CENTRISM

The question remains: Why?

Why did a president who had won the White House with a majority of independent voters, who was (by far) the most admired politician in the country, and who had the political power to stand up to hardcore ideologues to his left and right, veer so sharply leftward?

The answer is that Team Obama vastly misinterpreted its mandate, and has continued to misinterpret the sentiments driving the American electorate. And that sentiment has been, overwhelmingly, that the political class must go, because it has failed to listen to and meet the needs of the American mainstream.

The vicious convergence of globalization, economic dislocation, government malfunction, sharp declines in trust, belief in the future, and overall contentedness, have led to the perfect storm that is this new populist revolt. The impact of these forces is felt all the more acutely thanks to the digital age in which we live. Combined with the utter failure of government to protect ordinary Americans from devastating change, it is clear that populism is simply more profound and more powerful than populist movements of the past.

This is a difference not in tone but in scale. As we've demonstrated, populism has been part and parcel of our politics since the founding of the Union. But imagine populism of the past as a flashlight, illuminating previous crisis moments in American life. Now imagine the new populist revolt of the 21st century as a laser beam, ripping through the fabric of American politics. There is an energy, an intensity, and a forcefulness of populism that is a direct result of the forces described above, and that makes it fundamentally different than 20th-century populism.

Populism has always existed in American politics, but for the first time it is becoming the dominant force in Washington, in state capitals across the country, and at the ballot box. Left and right populist strains in the American electorate are nothing new. But today they have and will continue to become more prominent than ever.

The dominance of populism is just beginning to become apparent. But as we will demonstrate in the following chapters, new populism will play an outsized role in party politics for the foreseeable future. The impact will be staggering and generational.

THE MAINSTREAM VS. THE POLITICAL CLASS

I think that the political system has gotten so big, that it's turned into its own big business. I don't feel like politicians from either party are really working for the people. I think they're very self-serving. They get in there for these fifteen-year loops where they're getting rich and living an elite lifestyle. To be honest with you, I feel like the government and big business have cooked the books. That it's all a big spin. And the little guys are losing our pensions. My mom? Her pension is shot. She worked her whole life and has lost so much money. The senior citizens and the veterans are getting raw deals. And the bureaucratic spin is so complex that the lawyers can't even figure it out. That's the game.

It seems like a game of musical chairs. And all of the insiders have a chair, and the mom and pops are kept out. The middle class gets stuck paying for the lower class, while the class uses their connections to beat the system. If you're not on the side of the haves or the have-nots, you're *done*.

—Anonymous, Tea Party Express Rally,
Griffith Park, Los Angeles, CA, October 25, 2009

I've probably never been more disenchanted with Washington. And I do think that the Bush administration really extenuated and kind of polarized both parties. I really don't like Nancy Pelosi. I don't think that she works well as Speaker. It seems like her position is: It's our time in the sun and we're going to stick it to the Republicans. I think that there's too much partisanship. It doesn't seem like anyone works together anymore. It seems like basically, it's all about what they think, they're not willing to compromise on anything. And I just think that you have Washington stuck in the mud.

Obviously, I'm a little worried that the Democrats have both majorities, especially in the Senate. Where they can basically pass anything they want, any bill or anything else that they want to put through there. So I'm kind of worried about that.

But I also think that the way that the Bush Administration handled Iraq and some other things, basically rubber-stamping them all the way through, railroading Congress. I think it's led to partisanship that's really inefficient and holding the country back.

—Jack Sadick, anesthesiologist, 37, Chicago, Illinois

Despite the catastrophic blows dealt in recent years to our economic, political, and social systems—or perhaps, more appropriate, because of them—a very small yet very powerful segment of the American population has grown increasingly wealthy and influential. While millions of workers have been forced out of their jobs, while unemployment has skyrocketed and the economy has tanked, this tiny sliver of American society has managed not only to keep its collective head above water, but also to thrive.

Indeed, for this all-important segment of American society—the political elite—things have almost never been better.

Mainstream Americans have grown increasingly aware of the political elite in the wake of the economic crisis of 2008. This exclusive club comprises chieftains in business, government, and the media, who manage the public and private sectors, and for whom our system is fundamentally rigged. They control the nation's banks, think tanks, the flows of news and information, and virtually every lever of power and influence across society. They attend elite schools, are members of elite organizations, and operate within insular social circles.

Because of their extraordinary and concentrated power, and the sophistication of the industries they manage, the odds are tilted obscenely in favor of the political elite. Their top-rate educations provide them with access to sophisticated careers. Their managerial positions in technologically complex sectors in government and business allow them to game the system they control to their own self-interest. And their wealth and social status insulates them from the forces of globalization and economic decline that have ravaged most everyone else.

On the other hand, the American mainstream—by which we mean virtually everyone existing outside of the political elite—has been left out in the rain without so much as a plastic bag to keep them dry. These are ordinary people who come from across the political spectrum, left, right, and center; they are the forgotten majority among whom the inequities of our elite-driven system have inspired broad-based anger. And unlike past anti-elite populist movements, it is not just blue-collar workers and the agrarian poor who have been overcome by anger, fear, and an all-pervasive sense of despair.

Instead, as columnist Frank Rich noted in his December 2009 column for the *New York Times*, the members of this deprived segment are "mostly middle-class refugees from the suburban good life depicted in credit card ads. Their correlative to the Dust Bowl is a coast-to-coast wasteland of foreclosed office spaces where desk chairs and knots of dead phones lie abandoned in a fluorescent half-light."[1]

Yet Rich insists that the differences between the American mainstream and the political elite extend beyond the obvious disparities of privilege, power, and wealth. "This disconnect isn't just about the huge gap in income between the financial sector and the rest of America," Rich writes. "Nor is it just about the inequities of a government bailout that rescued the irresponsible bankers who helped crash the economy while shortchanging the innocent victim of their reckless gambles."[2]

We agree.

What most distinguishes the political elite from the American mainstream is how they fundamentally view the world around them, and their deeply held positions on virtually every major policy issue from global warming to foreign affairs. As David Brooks comments, "The public is not only shifting from left to right. Every single idea associated with the educated class has grown more unpopular." Brooks notes that while the "educated class" (what we call the political elite) believe in global warming, "public skepticism about global warming is on the rise." While the political elite believes in international intervention, the American mainstream has become more isolationist.[3]

Indeed, our own data support Brooks' thesis. Scott's polling at the end of 2009 showed a wide and radical disjunction. By identifying the qualities and characteristics that typify the elite—mainstream divide, Scott was able to demonstrate the growing chasm between these two groups.

Fifty-five percent of Americans overall report that they have grown more conservative in the last year, including 66 percent of the mainstream saying that they have become more conservative (27 percent say they have not). These findings compare to only 24 percent of the political class, which says it has gotten more conservative (with 74 percent saying that they have not).

Two-thirds of all Americans support income tax cuts to spur economic growth, with 80 percent of the mainstream supporting the idea. However, only one-third of the political class supports these cuts.

Eighty percent of mainstream respondents believe the media has become part of the political establishment, while only 4 percent of the political elite agrees with this assessment.

Ninety percent of the mainstream believes that our leaders in D.C. have abandoned their commitment to freedom and liberty, while a mere 24 percent of elites share the same opinion.

We believe this attitudinal divide, in addition to the historic forces previously described earlier is driving the new populist revolt. In this chapter we will precisely define who and what we mean by the divide between the elite and mainstream, as well as analyze and systematically document this growing chasm in American political life. We will show how the future of American politics will be less about what side of the partisan divide one is one, and more about whether one identifies with big government and big business or with ordinary American workers and entrepreneurs. We will explore this polarization through a combination of poll data and narrative to describe how the most significant political battle of the 21st century pits the American mainstream against the political class.

DEFINING THE POLITICAL CLASS

The culture and interests of what we call the political elite have overrun Washington. A self-selecting group of influencers from business, government, academia, and the media now occupy the most prestigious institutional positions in American society and in power centers in Washington.

Membership in the political class is not at all restricted to career politicians. In addition to the countless bureaucrats and policymakers who fill its ranks are people like Roger Altman and Robert Rubin, masters of business who then enter politics; media pundits such as Andrea Mitchell and David Brooks, who shape the manner in which news is presented and analyzed; and corporate moguls from Silicon Valley to Wall Street, who have an outsized influence on policymaking, and who filter through the revolving door between big business and big government.

How do you know whether you're in one group or another? Members of the political class might be tempted to respond, "Well, if you have to ask . . ." But to leave no doubt, Scott Rasmussen has developed an indispensable Political Class Index to identify who belongs in the political class and those who would be classified as mainstream Americans. He posed three questions to survey respondents:

1. Generally speaking, when it comes to important national issues, whose judgment do you trust more, the American people or America's political leaders?
   Those in the mainstream say the American people; those in the political elite say political leaders.

2. Some people believe that the federal government has become a special-interest group that looks out primarily for its own interests. Has the federal government become a special interest group?
   Mainstreamers say yes; the political elite says no.

3. Do government and big business often work together in ways that hurt consumers and investors?
   Mainstreamers say yes; the political elite says no.

Based on exhaustive research, Scott determined that 55 percent Americans could be classified on the mainstream side of the political divide, while only 7 percent make up the elite. When "leaners" were included, those figures increased to 75 percent and 14 percent respectively. It's particularly notable that these figures cut across political parties: an even percentage of Republicans and Democrats are identified as mainstream, along with large numbers of unaffiliated voters. Moreover, the telling factor here is that according to Scott's polling, the mainstream is growing.

When we describe the political elite as a "self-selecting group of influencers," we largely agree with the characterization offered in a 1995 *Harper's* article by Michael Lind, who wrote: "The closer you come to the centers of American politics and society, the more everyone begins to look the same. . . . The people who run big business bear a remarkable resemblance to the people who run big labor, who in turn might be mistaken for the people in charge of the media and the universities. They are the same people . . . most of the members of the American elites went to one of a dozen Ivy League colleges or top state universities. . . . They talk the same. They walk the same."[4]

This is one of the crucial reasons why the political class includes Democrats and Republicans and Independents, and why this political class tends to agree on the questions Scott posed as well as on specific policy issues. They are united by goals and outlooks more than partisan policy differences.

Above all, they are united in the common conviction that they are the people best suited to run America's government, to make political decisions, and to affect social change. They differ on specifics, but they all agree on a crucial issue: "ordinary" Americans possess neither the talent nor the temperament to make these decisions.

As a result, they regard the current populist upswing with dread, if not terror.

A Brief History of the Political Elite in America

The idea of the political class did not begin with Scott's Political Class Index, though he is the first to measure the cleavage between this specialized group and ordinary Americans on specific questions and issues. Nevertheless, the idea of an American political elite has been around for some time.

In the 19th century, when the country had much more stringent class lines than it does now, membership in the ruling elite was gener-ally dictated by family. Upward mobility always existed, but it wasn't so easy back then to crack into the upper tier occupied by the old blue-blood families of New York and New England, families like the Roo-sevelts and Vanderbilts. As the country opened up and became more democratic, and as society became more technologically complex, the notion of a political class became less about one's ancestors and more about one's talents. In this way, the notion of the meritocratic elite was born.

Today, as David Brooks has written, the American meritocratic elite is more concerned with occupational and intellectual distinction than with bloodlines, though family still counts for something. Brooks de-scribed what he saw as one of the staging grounds for the new political and occupational elite: the *New York Times* wedding page. "The *Times* emphasizes four things about a person—college degrees, graduate de-grees, career path, and parents' profession—for these are the markers of upscale Americans today. . . . And when you look at the *Times* wed-dings page, you can almost feel the force of the mingling SAT scores. It's Dartmouth marries Berkeley, MBA weds Ph.D., Fulbright hitches with Rhodes, Lazard Frères joins with CBS, and summa cum laude embraces summa cum laude."[5]

In place of the old Protestant Establishment, the new educated establishment has set down its own rules and standards. And since it tends to be populated by people with the same backgrounds and attainments, it shares broad values in common. The elite have even transcended old prejudices about race and gender, so that someone like Franklin Raines, son of a janitor, Harvard grad and Rhodes Scholar, or Carly Fiorina, are as much a part of the elite as Paulson et al.

This goes for conservatives and liberals—an important point to bear in mind. As Noam Scheiber, editor of *The New Republic* admit-ted, despite ideological differences and partisan bickering among the elite, "conservative elites are frequently as credentialist, even snobbish, as the liberal elites they scorn. Many conservative pundits and wonks attended top schools, read highbrow publications, and belong to ex-clusive professional societies. They firmly believe that elite credentials signify merit."[6]

They also tend to walk on the exact same turf—geographic turf, that is. The leading political pundits in print and TV, for example, overwhelmingly come from New York or Washington, D.C. Few voices from outside the main political and media centers have a national voice in the mainstream media.

The advent of blogs has leveled the playing field somewhat, but within the main organs of media power today, the range of back-grounds and opinions is vanishingly small. No wonder polls show that ordinary Americans tend to have little or no faith left in mainstream media outlets; the pundits who put forth in columns and Sunday morn-ing panels are often describing a world that mainstream Americans don't recognize.

This homogeneity of background and views might be a mere cos-metic distraction if the political class made decisions that enjoyed public support and supported the public good. But the political elite is un-popular for more than just its insularity; as we will show below, it is unpopular because their decision making has been so often destructive and self-serving. The result of which has been the popular uprising we are witnessing today and which is reshaping our politics.

Notable Elites

It is worth taking a moment not only to describe the political elite, but also to identify a few of the individuals who typify this incredibly influ-ential segment of society. Largely, those who make up the political elite are highly educated, incredibly motivated, and more or less decent people. What sets them apart is the fact that they went to elite schools; held key positions in government, business, and the media; and by dint of their education, power, and insularity have become fabulously wealthy.

There is nothing wrong with being successful—nothing is more American, after all, than craving and achieving wealth and fame. However, the political elite is shockingly out of touch with mainstream America. And the brief biographies below illustrate why this is the case.

Rahm Emanuel is perhaps the quintessential political elite. Emanuel earned degrees from Sarah Lawrence College and Northwestern University before embarking on a political career working for the Democratic Congressional Campaign Committee, Chicago Mayor Richard M. Daley, and President Bill Clinton. After serving as a senior adviser in the Clinton White House, Emanuel did a brief stint as an investment banker at Wasserstein Perella (Dresdner Kleinwort), earning $16.2 million in less than four years. In 2000, Clinton named Emanuel to the Board of Directors of Freddie Mac, and, in 2003, Emanuel used his extraordinary wealth and connections to win election to Congress representing Illinois' 5th District. In 2006, Emanuel was elected chairman of the Democratic Caucus, and, in 2008, he was tapped by Barack Obama as White House Chief of Staff, making him one of the most influential political elites in Washington.

Both Bush and Obama exacerbated the perception of the Washington–Wall Street "revolving door" by filling their Cabinets with quintessential Wall Street insiders who personify the qualities associated with the insular and hyper-connected world of the political elite.

In the Obama administration, economic adviser Larry Summers and Treasury Secretary Tim Geithner have become the whipping boys from both the right- and left-wing strands of the new populist revolt.

Tim Geithner comes from a long line of political class power holders. His maternal grandfather served as a speechwriter and adviser for President Eisenhower; his maternal uncle worked for the State Department; and his father, Peter Geithner, was a specialist in international development, United States Agency for International Development and later, the Ford Foundation. After graduating from Dartmouth University in 1983, having majored in Government, Geithner went on to receive his Masters at the Johns Hopkins School of Advanced International Studies. After receiving his Masters, Geithner began his career in politics at Kissinger Associates, working directly for Henry Kissinger as a book researcher, having been recommended by the dean of Johns Hopkins.

Geithner joined the Treasury Department in 1988 as an attaché to the U.S. Embassy in Tokyo. Between 1998 and 2001, he served as Under Secretary of Treasury for International Affairs under Robert Rubin and Lawrence Summers, and in 2002 became the Director of the International Monetary Fund's policy development and review department. In 2003, he was named President of the Federal Reserve Bank of New York, and presided over the New York Fed, until assuming his post in President Obama's Cabinet as Treasury Secretary.

Geithner has come under fire for his role in overseeing the handling of the collapse of Lehman brothers and the Wall Street and AIG bailouts as Chairman of the New York Fed, and for serving the interests of Wall Street as Secretary of the Treasury. As Jo Becker and Gretchen Morgenson of the *New York Times* point out: "he forged unusually close relationships with executives of Wall Street's giant financial institutions. His actions, as a regulator and later a bailout king, often aligned with the industry's interests and desires, according to interviews with financiers, regulators and analysts and a review of Federal Reserve records."[7]

And Geithner brought his relationships with Wall Street with him when he went to Washington. In the fall of 2009, the Associated Press obtained Geithner's calendars under the Freedom of Information Act. What they found only confirmed these suspicions. As Matt Apuzzo and Daniel Wagner of the Associate Press reported: "Not all players in the market enjoy the same access. In the first seven months of Geithner's tenure, his calendars reflect at least 80 contacts with Blankfein, Dimon, Citigroup Chairman Richard Parsons or Citigroup

CEO Vikram Pandit. . . . *Dimon and Blankfein are members of an exclusive club: Along with executives at Citigroup Inc., they are among a cadre of Wall Street executives who have known Geithner for years, whose multibillion-dollar companies survived the economic crisis with his help, and who can pick up the phone and reach the nation's most powerful economic official. . . .* 'They're people he has relationships with and who he can trust,' said Taylor Griffin, a Treasury Department spokesman during the George W. Bush administration and an adviser to the 2008 presidential campaign of John McCain. Griffin defended Geithner's relationships with industry executives. 'There's only so much time in the day and you can only talk to so many people. You choose the people whose point of view you value.'"[8]

Larry Summers, who Henry Kissinger once said should have a permanent White House office, epitomizes the elite career politician that populists loathe. Upon his graduation from MIT, Summers, the son of two economists and professors at the University of Pennsylvania, and nephew of two Nobel Laureates in economics, went on to Harvard, receiving his Ph.D. in 1982.

In 1983, Summers became one of the youngest tenured professors in Harvard history. He served as a chief economist for the World Bank from 1991 until 1993 when he was appointed Under Secretary for International Affairs and later in the U.S. Department of the Treasury under the Clinton administration. He was appointed Deputy Secretary of the Treasury under Robert Rubin in 1995, succeeding him as Secretary in 1999.

He served as the twenty-seventh president of Harvard University between 2001 and 2006, resigning over the controversy surrounding allegedly sexists comments about why women were underrepresented that he made during a January 2005 Conference on Diversifying the Science and Engineering Workforce. Shortly after his resignation, he joined the hedge fund D. E. Shaw as a part-time managing director.

"Lawrence H. Summers, one of President Obama's top economic

advisers, collected roughly $5.2 million in compensation from hedge fund D. E. Shaw over the past year and was paid more than $2.7 million in speaking fees by several troubled Wall Street firms and other organizations. . . .

"Financial institutions including JPMorgan Chase, Citigroup, Goldman Sachs, Lehman Brothers and Merrill Lynch paid Summers for speaking appearances in 2008. Fees ranged from $45,000 for a Nov. 12 Merrill Lynch appearance to *$135,000 for an April 16 visit to Goldman Sachs*, according to his disclosure form." [9]

Members of the political class can be found in both political parties.

There is no better example of the revolving door between business and government among the political elite than Hank Paulson. Paulson graduated Phi Beta Kappa from Dartmouth College in 1968, and received his MBA from Harvard Business School in 1970. From 1970 to 1972, Paulson served as Staff Assistant to the Assistant Secretary of Defense, and then as Staff Assistant to President Nixon from 1972 to 1973. In 1974, Paulson began a long career at Goldman Sachs. He became Goldman's CEO in 1999. His compensation package, according to reports, was $37 million in 2005, and $16.4 million projected for 2006. His net worth has been estimated at over $700 million.[10] Paulson served as President Bush's Secretary of the Treasury from 2005 to the end of the Bush administration, during which time he orchestrated the historic bailout of the financial industry—including, not surprising, Goldman Sachs.

Kenneth M. Duberstein is often referred to as "Counselor to the Presidents,"[11] in reference to over three decades that he has spent inside the beltway, influencing domestic and foreign policy, as well as providing strategic counsel to the private sector. He graduated from Franklin & Marshall College in 1965, after which he worked as an assistant for Senator Jacob Javits of New York. After receiving his Masters from American University in 1967, he worked in a variety of capacities in the Ford and Reagan administrations, including as President Reagan's chief of staff. Duberstein perfectly illustrates the nexus between business, government, and the media that characterizes the political elite.

Duberstein lives in Washington, D.C., with his wife, Jacqueline Duberstein, a producer of the *Charlie Rose Show*. He is a director of several major corporations, including Boeing and Travelers, and has previously sat on the board of Fannie Mae. Duberstein is also a trustee of the powerful, elite think tank, the Brookings Institution.

Most notable, however, these men move easily between the public sector, epicenters of power in Washington, and important posts in the mass media. We describe this flow as the "revolving door" by which the elite maintains the status quo, enriches itself, and perpetuates the policies that have been disastrous to mainstream America.

Collusion Among the Political Elite and the Revolving Door

I think that leaders in Washington are totally tuned out. I think that they're totally bought out by special interests and lobbyists. All those people in Washington are getting campaign money some way or another—and it's influencing how they handle their positions and the bills that they're supporting. It's bad. And it really validates my concern that less government is better. I think they should be seen and not heard. I think they should have a low profile.

—Ralph Sproveer, Chicago

Left- and right-wing populists are united by a general anger that has erupted over what they perceive as the collusion of the political class, in Washington and on Wall Street.

On the right, writes *New York Times* columnist Ross Douthat, the Tea Party movement has "become the vessel for a year's worth of anxieties about bailouts, deficits and Beltway incompetence. This August's town-hall fury wasn't just about the details of health care. Neither were the anti-Obama protests that crowded Washington over the weekend. They were about the Wall Street bailout, the G.M. takeover, the A.I.G. bonuses, and countless smaller examples of middle-income Americans' 'playing by the rules,' as [GOP pollster Frank] Luntz puts it, 'and having someone else benefit.'"[12]

On the left, writes *Salon's* Glenn Greenwald, "It is true that the federal government embraces redistributive policies and that middle-class income is seized in order that 'someone else benefits.' But so obviously, that 'someone else' who is benefiting is not the poor and lower classes— who continue to get poorer as the numbers living below the poverty line expand and the rich-poor gap grows in the U.S. to unprecedented proportions. The 'someone else' that is benefiting from Washington policies are—as usual—the super-rich, the tiny number of huge corporations which literally own and control the Government." [13]

The close ties among the political elite in business, government, and the media is a defining aspect of this incredibly powerful minority. And it allows them to collude in ways that infuriate the public.

As Simon Johnson pointed out in May 2009, just consider the power of Goldman Sachs to infiltrate the corridors of Washington: "The flow of Goldman alumni—including Jon Corzine, now the governor of New Jersey, along with Rubin and Paulson—not only placed people with Wall Street's worldview in the halls of power; it also helped create an image of Goldman (inside the Beltway, at least) as an institution that was itself almost a form of public service." [14]

Rubin had been co-chairman of Goldman Sachs before becoming President Clinton's Treasury Secretary. He later became chairman of Citigroup's executive committee. Another former CEO of Goldman— Hank Paulson, who presided over the investment bank during the long boom—later became George W. Bush's Treasury Secretary. After leaving the Fed, Greenspan himself became a consultant to Pimco, perhaps the biggest player in international bond markets. Jamie Dimon, JPMorgan's CEO, sits on the board of directors of the Federal Reserve Bank of New York, which, along with the Treasury Department, brokered the deal for JPMorgan to buy out Bear Stearns.

The list goes on and on like this, and not just at Treasury but at virtually all the major Washington power centers. It provides an incredibly close linkage between government and business, entrenching the political elite and concentrating their power.

The elite, of course, see nothing wrong with this picture. Americans saw yet another example of this at the outset of President Obama's term, when former Senate Democratic leader Tom Daschle was poised to become Health and Human Services Secretary, a post from which he would lead the president's healthcare reform efforts.

Daschle, however, soon ran into trouble with a variety of tax problems—including failure to pay at least $128,000 in back taxes— and withdrew his nomination to avoid causing controversy for the president. It's striking, though, what wasn't considered controversial: that Daschle had, since leaving the Senate, served as a corporate lobbyist, in which, as Glenn Greenwald described it, he earned huge sums by "telling large corporations and wealthy individuals how they can get the legislation that they want from the Congress, including giving advice to the very companies and giving speeches to the very companies that he would have ended up regulating as part of his duties as Health and Human Services secretary."[15]

Daschle made at least $5 million lending his name and influence to businesses, including at least a quarter-million from healthcare companies. But New York Times columnist David Brooks, a charter member of the political class, dismissed concerns about Daschle's lobbying work, painting Obama and his supporters as naïve idealists who didn't understand how Washington works.

In sum, in the insular world of the political elite, the revolving door between business, government, and the media provides a means by which the elite can collude with something approaching impunity.

DEFINING THE AMERICAN MAINSTREAM

The American mainstream is comprised of ordinary people from across the political spectrum, left, right, and center. These Americans have always believed that if they worked hard and paid their taxes, things would work out in the end and they would get ahead. They'd do better than their parents and set their children on a path to greater opportunities. Now they feel that the traditional hard-work mantra hasn't paid off, and they blame the political elite for what has gone wrong with the American Dream.

Mainstream Americans are profoundly disillusioned by the actions of the political elite, which they view—rightly so—as out of touch with their needs and concerns. These everyday Americans value the principles of self-governance and personal freedom. They believe in opportunity, fair reward for effort, and the centrality of hard work. Individual achievement and social commitment are fundamental to the pursuit of happiness, and they believe that members of the political elite have violated these principles at the expense of ordinary American citizens.

Generally speaking, mainstream Americans are offended by the cronyism and nepotism of those in elite circles, who play by a different set of rules. In fact, a recent Rasmussen Reports survey found that 57 percent of the American mainstream would like to replace the entire Congress, and 74 percent trust their own economic judgment more than that of their duly elected representatives in Washington.

And it's easy to see why. Mainstream America has taken it on the chin over the last several decades. As Ruy A. Teixeira and Joel Rogers wrote in "America's Forgotten Majority," published in the June 2000 edition of the *Atlantic Monthly*, "From 1979 to 1999, the average real hourly wage rose 14 percent for those with college degrees and 19 percent for those with advanced degrees. In contrast, average wages fell by four percent for those with only some college, 10 percent for those with only a high school diploma, and a stunning 24 percent for high school dropouts. Men among the latter three groups did even worse: they were down seven, 15, and 27 percent respectively." [16]

Amid all the economic euphoria of the two decades before the Great Recession, this largest segment of the American electorate didn't see itself going forward, but backward, losing ground while the political elite celebrated the glories of untrammeled free markets.

Neither Republican nor Democratic economic policies have done a whole lot to address the economic anxieties and struggles of this group, and, in part, that may have to do with the fact that they're not well understood by the political elite, who are rather well-to-do. Case in point: the median household income in 2000 was $42,000; about two-thirds of Americans had incomes between $15,000 and $75,000.

Clearly, the American mainstream is far removed from the power suites of the political elite. And the political elite has little interaction with or knowledge of the true lives that most Americans lead. This chasm has exacerbated the forces that are stoking the populist fires across the country—a dynamic we will explore below.

The Great Divide (aka, the Palin Effect)

Despite what the mainstream media has to say, the divide between Democrats and Republicans is not the most important or the most interesting dynamic in American politics today. Far more important is the widening gulf between the beliefs and attitudes of the political elite and those of mainstream America. Consider that according to Scott's polling:

- Eighty-six percent of the political elite believes that the nation is heading in the right direction, while only 19 percent of mainstream Americans agree.
- A plurality of political elite respondents believe that the economy is improving, while 66 percent of mainstream Americans believe that it's getting worse.
- By a 62–10 margin, the political elite believe that government today reflects the will of the people; by a 79–10 margin, mainstream Americans disagree.
- Seventy-four percent of mainstream Americans say that the political system is badly broken, while almost the exact same number of the political elite—77 percent—say that it is not.
- Moreover, 61 percent of mainstream Americans believe a political class dominates government; meanwhile, 74 percent of the political class say there is no political class!

Is it no wonder, then, that a politician like Sarah Palin has aroused the level of public support that she did. Palin was a polarizing figure in the 2008 presidential race, to be sure, with negatives almost as high as her positives. But she was also the biggest crowd draw on the campaign trail next to Barack Obama, and to this day has maintained her rock-star status in the Heartland.

When Palin spoke out against "elites," when she pledged to fight for "Joe Six Pack" and "Hockey moms across the nation," the political class snickered and derided her. But millions of other Americans felt that they had finally found someone like them, someone who knew what it was like to live the way they did.

True to its insular nature, the political class demonstrated bewilderment about Palin from the outset. Yes, she was deeply flawed as a vice-presidential candidate, and, in our opinion, not close to being qualified for the number-two job. But the mainstream media and the political class seemed not even to attempt to understand what her appeal might be. The more the media attacked her, of course, the more a segment of the American electorate identified with her.

Palin almost seemed to set off a certain trip wire within the political class regarding access to power: she didn't meet their standards, and they felt threatened by her. Even when she stepped down as Alaska governor and announced that she had a book deal—hardly unusual for a politician with her national name recognition—pundits couldn't resist being dismissive. In an entry on the *Huffington Post*, CNN political commentator Paul Begala asked his readers to "ponder the fact that Rupert Murdoch's HarperCollins publishing house is paying this, umm, writer $11 million for a book." [17]

The way many mainstream Americans see it, the political elite is engaged in an active effort to close off opportunities and advancement to all but those who belong to the exclusive ranks of that same elite. As their resentment grows, so does the divide on issues, big and small, driving populism in America to new heights.

ON THE ISSUES

In June 2009, at a 35th anniversary class reunion of the Harvard Class of 1974, alumni were asked to fill out a questionnaire on their lives and attitudes. Their answers provide a useful insight into the outlook of the political class on how they see their lives and how they see the country:

* Eighty-six percent said Harvard opened doors for them that would not have opened otherwise.
* Eighty percent felt that their career was on the right track, and 92 percent felt the same way about their personal lives.
* Seventy-eight percent believed that the United States was on the right track.
* Confidence in President Obama was high: 83 percent on the economy and 86 percent on foreign policy.
* Seventy-five percent said that their best years were ahead.

Now consider some recent polling data of the broader American population: A Pew survey in May 2009 found that 71 percent agreed, "today it's really true that the rich just get richer while the poor get poorer."

Scott's polling has revealed a whole set of issues on which the American people's outlook is much less rosy than the Harvard Class of 1974. Only 27 percent of Americans now think that the next generation will be better off than their parents. And just 33 percent of workers believe their next job will be better than the one they currently have.

Doug's Aspen research revealed that just two in ten Americans think of the American Dream as "alive and well."

The philosophical divide that Scott identified with his Political Class Index takes on substantive form when applied to current policy debates, but it's important to remember that it goes deeper than public policy. It really reflects fundamentally different ways of looking at the world by two groups of people who have less and less in common with one another.

On many issues, there is a bigger gap between the political elite and mainstream Americans than between mainstream Republicans and mainstream Democrats. Before getting to specific policy positions, though, consider the gulf between the two groups on broader, perceptual issues. They give a good indication of how differently the two groups see the world. Here's a small sample:

- By a 69–15 margin, mainstream Americans believe that voter approval should be required for all tax increases; 74 percent of the political class disagrees.
- Eighty-five percent of mainstream Americans say that the two parties should pay for their own primaries and conventions; just 45 percent of the political class agrees.
- Seventy-six percent of mainstream Americans believe that members of Congress are overpaid; most in the political class say they're paid about the right amount.

At the same time, a shocking amount of agreement exists between mainstream Americans on key issues, regardless of party affiliation. Consider the following statistic. Seventy percent of U.S. voters believe that big business and big government generally work together against the interests of investors and consumers, according to Rasmussen Reports.

This figure includes equal numbers of Democrats and Republicans: 71 percent of Democrats believe big government and big business are on the same team, as do 69 percent of Republicans and 69 percent of those not affiliated with either major party. In other words, there are no significant differences to be found by gender, age, race, or ideology on this point.

This divide is present across a range of issues.

Taxes

A profound majority of mainstream Americans believes that tax increases hurt the economy and that tax cuts help the economy. Members of the political class believe exactly the opposite. Mainstream Americans strongly believe that more taxation is harmful to the economy (74 percent) and that tax cuts are beneficial (69 percent). By contrast, the political class doesn't see it that way at all; just 19 percent worry that tax increases hurt the economy, and a mere 33 percent think cutting people's taxes does much good for the economy. Again, these mainstream and political class responses cut across party lines.

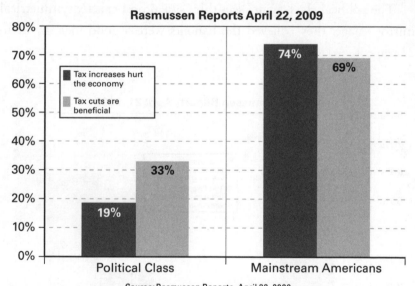

Source: Rasmussen Reports, April 22, 2009.

Government Bailouts

The financial emergencies of 2008 and 2009 also drew clear lines in the sand between the American mainstream and the political class. The two groups disagree fundamentally on government bailouts of

financial institutions. Mainstream Americans tend to see powerful institutions like AIG, Citigroup, and Bear Stearns as part of the problem
that created the mess, not institutions worthy of blank checks from
the federal government. Eighty percent of respondents told Rasmussen Reports that the bailout money was going to the very firms that
caused the financial crisis in the first place. By a 59–26 margin, they
believed that the financial-industry bailouts were a bad idea. This of
course explains their distaste for the obscene bonuses these firms paid
out with taxpayer dollars (bonuses that, for the record, wouldn't have
been an issue if the markets had ruled; AIG would simply have gone
out of business. Though, to be fair, much of the American economy
might have followed).

The political class, again, sees things in almost exactly symmetrical
mirror image: they believed the bailouts were a good idea, by 61 to
23 percent.

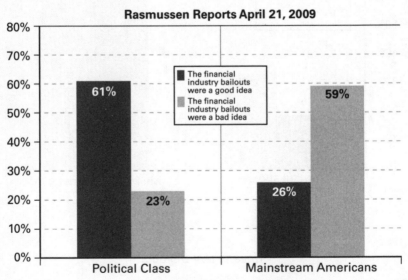

Source: Rasmussen Reports, April 21, 2009.

Government-Business Collusion

The political elite and mainstream Americans disagree fundamentally on whether or not politicians should return campaign contributions that they had received from bailed-out financial giant AIG. Seventy-seven percent of mainstream Americans said that politicians should return such contributions, while the exact same percentage of the political class disagreed. Again, the party lines don't matter much here: 74 percent of mainstream Democrats believe the campaign cash should be returned. So did 78 percent of mainstream Republicans, as well as 78 percent of those mainstreamers not affiliated with either major party.

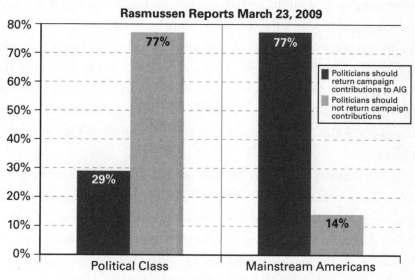

Source: Rasmussen Reports, March 23, 2009.

Immigration

The immigration debate also shows the gulf between ordinary Americans and elites. According to a Rasmussen poll in April 2009, 66 percent of likely voters nationwide said that it was "very important" for the government to improve its enforcement of the borders and reduce illegal immigration, but only 32 percent of the political elite agreed.

An even more dramatic gap has opened up on the question of legalizing the status of illegal aliens. Voters nationwide were evenly divided on whether this issue was an important part of immigration reform: 48 percent said it was important while 45 percent said it wasn't. By contrast, a whopping 74 percent of the political class considered legalizing the status of illegal residents important and worthwhile.

THE RIGGED SYSTEM

As demonstrated above, the estrangement that mainstream Americans feel from the political elite has nothing to do with partisan politics, and everything to do with the everyday reality that the mainstream is experiencing, and to which the elite are essentially blind.

In the previous chapter, we identified several main forces that are driving the populist revolt: globalization, economic collapse, and political stagnation. These forces have devastated the lives of tens of millions of hardworking Americans. However, in a perverse way, members of the political elite have benefited enormously from these systemic cataclysms.

Globalization has led to the loss of 5 million manufacturing jobs since the inception of NAFTA in 1997. While millions of mainstream American families contend with these extraordinary losses, the political elite in business and government have benefited from increased corporate profits and decreased tax liabilities. Political stagnation has frustrated the electorate to no end, but it has kept the political elite in power and preserved the status quo. This has locked mainstream Americans out of their own government, while allowing the elite to continue to enrich and entrench themselves.

The result of these gross inequities is the pervasive sense among mainstream Americans that the system is rigged. We do not use this word to be provocative or bombastic. We use it because, in Scott's polling, most Americans feel this way. And, indeed, in many ways they are right: the system is rigged against them.

The truth of the matter is, not only have the political elite benefited from the forces that have destroyed the lives of so many Americans. In many ways, *they are responsible for the creation of this crisis in the first place.*

The financial downturn that exploded during the fall of 2008 was preceded by two decades of deregulation and irresponsibility on the part of the political elite members on Wall Street and in Washington. Prior to the economic downturn, the political class as a whole was overwhelmingly "mesmerized by Wall Street, always and utterly convinced that whatever the banks said was true,"[18] wrote Simon Johnson, a former chief economist of the International Monetary Fund. Financial elites in both the government and Wall Street, Johnson argued, had become so powerful as to give the "financial sector a veto over public policy."

Johnson's argument is crucial in pointing not just to Wall Street, but also to Washington: the typical line of defense after the market meltdown and financial crisis was that Washington regulators had been muzzled by the overpowering political clout of the Wall Streeters, but that isn't what happened. For the most part, Washington happily went along with the deregulatory ride.

You can literally take your pick of any number of destructive policy choices that over the past ten years have enriched the political elite and damaged the lives of the mainstream.

The Gramm-Leach-Bliley Act of 1999 repealed the Glass-Steagall Act and allowed, for the first time, commercial and investment banks to merge. There is no telling how many millionaires were made among the political elite in the years that followed. This policy reversal was strictly meant to benefit the elite, at the expense of mainstream America.

Fannie Mae and Freddie Mac spurred by perverse incentives, such as lending to "sub-prime" mortgage holders, soon grew "too big to fail." When they did, it wasn't the elite that paid the biggest prices. Sure, some rich people lost some money. But they were immediately bailed out by Washington, and quickly recovered their losses. Meanwhile, millions of ordinary Americans lost their homes, lost their jobs, and will likely never recover from these disastrous loses.

The Federal Reserve, the SEC, and private Wall Street regulators all failed—or perhaps it should be said, flat-out refused—to monitor the risks associated with the derivatives market adequately. The Fed kept lowering interest rates, prompting a marked increase in unchecked subprime-mortgage lending, which led to a housing bubble that proved nearly fatal for the U.S. economic system. Again, this further enriched the political class, and terribly damaged the mainstream.

While all of this went on, the political class in Washington and on Wall Street—and their enablers in the mainstream media—cheered on the brave new market. Only a few intrepid souls, like Brooklsey Born at the Commodity Futures Trading Commission, dared to question the fierce logic of the deregulatory climate. Born pushed in 1998 for regulation of over-the-counter derivatives, particularly the highly complex instruments known as credit default swaps (which would later play such an important role in the downfall of AIG).

But Born's concerns and recommendations were set aside, quashed by the most powerful of elite trios: SEC Chairman Arthur Levitt, Fed Chairman Alan Greenspan, and Treasury Secretary Robert Rubin. Other efforts were similarly thwarted by political elites in Washington and the financial sector. Greenspan led the way, opposing regulation, lowering interest rates to make borrowing money ever easier, and continually preaching the value of market innovation. Fannie and Freddie, for their parts, were protected from stricter regulation of their loose lending practices by a number of Democrats with ties to the banking industry, including Representative Barney Frank and Senator Chris Dodd.

The prevailing political-class attitude may have been best summed up by assistant Treasury Secretary Darcy E. Bradbury, who said in 1994 that the Treasury had "no intention of telling corporate America that they can't make or lose money any way they want." It doesn't get much blunter than that. Washington insiders—liberal and conservative, Democrat and Republican—were convinced that the free flow of capital and a free hand for major financial institutions in creating financial products were the right policies for the U.S. economy and would regulate themselves.

We all know it didn't work out that way. But the banks didn't suffer the consequences; mainstream America did. Look no further than the banks that were seized by the federal government during the financial crisis. As Simon Johnson smartly notes, these banks are stronger and more powerful than ever: "Big banks, it seems, have only gained political strength since the crisis began. And this is not surprising. With the financial system so fragile, the damage that a major bank failure could cause—Lehman was small relative to Citigroup or Bank of America—is much greater than it would be during ordinary times. The banks have been exploiting this fear as they wring favorable deals out of Washington. Bank of America obtained its second bailout package (in January) after warning the government that it might not be able to go through with the acquisition of Merrill Lynch, a prospect that Treasury did not want to consider." [19]

There are any number of examples that demonstrate how the system is fundamentally rigged *by* the political class to *benefit* the political class. And it comes as no surprise that this rigging has resulted, over time, in fabulous wealth for the elite and tremendous economic pain for the mainstream.

But the mainstream can only endure so much pain from this rigged system before it comes crashing down around the heads of the political elite. And that is precisely what we are experiencing today with the explosion of new populism.

POPULISM RISING

We constantly hear about the divide between Republicans and Democrats on issue after issue. In some areas, like health care, there are legitimate grounds for looking at things through that traditional partisan lens. But as our polling data shows, in many cases the starkest divide on issues, attitudes, and outlooks is not between conservative and liberal, Republican and Democrat, but between mainstream Americans and the political class.

The political class stands alone, separate and divorced from every other American group; you're either in the meritocratic elite, or you're not; you're either one of the influencers of opinion, one of the power brokers in Washington or Wall Street, one of the technocratic elite with Ivy League pedigree and a lifestyle comfortable and affluent, or you're not. And if you're not, you have that in common with everyone else.

That makes the mainstream an enormous—but also sometimes amorphous—group. As we've shown, there are certain broad attitudes they share toward Washington and toward big business, toward corporate greed and political self-seeking. In the broadest sense, the political class tends to trust power, and why not, since they're the ones wielding it and benefiting from it. Meanwhile, the American mainstream tends to be much more skeptical of it. After all, they've seen the consequences of the system that is rigged against them in so many areas of their lives.

As a result, a resurgent populism has surfaced within the broad mainstream that seems clearly to be more than a passing trend. Born of the very mainstream-political class divide that we've described in this chapter, it has shot off into two distinct and potent directions: left-wing populism, which pushes for a redistribution of wealth, higher taxes for the wealthy, confiscatory taxation of executive bonuses, and universal health care; and right-wing populism, which seeks smaller government, stronger states' rights, less taxation, and market-based solutions to the problems of health care and education.

These are the twin engines driving the mainstream-political class breakdown in American life today; the most politically motivated and determined members of the American mainstream. They're having an impact on the policy debate and the way politics is done in Washington, and they aren't just going to go away, as the political elite might hope, anytime soon.

These populist movements deserve our detailed attention, and they are the focus of the next four chapters.

THE EVOLUTION OF THE TEA PARTY MOVEMENT

"When we finished our last tour, we weren't going to go on another tour until 2010, and then one week later they announced that we're doing another tour. I think we're going to keep the momentum going. I think that it's what we need to do for our country. Keep people inspired. People in Washington think that we're just going to die out. . . . One of the people who started that organization started the TPX, so they asked me to come on board. I'd say that I'm probably more of a social issue person. I'm more concerned about abortion. But I believe in the movement," said singer Diana Nagy on board one of the two Tea Party Express coach buses. Nagy traveled with the first TPX tour as well, performing "When Freedom Flies," an original song that she wrote honoring American troops while working with Move America Forward, the nation's largest grassroots pro-troop organization.

There were two mass gatherings of people in 2009. The first was expected and universally applauded; the second was unrecognized, misunderstood, and not even fully documented.

The first event was, of course, Barack Obama's inauguration on January 20, 2009, when 1.8 million people amassed on the National Mall to hear the President's ringing speech, in which he said: "On this day, we gather because we have chosen hope over fear, unity of purpose over conflict and discord. On this day, we come to proclaim an end to the petty grievances and false promises, the recriminations and worn-out dogmas, that for far too long have strangled our politics."[1]

Quite justifiably, it was seen as one of the great inaugural turnouts in American political history, a validation of his historic campaign.

But the other gathering, which perhaps did not have as many people, was the march on Washington on September 12, 2009, when tens if not hundreds of thousands of people traveled to Washington, D.C., where they gathered near the steps of the capital to hear speakers, including FreedomWorks' Dick Armey and Brendan Steinhauser, the Tea Party Patriots' Jenny Beth Martin, and the Tea Party Express' Lloyd Marcus.

Unlike the Obama inauguration, which was a centrally organized state-sponsored event, this was a spontaneous outpouring of support. While it was mobilized in part by Fox News host Glenn Beck, it also reflected deep-seated anger about the direction and shape of government and extraordinary outpourings of spontaneous support, which led organizers to say that their movement was at least as strong and at least as powerful as the one that elected Barack Obama.

And while that may be a bit of an exaggeration, it's not by much.

How did this all happen? It began with thousands of small gatherings, many of them spontaneous, over the course of 2009. This chapter looks at how the movement developed, why it developed, and results the political world is still reeling from today.

The question has been asked of whether the Tea Party is an authentic national movement with broad-based support, or a more limited narrow movement that has only been able to produce real crowds and real enthusiasm because of so-called Astroturf.

Fortunately, a large amount of research has been done by a wide variety of organizations that answer the question definitively.

First, the Tea Party movement is broad-based with wide support. As we will discuss in depth in Chapter 7, over half of the electorate now say they favor the Tea Party movement, around 35 percent say they support the movement, 20 to 25 percent self-identify as members of the movement, and 2 to 7% say they are activists.

And Tea Party protesters see themselves as being part of the major-ity in America. Eight-eight percent of self-identified tea partiers think most Americans view the Tea Party movement favorably.

Indeed, in our February 2010 survey, 49 percent of respondents said that more people should get involved in the Tea Party movement, while only 34 percent said they should not.

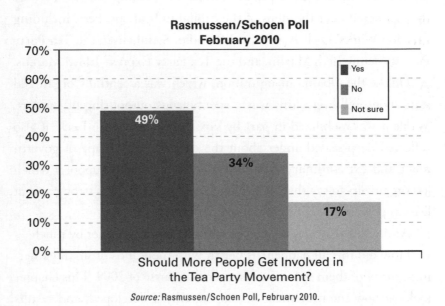

Source: Rasmussen/Schoen Poll, February 2010.

The data is particularly clear, and some polls have shown that the Tea Party movement is the most popular force in American politics.

A REAL MOVEMENT

Approaching the New York State capital building, the chanting of the crowd grew louder. The New York State Tea Party Convention was scheduled to begin at noon, but the park in front of the capital was teeming with more than one thousand protestors well beforehand.

Nancy Pelosi famously dismissed the April 15, 2009, Tea Parties as "Astroturf"—fake grassroots events. But at the right-wing rally in Albany on June 16, one thing was immediately clear: the protesters were loud, they were impassioned, and, most of all, they were angry.

This was no perfunctory rally for the sake of putting on a good show. This was no Astroturf event masquerading as a popular uprising. This was the real deal.

As the clock struck noon, a folk band broke into "Proud to Be an American." Erik Anderson, president of the We Surround Rochester organization and chief organizer of the day's event, took the stage, megaphone in tow.

"Think about our United States Senators, Gillibrand and Schumer," Anderson bellowed. "Do you think they're representing you?" The crowd responded with a unanimous chorus of "NOOOOOOOOOO!" as the band launched into "Blowin' in the Wind."

Many protestors had taken a day off work to attend the Albany rally, traveling by bus, plane, and train from as far away as Long Island and Buffalo. Some in the crowd were dressed in colonial garb, others sported feathers in their hair, and many were wearing T-shirts that had been custom-made by local organizations. Nearly everyone in sight was waving homemade signs with slogans such as: GIVE ME LIBERTY NO DEBT, CAR CZARS AND INTERNET CZARS, and WE THE PEOPLE ARE NOT HAPPY—NO NATIONAL HEALTH CARE.

What united every Tea Party protestor in East Capitol Park was a profound sense of anger at the mega bailouts for corporate America, at economic policies that failed to produce tangible benefits for workers and families, at a ballooning federal deficit and ever-expanding size and scope of the federal government, and at elected leaders both in Albany and in Washington.

"It has nothing to do with Democrat or Republican, what it comes down to is *representation*," explained Lisa, a Tea Party organizer from Rochester. "Our voices aren't being heard by our president and legislators, both here in Albany or in Washington, D.C. They are *absolutely* out of touch. Trust me, I've tried everything I could think of to reach out to the people who are supposed to be representing me. I've called

Schumer's office. I've emailed [Governor] Paterson. What do I get back? Automated emails. They just do not care what I have to say."

In interview after interview in Albany, we heard the same thing. An unresponsive state and federal government. Policymakers simply ignoring their constituents. Taxpayers picking up the tab for costly legislative initiatives. The deck stacked against ordinary Americans.

"Frankly I'm tired of being taxed," explained Jen, a protestor from Syracuse who took off a day from work to make the trip to the Tea Party convention. "I'm tired of the nonsense that goes on in Albany, disgusted by the fact that they behave like babies. . . . I want to see a lot less government in my life, period.

"I don't think that they have a constitutional right to take someone's money and give it to someone else," Jen told us. "It is absolutely a redistribution of wealth and I am *absolutely* against it."

In the background, Anderson continues his speech to the crowd.

"The Bush and now Obama administration," Anderson chants, have allowed "unelected car czars and Internet czars" to control the lives and livelihoods of hardworking Americans.

"New York," Anderson decrees, "is run by a gang of three: the Governor, the Senate Majority Leader, and the Assembly Majority leader. This is *not* a constitutional governing system," he continues, as the crowd becomes increasingly raucous with each word he speaks. "This isn't even socialism. *This is tyranny*," he concludes; the crowd erupts in a chorus of *"Booooo!"*

Hundreds of protesters turn toward the capital and begin to chant: "Kick them out! Kick them out!"

At a table near the side of the stage, is an Albany native named Hal, in his early 50s and sporting an American flag ball cap. Hal was selling Tea Party Patriot T-shirts with his wife and daughter. Asked why his family decided to attend the rally, he didn't miss a beat: "What we are protesting are corrupt career politicians, tax increases, excessive and wasteful government and intrusive government policies. Democrats *and* Republicans are at fault. These things have been accelerated by Obama certainly, but both Clinton and Bush are to blame too."

What happened in Albany in June 2009 was no anomaly. Over the course of 2009, we were on hand to witness the emergence of a powerful new political movement in American politics: right-wing populism.

Nobody saw it coming.

Some in this movement are first-time political activists. Some are old-school populist crusaders from previous conservative movements, such as Prop13 and Contract With America. Together, they are a diverse group of angry, frustrated, and mobilized conservatives. Their movement is historic because it is unprecedented.

Never before has the different strands of the conservative movement been united under one roof. The Tea Party movement has given voice to an incredible spectrum of voices on the right: economic conservatives, small government libertarians, social conservatives, and the religious right. Over the years, each of these right-wing blocs has had their moment in the sun. During the 1980s, economic conservatives brought about the Reagan revolution. During the '90s, social conservatives and the Christian right swept in the Gingrich revolution.

The 2010s, however, could well be defined by the Tea Party revolution: the first broad-based conservative movement to unify the three strands of the American right.

This is a historic development overlooked by pundits and prognosticators. Indeed, the Tea Party movement is real and continues to grow exponentially. It is not simply an equal and opposite reaction to the Obama administration and its liberal leaning policies. It is a movement with deep roots accelerated by economic, social, and political exigencies. The result is that a new conservative populist force in American politics has begun to influence and decide local elections, for example, in New York's 23rd District, as we will discuss below.

The movement has been underestimated, under-appreciated and

under-acknowledged. But through our firsthand experience on Tea Party bus tours, at Tea Party rallies, and in one-on-one conversations with right-wing populist activists, we have seen this movement coalesce and grow over the course of 2009. And after spending dozens of hours on the road with the Tea Party movement, we know that it is real, it is powerful, and we believe it will play a major role in the 2010-midterm elections and beyond.

THE ORIGINS OF THE TEA PARTY MOVEMENT

Contrary to popular belief, the Tea Party movement didn't begin in Washington, D.C., in 2009 with the inauguration of Barack Obama. As we noted in Chapter 2, we believe it began in 1992, with unprecedented electoral success of Ross Perot, around whom a new populist movement coalesced and has never truly dissipated. Quite the opposite; it is now, almost two decades later, on the ascent.

One could see the beginning of this resurgence on December 16, 2007, in Boston. On that day—the 234th anniversary of the Boston Tea Party—2008 presidential candidate and right-wing populist leader Ron Paul led supporters from the State House to Faneuil Hall.

A little-known libertarian Texas congressman, Paul had inhabited the political fringe. He had formerly attracted the most notice for authoring a raft of radical legislation that never passed committee, such as bills to abolish the federal income tax and the Federal Reserve and to repeal the 1973 war powers resolution that let the president initiate hostilities without a formal declaration of war from congress. His main platform plank was to return America to the gold standard, the last vestige of which was ended by President Nixon in 1971. But Paul was on to something.

In 2007, according to the *Boston Globe*, Paul and his compatriots "re-enacted the dumping of tea in Boston Harbor, by tossing banners that read 'tyranny' and 'no taxation without representation' into boxes that were placed in front of an image of the harbor."[2]

It's worth recalling that this was a year before the 2008 presidential election, and at the end of two terms of the Bush administration and six years of Republican control of Congress. Paul and his supporters were reacting to the dramatic increase in federal spending that occurred under President Bush, and the federal deficit that ballooned along with that spending.

In fact, it's clear today that George W. Bush was no small government, Reagan-era conservative. Any number of independent analyses show that Bush spent more than any other modern-era president, all the way back to LBJ. A few highlights, according to the conservative think tank the Heritage Foundation include:

- Expanding the federal budget by $700 billion.
- A Medicare prescription drug entitlement that will cost $800 billion over ten years.
- Increasing the federal debt by some $2.5 trillion.
- Running budget deficits of $300 billion each year of his presidency.[3]

Say what you will about Bill Clinton, but his fiscally conservative policies, which left the nation a several hundred billion dollar surplus, were thrown out the window by George Bush and an extremely complicit Republican congress.

Certainly, anger over this disastrous level of spending came to a head when the economy imploded at the end of Bush's presidency, fueling a nascent conservative populist movement.

Even conservative commentators like David Boaz have begun to opine for the bygone Clinton-era. Boaz recently wrote, "Suddenly, I find myself nostalgic for Bill Clinton. It comes as a shock. Back in 1996, I denounced his 'breathtaking view of the ability and obligation of government to plan the economy' and his 'profoundly anti-individualist ideas.' But now I have a hazy memory of the Clinton years as a sort of Golden Age. Government spending was growing only slowly, the bad ideas were mostly small, and we bombed a lot of countries but didn't put American troops at risk."[4]

But it's not just conservative commentators. We heard this refrain time and again at Tea Party events throughout 2009. Joe Wierzbicki, on the road with the Tea Party Express bus tour in 2009, had more ire for Bush than Obama: "The problem that people have is eight years of Bush who was supposed to stand for limited government going into out-of-control deficit spending. In the end throwing in the towel on free market principles saying that we have to have bailouts 'for the good of capitalism' which makes no sense."

Mark Williams, an organizer with Our Country Deserves Better PAC, also suggested the right-wing populist movement was really begun as a reaction to the Republican Party betraying its core economic principles: "There was nothing [fiscally] conservative about the Bush administration. . . . I was working up in upstate New York during the last election, and during those last few days of the Bush administration that's when it really started to smolder big time. And when that bailout, that TARP program, I think that's when conservatives truly parted company with W. . . ."

And while Ron Paul, a staunch libertarian, may disagree with the Tea Party movement on a number of social issues, linking the two is the fact that they are constitutionally based, driven by fiscal conservatism, constitutionalism, and States rights.

As Adam Liptak of the *New York Times* explains: "The content of the movement's understanding of the Constitution is not always easy to nail down, and it is almost always arguable. But it certainly includes particular attention to the Constitution's constraints on federal power (as reflected in the limited list of powers granted to Congress in Article I and reserved to the states and the people the 10th Amendment) and on government power generally (the Second Amendment's protection of gun rights, the Fifth Amendment's limits on the government's taking of private property). . . . [I]f there is a central theme to its understanding of the Constitution, it is that the nation's founders knew what they were doing and that their work must be protected."[5]

As Richard Viguerie noted in a December 2009 piece for *American Thinker*:

> The Tea Party Movement, however, is about more than electing new politicians. . . . What's happening in the tea parties is that people are actually using the Constitution to ground and form policy choices, and as a constructive means to hold the political establishment accountable.
>
> Our constitutional system of checks and balances is currently in shambles. Congress refuses to hold the president accountable constitutionally, and the courts refuse to hold the other two branches accountable. . . . The 10th Amendment, intended as a fundamental, "systemic" protection of our constitutional form of government, says that all powers not given expressly to the federal government by the text of the Constitution are reserved to the States or to the people. It is a fail-safe against tyranny.
>
> The 10th Amendment, which has been collecting dust in the closet, is a natural resource for the "leaderless" Tea Party Movement. The way to restrain the abuses of power and create a culture of freedom and economic prosperity lies within the Constitution itself. Tea partiers will use the Constitution, which has been so disregarded by the three branches of government, to tame the beast of tyrannical big government.[6]

In this context, it's important to understand that right-wing populism didn't simply come out of the woodwork in 2009. The seeds of the movement were planted long before. And in the wake of Ron Paul's initial Tea Party, a number of events caused the right-wing populist movement to crystallize and take shape.

RIGHT-WING POPULISM ON THE RISE

On February 16, 2009, Keli Carender, a nose-ring sporting actress used her conservative blog Liberty Belle to organize an anti-stimulus protest rally, which she coined "the porkulus," drawing a crowd of 120 in her home state of Washington.

"I basically thought to myself: 'I have two courses. I can give up, go home, crawl into bed and be really depressed and let it happen,' . . . 'Or I can do something different, and I can find a new avenue to have my voice get out."[7]

"The Porkulus" was a spontaneous, grassroots rebellion, driven by anger and fear of the implications of President Obama's excessive government spending initiatives and frustration with a seemingly out-of-touch and ineffective government. In other words, it was a modern-day Tea Party three days ahead of its time.

The Tea Party movement as we know it today was set in motion on February 19, 2009, when CNBC financial analyst Rick Santelli made an impromptu speech on the floor of the Chicago Mercantile Exchange that became an instant YouTube classic. After voicing his opposition to the "proposed $275 billion deficit-financed homeowner bailout plan and other massive spending measures," Santelli called upon like-minded Americans to make their voices heard with a 21st-century revival of the Boston Tea Party.

"This is America! How many of you people want to pay for your neighbor's mortgage that has an extra bathroom and can't pay their bills?"[8]

Santelli gave voice to a growing sentiment among independent-minded voters in the wake of the bailouts. It wasn't just the sheer size of government spending; it was where those tax dollars were headed. And in the minds of many, they were headed to the undeserving at best, and those who had in fact caused the economic crisis at worst.

What made Santelli's rant so powerful was that it spoke directly to an all-pervasive sense of anger at government spending in general, and those who were receiving it in specific, particularly with respect to Obama's stimulus package and budget, which had been brewing for quite some time.

The bailout of AIG and the creation of the TARP program under Bush were followed by the auto industry bailout under Obama— in effect, a bipartisan government takeover of huge segments of the economy. Obama then followed the auto bailout with a $787 billion economic stimulus program that some right-wing populists dubbed the "porkulus bill": a bailout of profligate state governments and the Democratic interest groups feeding at their troughs that the populists contended would not stimulate the economy or save any private sector jobs. All told, an estimated $2 trillion in government spending added up not only to record deficits, but also to record resentment of the political elite and politicians of both parties in Washington.

Santelli called for a "Chicago tea party" to protest this unprecedented government intervention. His on-air rant was soon a highlight on the Drudge Report. It played on all the cable networks throughout the day, and it was seen more than a million times on YouTube.[9]

Within hours, as the *Weekly Standard*'s John Last noted, Santelli-inspired Tea Party organizing websites sprouted up across the Web, and "on Facebook, dozens of Santelli groups formed, ranging from fan clubs to draft-president movements to tea party plans for Chicago, Texas, New York, and Los Angeles."[10] As Last reported: "ChicagoTea Party.com bills itself as the official home of Santelli's tea party. The site belongs to Zack Christenson, a Chicago radio producer. Christenson had bought the domain last August, thinking it might be a good name for a group. Within 12 hours of Santelli's rant, Christenson had retooled the site, and 4,000 people quickly signed up."[11]

The movement quickly picked up steam with the help of several national conservative organizations. In the weeks that followed, local protests erupted in Cincinnati, Green Bay, and Harrisburg. The mounting Tea Party movement reached its first crescendo on April 15, when over 750 tea parties were held in cities and towns from coast to coast in honor of Tax Day.

In Washington, protestors tossed teabags onto the White House lawn. In Austin, Texas, Gov. Rick Perry energized a crowd of about one thousand, accusing the Obama administration of restricting states' rights and vaguely suggesting that Texas might want to secede from the union.

SUMMER 2009: THE TEA PARTY RESPONSE TO THE HEALTHCARE OVERHAUL

While the Tea Party protest movement was initially focused primarily on President Obama's budget and spending initiatives, as efforts to pass healthcare reform legislation heightened in Washington, President Obama's proposed healthcare reform plan soon became another focal point of the Tea Party movement. The movement saw the proposed legislation as more evidence of Obama's supposed socialism, as a government takeover of one-sixth of the economy that would tax and fine Americans, and curtail their individual rights. On July 17, the Tea Party Patriots organized nationwide events specifically targeting the Obama administration's proposed reform plan, which they referred to as "socialized medicine."

The healthcare debate became a vessel for a series of frustrations. Voters opposed the bailouts that were started by President Bush. They opposed them when continued by Obama, who then upset the populist applecart further by bailing out the auto industry, taking over GM, spending two billion dollars on "cash for clunkers," and failed to achieve quick results with the government stimulus. The sum total of frustration from these and other administration policies and initiatives became rolled up in the healthcare debate. At a fundamental level, the American people felt they simply weren't being listened to.

In this way, right-wing populism came to a head in the summer of 2009. Every year, during the Congressional Recess in August, members of Congress return to their districts to meet face-to-face with their constituents. Oftentimes, members hold town-hall style meetings. In August 2009, anti-healthcare reform protesters flocked to town-hall meetings throughout the country, and these meetings became explosive venues for right-wing populists furious with the economic and social policies of the Obama administration.

The scene was best summarized by *Politico*, as the 2009 Congressional summer recess got under way: "Screaming constituents, protesters dragged out by the cops, congressmen fearful for their safety—welcome to the new town-hall-style meeting, the once-staid forum that is rapidly turning into a house of horrors for members of Congress. On the eve of the August recess, members are reporting meetings that have gone terribly awry, marked by angry, sign-carrying mobs and disruptive behavior. In at least one case, a congressman has stopped holding town hall events because the situation has spiraled so far out of control. 'I had felt they would be pointless,' Rep. Tim Bishop (D-N.Y.) told POLITICO, referring to his recent decision to temporarily suspend the events in his Long Island district. 'There is no point in meeting with my constituents and [to] listen to them and have them listen to you if what is basically an unruly mob prevents you from having an intelligent conversation.' " [12]

Leading many of these heated protests were local and national Tea Party groups, as well as their interest group supporters. A nationwide Tea Party Day was organized to take place on August 22 by right-wing national political organizations, such as American Liberty Alliance, FreedomWorks, and Americans for Prosperity, as well as the new media-community organizing group, The Sam Adams Alliance, and political training institute, American Majority.[13]

Behind the scenes, many of the national conservative interest groups, which we will profile in-depth in the following chapter, were attempting to use the town-hall meetings to their own end.

As Lee Fang of *Think Progress*, described: "The lobbyist-run groups Americans for Prosperity and FreedomWorks, which orchestrated the anti-Obama tea parties earlier this year, are now pursuing an aggressive strategy to create an image of mass public opposition to health care and clean energy reform. A leaked memo from Bob MacGuffie, a volunteer with the FreedomWorks website Tea Party Patriots, details how members should be infiltrating town halls and harassing Democratic members of Congress."[14]

Indeed, the leaked memo makes no bones about the fact that these national conservative organizations were attempting to seed the town-hall meetings with angry mobs. The memo encouraged participants to "Artificially Inflate Your Numbers" and "Be Disruptive Early And Often." But in truth, there was little need for these directives. The fact of the matter is that thousands of everyday Americans showed up to express their deeply held emotions about the state of the nation. We were there, and we witnessed the real anger expressed by real people across the political spectrum.

On September 9, 2009, after a difficult summer in which he had seen his poll numbers drop as more Americans expressed opposition to his healthcare reform plans, President Obama delivered a comprehensive speech on the issue to a joint session of Congress. Though the address was generally well received, it was soon overshadowed by what happened while Obama was speaking. The president had just finished reassuring his listeners that, contrary to what some of his adversaries alleged, his health plan would not extend coverage to illegal immigrants.

"You lie!" thundered a voice within the chamber. The president paused a moment and proceeded with his speech. House Speaker Nancy Pelosi and Vice President Joe Biden, seated behind the president, looked surprised and then disgusted. Others in the media and at home asked themselves, "Who said that?"

The answer was Joe Wilson, an obscure Republican congressman from South Carolina. Wilson became an instant celebrity after his outburst, the likes of which no one could recall happening before during a presidential address to Congress. Though his office issued a statement of apology, which the president accepted, the furor did not die down. Democrats in the House of Representatives publicly rebuked him a week later, demanding that he deliver his apology on the House chamber. Wilson refused. He was done apologizing, he said, and he soon emerged as a hot figure on the populist right, a new hero for all those who oppose big government, taxes, stimulus bills, bailouts, and a "government takeover" of the healthcare system. In the span of a week following his outburst, Wilson raised close to $2 million—an astonishing sum for a figure so unknown outside of his home state.

Wilson's outburst was reflective of the disruptive and oftentimes disrespectful conduct exhibited by conservative protestors at town-hall meetings on healthcare reform. But even this incredible display of aggression and anger was not the height of right-wing populism in 2009. Indeed, right-wing populism reached a fever pitch during the September 12 March on Washington.

THE 912 PROJECT

As we discussed in the beginning of the chapter, two mass gatherings occurred in Washington, D.C., in 2009: President Obama's Inauguration and the 912 Project.

On September 12, 2009, hundreds of thousands of protestors marched down Pennsylvania Avenue in Washington, D.C., as part of the 912 Project's Taxpayer March on Washington. The 912 Project was first conceptualized in March 2009, when conservative television host and right-wing populist champion Glenn Beck, known for his hectoring arguments and colorful denunciations of the administration, called upon his viewers to take their country back on an episode of his Fox talk show. The rally was subsequently organized by FreedomWorks, as well as local and national Tea Party groups. It targeted President

Obama's "tax-and-spend" fiscal policies as well as "government-run health care."

We were on hand for the entire march, and what we witnessed was illuminating.

A group of five people huddled together in front of the White House waiting for the sixth member of their group to snap a photo. They were all dressed for the occasion in matching custom made red T-shirts that said "Don't Tread on My Rights" on the front, and "I'm Not Your ATM" on the back, while waving flags and holding their handmade signs with slogans such as "Member of the Mob" and "HR 3200: Kill the Bill" in the air for all to see.

"Everybody say tax cuts!" yelled the woman before snapping the picture. The group then set out on the fifteen-block trek toward Capitol Hill, joining fellow marchers in a boisterous chant of "USA! USA!"

While the 912 Project has been promoted by Glenn Beck and a number of conservative organizations, such as FreedomWorks, the tens of thousands of enthusiastic members of the crowd, who had traveled by car, train, plane, and even motorcycle to attend the event, were adamant that they were attending the event on their own accord, united by a shared anger at the actions of policymakers in Washington, and a passionate dedication to making their voices heard.

"We're not sponsored by anybody!" explained Jackie Doyle, a middle-aged woman holding a sign that said, "How much are you getting paid to be here? Me = $0.00." Ms. Doyle had flown in with her husband from Chicago for the event. "We came here on our own to protest big government spending in general. It's not only healthcare reform and it's not only [Obama], it's *all* of them up there on that hill. They're just not listening to us anymore, but if we don't stand up and do something to make our voices heard, then it's our *own* fault!"

When asked if Ms. Doyle had tried to get in touch with her state's congressional delegation through other means, she replied: "Of course! I'd say I send Senator Durbin about one or two emails a week trying to tell him what I don't like about what he and his colleagues are doing, and guess what? They get sent back to me. I'll call his office, neither he nor his aides will see us. Well, I'm not going *anywhere*. I will keep repeating my message until my voice is heard. We have to be heard, we're not *heard* anymore!"

Nearby, a man dressed in a Ronald Reagan costume with a megaphone was standing on a sailboat that was being pulled by a pickup truck. A sizable audience had clustered around the boat to cheer in response to the Reagan impersonator's speech: "All you politicians voting for healthcare reforms that go against the will of the American people, I have some advice for you: Dust off your résumés, because you're going to need them in 2010!"

This scene was reflective of a belief that asserted itself time and again throughout the day: the belief that the era in which small-government politicians such as Reagan could be counted on to defend the freedom and liberty of the American people was long gone.

Another common belief harbored by the marchers was that policymakers in Washington sought to marginalize and exploit the hardworking American taxpayers, while they personally partake in corruption. Walking near the Treasury Building, which is nearby the White House, a woman turned to her young daughter and said: "Look honey, that's where Tim Geithner lives . . . he doesn't pay his taxes!"

While some protestors targeted healthcare reform in particular, for others, their issue of choice was abortion, offshore drilling, taxation, or the stimulus bill and bailouts. It was clear from the STOP OBAMANATION slogans, to the numerous protestors who were dressed as Ben Franklin, George Washington, and other recognizable leaders of the American Revolution, that the protesters felt their very liberty was at stake. Their fear was palpable, and it was in response to social and economic policies and actions of a government whose size and scope appeared to be increasing on a daily basis.

"We're here to support our hero Glenn Beck," said Suzanne Pabst, dressed in full patriot attire: navy pants with white stars, a white T-shirt, and a large red hat. Pabst, who had driven from Missouri, continued: "Thank God for Glenn, he truly understands. The number one reason we're here is that we are *patriot*s. The Constitution was written for the people by the people. Above all, I'm here for my kids and my grandkids. I want them to have the same opportunities that I did. Their freedom is at stake."

A leather-clad couple, Laura and Hank, were dressed in head-to-toe biker gear, each waving a massive American flag while blasting "Proud to Be an American" from a boom box. This display of patriotism prompted a hug or handshake from every protestor who marched by. Laura and Hank had traveled by motorcycle from Erie, Pennsylvania, to make their voices heard in Washington. Like everyone else I spoke to, they vehemently insisted that while they were inspired by and agreed with Glenn Beck, they were there on their own accord.

As Laura explained, "The second we heard about the 912 Project I said to Hank, 'Well we're going to have to hop on our bikes and head down to D.C.!' I'm so angry about big government. It's just too big. I don't want special interests and lobbyists buying control over *my* life. The government needs to get out of health care, and stay out! Our Representatives aren't listening to us, so we're here to take things in our own hands!"

Tributes to Joe Wilson could be seen everywhere, as well. Scattered throughout the posters condemning "socialized medicine," demonizing "tax and spend" fiscal policies, and, of course, the "don't tread on me" flags, were signs quoting Wilson with slogans such as LIAR or YOU LIE. Some carried JOE WAS RIGHT, STAND WITH JOE, and JOE 2012 signs and banners. Others chanted "Liar!" whenever they got the opportunity.

NOVEMBER 2009

The November 2009 elections were a showcase for the emerging prominence of right-wing populism and the Tea Party movement. And the special election in New York's 23rd Congressional District was perhaps a harbinger for future elections in the age of the new populism.

In New York's 23rd, a special election was required to fill the seat of moderate Republican John McHugh, who had been appointed Secretary of the Army by President Obama, after serving eight terms in the House.

Since the late 1800s, moderate and centrist Republicans, including McHugh, had represented the 23rd. In keeping with tradition, local Democrats nominated a moderate, pro-business attorney, Bill Owens, as their candidate. Meanwhile, local county GOP leaders chose as its candidate a moderate Republican state assemblywoman, Dede Scozzafava, who espoused abortion rights and had many ties to organized labor.

Scozzafava received official endorsements from national GOP leadership, including House minority leader John Boehner and RNC chairman Michael Steele.

Scozzafava should have gone on to a clear and decisive victory, given the demographics of the district, a distinctly working-class area in upstate New York that for a century had sent a Republican to Congress. However, a right-wing populist, Doug Hoffman, decided to run as a third-party candidate on the Conservative Party ticket.

Perhaps if the special election had been a primary election, Republican voters in Upstate New York would have nominated Hoffman. However, since local party officials picked a candidate absolutely designed to provoke a fight with the party base (Scozzafava wouldn't even commit to voting against the Obama health plan, the hottest issue on the agenda at the time), a fight is exactly what they got.

Hoffman became a cause célèbre of the Tea Party movement, not for his qualifications, which were tremendously lacking, but for the right-wing populist ideology he espoused. He received the endorsement of economic and social right-wing populists including Sarah Palin, Glenn Beck, Rush Limbaugh, Michele Bachmann, Dick Armey, the Club for Growth, the Susan B. Anthony List, and the conservative National Organization for Marriage.

Three days before the special election, Scozzafava suspended her campaign in response to national attention that Hoffman had received and the vilification she had endured from right-wing populists, who portrayed her as a stealth liberal and union cat's-paw. In a shocking turn of events, due to Hoffman's local and national support, there was simply no way for the Republican nominee to win this Republican district.

Ultimately, on Election Day, Bill Owens narrowly defeated Hoffman 49 to 46 percent, representing only a 4,300-vote margin.[15] However, Hoffman's candidacy and popularity is a clear indication of the extent to which the Tea Party movement can and just might influence the 2010-midterm elections. Notably, it appears at this time of writing that the right-wing populists were thinking longer-term and more strategically than their GOP counterparts. It is likely that Republicans will win back this seat in November 2010, in which case the Tea Party agitation will have been especially prescient and effective.

While New York's 23rd received the most media attention for the role that right-wing populists played, two additional elections in November 2009 show the growing power and prominence of right-wing populism and the possibility that they might augur tax revolts.

In New Jersey, Democratic Governor Jon Corzine was defeated handily by Republican Chris Christie. In a nasty campaign that featured endless ad hominem attacks by both candidates, at the end of the day, the race was decided by Independents who had swung suddenly and dramatically to the conservative populist cause.

Christie made two arguments that stoked this sentiment: that New Jerseyans were being taxed to death, driving business out of the state, and that Corzine, a former Goldman Sachs CEO, had managed the state's finances in the same disastrous way as Wall Street had ruined the national economy. "In exactly the same way that many of the bad actors on Wall Street used smoke and mirrors and gimmicks to run our national economy into the ground, Jon Corzine has brought that same style of leadership to New Jersey, and he has driven our economy into the economic ditch," Christie said in speech after speech.[16]

During the week preceding the election, a Quinnipiac University survey had Gov. Jon Corzine ahead of Republican Chris Christie by 43 percent to 38 percent, with independent Chris Daggett at 13 percent. But the right-wing populist fervor sweeping the country in the fall of 2009 changed the outcome of the race, and gave Christie a decisive five-point victory. In fact, Rasmussen Reports showed Corzine falling to his biggest deficit in the race shortly after announcing a big tax hike plan—a plan that clearly didn't fit populist mood of voters at the time.

In another telling election in New York's Nassau County, the long-time Democratic county executive, Thomas R. Suozzi, was narrowly defeated by Republican Edward P. Mangano, as Republicans took control of the county legislature. According to the *New York Times*, "Both [Republican] candidates . . . said that Democrats approached them in the days before the election and told them they were voting Republican for the first time." The *Times* noted that "frustration with the economy" and "outrage of high local property taxes" were the primary factors in this local upset. The election may portent bad news for incumbents, for Suozzi lost even though he had traveled the state championing the idea of a property-tax cap.

In the complicated and ever-changing world of politics, it is often a mistake to read too much into the events of a small number of election results, or isolated public opinion polls. Our national politics are defined by broad trend lines, not the outcome of a few isolated local campaigns and elections.

But the events of 2009 that we have described above were different. As we have noted in previous chapters, the fundamentals across several aspects of American life have shifted dramatically in recent years. And this shift is the rocket fuel that drove right-wing populism to extraordinary heights in 2009, and, as we will argue in Chapter 7, will continue to do so for the foreseeable future.

THE TEA PARTY MOVEMENT: REACTIONS AND REALITY

Questions were immediately raised by members of both the political and media establishment about the extent to which the Tea Parties could truly be considered a grassroots uprising, given the role that current and former Republican politicians, lobbyists, and media figures played in organizing, financing, publicizing and executing the events. From the beginning, critics questioned the extent to which the Tea Parties truly represented grievances shared by a majority of the American public, writing them off as an "Astroturf" movement organized by Republican politicians and right-wing media.

Let's quickly examine some of the claims made by the Tea Party movement's detractors in politics and the media.

The Tea Parties Aren't Really Grassroots; They're Just Astroturf

During an April 15, 2009, interview, House Speaker Nancy Pelosi (D-CA) famously dismissed the Tea Partiers saying, "This initiative is funded by the high end—we call it Astroturf, it's not really a grassroots movement. It's Astroturf by some of the wealthiest people in America to keep the focus on tax cuts for the rich instead of for the great middle class."[17]

This was the reaction of much of the mainstream media in response to the April 15 Tea Party protests. The *New York Times* suggested that perhaps the Tea Party detractors were correct in asserting that the Republican Party was really organizing the movement. They note that "Although organizers insisted they had created a nonpartisan grassroots movement, others argued that these parties were more of the Astroturf variety: an occasion largely created by the clamor of cable news and fueled by the financial and political support of current and former Republican leaders. . . . The Web site TaxDayTeaParty.com listed its sponsors, including FreedomWorks, a group founded by Dick

Armey, the former House majority leader; Top Conservatives on Twitter; and RFCRadio.com." [18]

Liberal commentator and *Times* columnist Paul Krugman quipped: "These parties—antitaxation demonstrations that are supposed to evoke the memory of the Boston Tea Party and the American Revolution—have been the subject of considerable mockery, and rightly so . . . it turns out that the tea parties don't represent a spontaneous outpouring of public sentiment. They're AstroTurf (fake grass roots) events, manufactured by the usual suspects. . . . And the parties are, of course, being promoted heavily by Fox News." [19]

The reality of the situation was much different from the initial reaction of the press. To be sure, national Republican organizations and politicians, capitalizing on the rising opposition to the president's policies, publically supported and in some ways facilitated the burgeoning Tea Party movement. But Tea Party attendees have staunchly maintained that their movement is a nonpartisan protest effort. As a Washington, D.C., Tea Party co-sponsor, Phil Keppen, told Fox News host Greta Van Susteren: "This is the kind of huge, large-scale event that only can come together when you have thousands of volunteers and you have thousands of activists and you have thousands of ordinary folks who are willing to step up and put it together. And right here in Washington, we have a great example of that. . . . This is about being Republican, Democrat, independent, Libertarian, conservative, anybody, anybody who's upset with the stimulus package." [20]

We heard this same sentiment at Tea Party events we personally attended. Doug Arcamone, a Tea Party attendee in Sacramento, CA, was impassioned about his independence and even his dislike of the Republican Party: "I am not an officer of the Republican Party. I am just a retired, working class stiff raised in a lower-middle class family who has worked since he was 13, a veteran and a patriot. . . . What I personally experienced in Sacramento were about 5,000 attendees of all political and socio-economic persuasions. We patriots had in common a desire to keep intact those principles upon which this country was

founded. . . . Make no mistake. I am equally unimpressed with politicians from the Republican Party, as were many others at the tea party I
attended. To many of us, it's just business as usual in Washington, D.C.,
regardless of which side of the aisle the politicians are on. They have
no regard for the thoughts or feelings of honest, hard-working people.
We've had enough of self-interested political agendas and grandstand-
ing from both sides and are all looking for a real 'hero.' Now we may
have to be our own heroes."

And indeed, our own poll data shows that the majority of the
American mainstream have not been swayed by elitist bias and 48 percent of respondents in a February 2010 poll conducted by Rasmussen
and Schoen said that the Tea Party movement is grassroots, while only
26 percent said it was Astroturf.

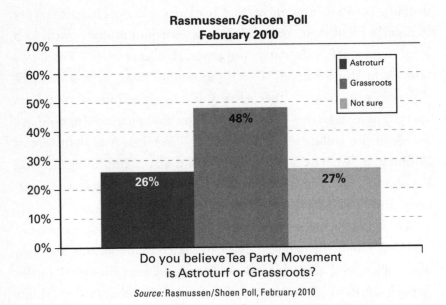

Source: Rasmussen/Shoen Poll, February 2010

Similarly, the public rejects the political class' depiction of the Tea Party
movement as representing the radical fringe.

The majority of Americans view Tea Party activists as concerned
citizens who are worried about the country's economic future, rather

than anger-driven, anti-government fringe people. In a January 2010 McLaughlin poll, 56.8 percent of respondents said that Tea Party activists were concerned citizens, 18.9 percent said they were members of an anti-government fringe group, and one-quarter didn't know.[21]

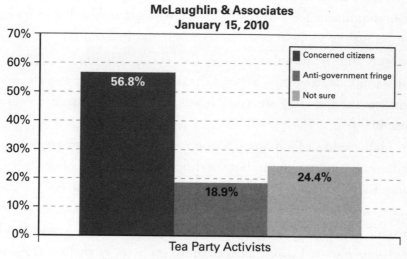

McLaughlin & Associates
January 15, 2010

- Concerned citizens
- Anti-government fringe
- Not sure

56.8%

18.9%

24.4%

Tea Party Activists

Source: McLaughlin & Associates, January 15, 2010

The Tea Party movement benefits from many of the advantages of social and political protest movements, not just a diffusion of organizations, but also the energizing presence of so many people who have never been politically active before. These first-time activists have often powered political change in the United States: They were the engine behind the Civil Rights movement and the antiwar movement, and, more recent, they were a central pillar of Barack Obama's presidential campaign in 2008.

Now, this same first-time enthusiasm has given its energies to the Tea Parties, and its newcomers come from all age groups. Some, like Matthew Clemente, fit the traditional profile of a young activist motivated by political developments. Clemente is just 20 years old and found the Tea Party movement after watching his father's food market struggle as the recession hit many of his regular customers. "The taxes my dad was paying were laying on him hard, and you see these failed banks getting billions in taxpayer money after making bad investments and not playing by the rules," he said. Clemente is now a state coordinator for FreedomWorks.[22]

Others are considerably older. Diana Reimer, 67, is a Pennsylvania state coordinator for a Tea Party group who got involved after trying unsuccessfully for years to sell her family home. Frustrated by the bank bailouts and the stimulus package, she tried contacting her representatives in Congress, but "When I'd make a call, I'd get an aide, and that was the end of it," she said. "It was frustrating. I wanted my voice heard."[23]

Idaho resident Pam Stout, 66, once worked for the government in federal housing programs, but she'd never been active politically. But since the foreclosure crisis—during which her son lost his job and home—she reached out to the Tea Party movement and has since become a committed activist. Now she maintains email contacts with over four hundred people in the Sandpoint area, as well as state and national Tea Party organizations.[24]

These people form the lifeblood of the movement, not the more attention-getting crackpots and racists who are a small but vocal minority and provide an easy target for those who, even now, wish to dismiss the movement's power and seriousness.

There is no question that the Tea Party movement, driven by these activists and concerned citizens, was and continues to be beyond the control of any one party, group, or leader. That said, a number of Republican leaders and organizations did publicly align themselves with the creation of the Tea Party movement, lending it legitimacy and fund-raising prowess in 2009. We will explore the connections between the national Republican Party and the Tea Party movement in detail in Chapter 7.

The April 15, 2009, Tea Parties Are Just a One-Time Phenomenon

In NBC's coverage of the April 15 Tea Parties, NBC News Political Director Chuck Todd typified the reaction across much of the mainstream media: "There's been some grassroots conservatives who have organized so-called 'tea parties' around the country hoping the historical reference will help galvanize Americans against the president's economic ideas. . . . But I tell you, the idea hasn't really caught on."[25]

As we now know, the idea that the Tea Party movement was ephemeral could not be further from the truth. Eight months after Todd's on-air comments, a December 2009 WSJ/NBC News poll found that 41 percent of respondents said they had a very or somewhat favorable view of the Tea Party movement, and only 24 percent said they had a somewhat or very negative view of the group.

And recent poll data suggests that Tea Party support has been on the rise.

As Scott's polling showed at the end of 2009, the Tea Party movement's strength was growing across the electorate. It's also achieved a higher level of respect among voters. A Fox News/Opinion Dynamics poll in February 2010 showed that 51 percent consider the Tea Party movement a "serious" group.

Following up on Scott's surveys, we did extensive national polling in February 2010 and found substantial Tea Party support among a broad-based cross section of the American public.

Tea Party affiliates in the general electorate can be broken down into four groups: Sympathizers, Supporters, Members, and Activists.

Sympathizers (favorables): Recent poll data shows that over half of the public now have a favorable impression of the Tea Party movement. In a February 2010 survey conducted by Schoen and Rasmussen, 55 percent of respondents said they had a favorable impression of the Tea Party movement. An Economist/YouGov poll conducted at the same time found a similar favorability rating of 53 percent.

And in a December 2009 WSJ/NBC News poll, the Tea Party Movement topped both the Democratic and Republican Parties: 41 percent of respondents said they had a positive opinion of the Tea Party movement, while only 35 percent said they had a positive opinion of the Democratic Party, and 28 percent for the Republican Party.

And, indeed, it is highly likely that the question used in the survey

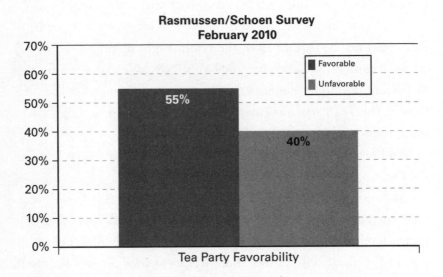

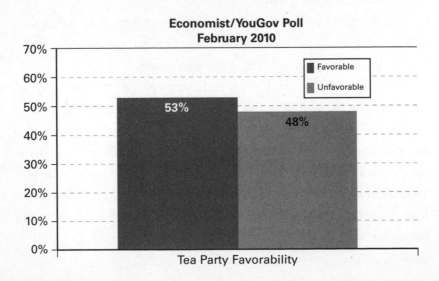

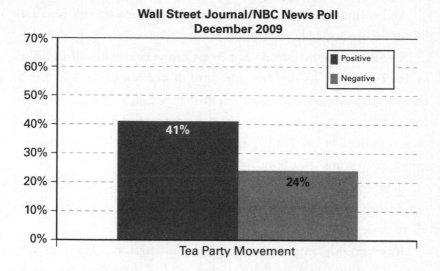

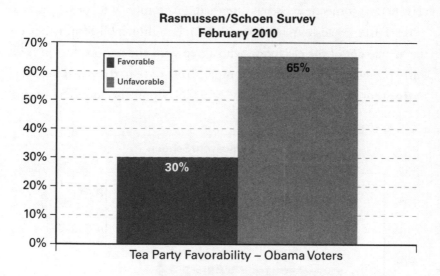

was biased against the Tea Party, using the terms "most of whom are conservative" and "any type of tax increases" in their description.

The Tea Parties have broad national support, appealing primarily but not exclusively to unaffiliated and Republican voters. In fact, in our own poll, 30 percent of Obama voters said they had a favorable impression of the Tea Party movement.

And within the American mainstream, the ideas that the Tea Party stands for are arguably more popular than the movement itself.

Supporters: Approximately 35 percent of the electorate self-identifies as Tea Party supporters. Over one-third of our respondents in a February 2010 survey—37 percent—said they are Tea Party supporters. Independents, again, were higher, at 42 percent. And Obama voters were considerably lower at 13 percent, though 21 percent were noncommittal, answering "Not Sure."

Members: A February 20, 2010, Economist/YouGov poll found that one in five Americans identify themselves as being part of the Tea Party movement.

Activists: Only a small percentage of Tea Party sympathizers, supporters, and members can be classified as activists. An activist can be classified as someone who has attended, given money to, or organized a Tea Party protest. A January 2010 McLaughlin poll found that of the 52 percent of the electorate who agree with the reasons for the Tea Party protest, only 5 percent of sympathizers have participated in a Tea Party event. Similarly, a February 2010 CNN poll also found 5 percent

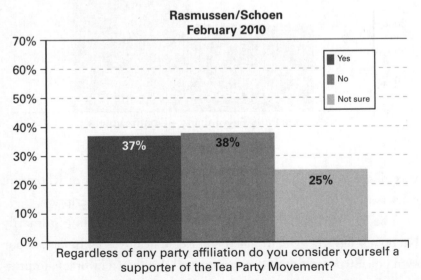

Rasmussen/Schoen February 2010

Regardless of any party affiliation do you consider yourself a supporter of the Tea Party Movement?

Source: Rasmussen/Schoen Poll, February 2010.

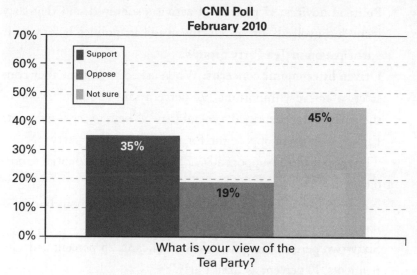

Source: CNN/Opinion Research Poll," February 17, 2010,
http://i2.cdn.turner.com/cnn/2010/images/02/17/rel4b.pdf.

of the electorate having attended a Tea Party rally. They also found that 2 percent had given money to a Tea Party organization and 7 percent had taken active steps to support the movement either in person, via email, or on the Internet.

McLaughlin Poll, January 2010	
I have participated in a tea party or similar protest myself.	5.6%
I have not participated in a tea party protest but I generally agree with the reasons for those protests.	46.9%
I do not agree with the tea party protests nor do I agree with the reasons for those protests.	29.7%
Don't know	17.7%

In early March 2010, the Sam Adams Alliance released a study on the motivations, values, beliefs, and goals of individual Tea Party activists called *The Early Adopters: Reading the Tea Leaves.* Below, are some of the key findings:

- **Political novices:** 47 percent of activists surveyed said that they were "uninvolved" or "rarely involved" in politics before their participation in Tea Party groups.
- **Driven by economic concerns:** When asked what issue they consider to be "very important" 92 percent said "budget." None of the participants identified a social issue as being very important.
- Eighty-six percent oppose the formation of a third party.
- Thirty-six percent support a 2012 Sarah Palin presidential candidacy.
- Ninety percent cited "to stand up for my beliefs" when characterizing their initial reason for involvement.
- Sixty-two percent identified as Republicans, 28 percent as Independents, 10 percent as "Tea Party." [26]

The Tea Party Movement Is Being Led
Top-Down by the Republican Party

Traditionally, the Republican Party has been associated with the economic and social conservative ideologies driving the Tea Party movement. But it would be wrong to write off the Tea Parties as being orchestrated by Republican politicians for the electoral benefit of the Party.

In fact, the Tea Party movement is comprised of voters who believe that the Republican Party as a whole has strayed far from its ideological roots and that Republican policymakers in Washington are no different from the Democrats.

As 2009 came to a close, a remarkable 23 percent of respondents in a December Rasmussen poll said they would vote for a Tea Party candidate in the 2010 midterm elections. Furthermore, according to Scott's polling, 41 percent of Americans no longer see a major difference between the Democratic and Republican parties. This is a shocking turn of events, just one year after a highly partisan presidential election that featured stark differences between deeply divided Democrats and Republicans.

As we will discuss in detail in Chapter 7, national Republican leaders have attempted to co-opt and use the surge in right-wing populism to their own end. But from our extensive interviews with right-wing populists, it's all too clear that the Tea Party movement is not a Republican-centric phenomenon in the least bit.

The Tea Party Movement Can't and Won't Influence Electoral Outcomes

David Brooks typifies the suspicion with which the media elite view insurgent right-wing populism in an October 2009 column: "It is the story of media mavens who claim to represent a hidden majority but who in fact represent a mere niche—even in the Republican Party. It is a story as old as *The Wizard of Oz*, of grand illusions and small men behind the curtain. . . . Over the years, I have asked many politicians what happens when Limbaugh and his colleagues attack. The story is always the same. Hundreds of calls come in. The receptionists are miserable. But the numbers back home do not move. There is no effect on the favorability rating or the re-election prospects." [27]

Our analysis shows that it is virtually inevitable that the Tea Party movement will be a driving force in determining the outcome of the 2010-midterm elections, with the potential to transform the country's political landscape in an unprecedented and irrevocable way. We will discuss the relationship between the Tea Party movement and the GOP at length in Chapter 7.

THE **STRUCTURE** OF THE **TEA PARTY MOVEMENT**

(Unidentified Tea Party protester on megaphone): WHAT DO WE SAY TO SOCIALISM? (Crowd): NOOOOO

WHAT DO WE SAY TO FREEDOM? YESSSSSSSS

WHAT DO WE SAY TO FREE MARKET? YES-SSSSSSSSS

WHO WANTS HIGHER TAXES: NOOONE

WHAT DO WE SAY TO HARD WORK? YESSSS

THIS IS ABOUT FREEDOM, THIS IS ABOUT LOWER TAXES, THIS IS ABOUT THE GOVERN-MENT TAKING AWAY WHAT WE HAVE— TAKING AWAY OUR FREEDOM

While the two 45-foot coaches, which transport the TPX organizers, rally speakers and performers, and the media were stuck in traffic en route from San Diego and running about hour late, the crowd of over one thousand Tea Party protesters congregating in Griffith Park on October 25, 2009, did not need Tea Party organizers to help them get riled up in support of their movement.

Some local Tea Party groups, identifiable by their matching T-shirts had set up small tables where they distributed literature and pamphlets and sold buttons, pins, and T-shirts. The majority of the crowd, however, was made up of ordinary California citizens who had come with their families, many with three generations in attendance. They sat on blankets or lawn chairs toting homemade signs, and breaking out in spontaneous chants and cheers as they waited for the TPX buses to arrive.

There is perhaps no more polarizing question in American politics today than the following:

What exactly is the Tea Party movement?

There is a certain and notable lack of national consensus. The political elite often deny that the Tea Party movement even exists. The Democratic establishment accuses the Republican establishment of manufacturing the Tea Party as a grassroots movement. The Republican establishment, in turn, claims Tea Party supporters as their own conservative base.

And yet, poll after poll of the American electorate throughout 2009 and 2010 has shown that the Tea Party has grown in its own right and now constitutes its own political entity, distinct from the major parties and arguably more popular as well.

This lack of consensus about what the Tea Party movement is and what it means for American politics is rooted in a lack of information and a lack of analysis.

A full accounting is needed for the simple and fundamental reason that right-wing populism could be the defining political movement of this decade, and possibly the foreseeable future.

Our goal is to provide that analysis in this chapter. We will identify the major players who are driving and leading the Tea Party movement, from well-known Tea Party political heroes like Sarah Palin, to lesser-known candidates who have allied with Tea Party groups, like Marco Rubio. We will describe the symbolic leaders, future political candidates, organizational backers, and individual organizers who together define this burgeoning national movement.

In addition, through our proprietary research and in-person interviews with Tea Party activists, we will explore the economic and political undercurrents of right-wing populism. And we will explore the dynamics that together explain the growing phenomenon of right-wing populism in America.

Through this analysis, for the first time, we will paint an accurate and unbiased picture of how the Tea Party movement—the manifestation of insurgent right-wing populism in America—is not only being led and organized, but also how it represents a major realignment of the U.S. electorate.

THE MAJOR PLAYERS

To the lay consumer of mainstream media content on cable TV or online, it's not difficult to see why the Tea Party movement is such a conundrum. It has no formal figurehead. There is no Tea Party headquarters in Washington. And the Tea Party is certainly not a registered political party. It is a network of political activists disconnected from the political establishment that, for historic reasons, is at the center of an unprecedented shift in American politics.

To that end, it is helpful to think of the Tea Party movement as having four distinct strands that we will explore here: organizational backers, individual organizers, symbolic leaders, and the Tea Party base.

Organizational Backers

In addition to these individual organizers who are giving voice to the views of Tea Party activists, a number of established organizations fall under the banner of the Tea Party movement. While the number of state and local Tea Party-affiliated organizations has already grown beyond number, five core organizations form the backbone of right-wing populist, Tea Party activity nationwide.

- **FreedomWorks** is an advocacy group founded to lead the fight for lower taxes, less government, and more liberty. The group is chaired by former former Texas congressman and House Majority Leader Dick Armey, a ten-gallon-hat-wearing, free-market economist, who joined FreedomWorks in 2003 and also sponsors the website TaxDayTeaParty.com. Its president is Matt Kibbe, a longtime advocate for less government regulation of business and a corporate lobbyist. In his own words, this is how Armey described the organization: "During my time as Majority Leader on Capitol Hill, I came to recognize that grassroots action is the most important factor to winning at politics. That's what FreedomWorks is all about. I know FreedomWorks and its members well from past campaigns on the Flat Tax, Social Security reform, and school choice. In every issue that matters to the U.S. economy, FreedomWorks is right there in the fight. I am very excited to be a part of this great organization."

Nancy Pelosi and other critics have accused the group of having close ties to the insurance industry, but according to the *New York Times*: "Armey and his organization have operated nimbly, seeding and supporting protests against policies of the Obama administration and the Democratic Congress while taking care not to be seen as controlling the dissent from on high. . . . Armey himself has been traveling the country in support of favored political candidates, not all of them running on the Republican line."[1] Indeed, at a news conference in January 2010, FreedomWorks put out a list of candidates it would back or oppose in key races in November. They announced that they would work against Charlie Crist in his race for the Florida Senate, Sen. Harry M. Reid (D-Nev.), and Rep. Alan Grayson (D-Fla.), each of whom the group labeled an "Enemy of Liberty." The group announced its support for GOP Senate candidates Marco Rubio (FL), Pat Toomey (PA), and Rand Paul (KY), each of whom it labeled a "Champion of Freedom."

- **Our Country Deserves Better,** a California-based PAC, was formed in August 2008 to oppose the presidential candidacy of

Barack Obama, whom the PAC portrays as a free-spending ul-
traliberal surrounded by corrupt aides and bent on instituting
socialism in the United States. Led by its chairman Howard
Kaloogian, a former Republican member of the California state
assembly, it launched a two-week "Stop Obama" bus tour beginning on October 15, 2008, hosting thirty-five rallies across the
country. Our Country Deserves Better stands for a number of
right-wing populist issues, including lower taxes, opposition to
bailouts, strong national defense, secure borders, sound energy
policy, and judges who "respect the Constitution."[2]

In 2009, the PAC raised approximately $585,000 over a period
of six months for bus tours, which became known as the Tea
Party Express. The tours have continued in 2010. The first tour
was launched on August 28, 2009, with a "caravan of vehicles"
that featured "two 45-foot buses along with several RVs and a
contingent of SUVs and support vehicles" on a mission east from
California "to unify, educate, and most importantly encourage
Americans to continue their opposition of deficit spending,
government-run health care, and irresponsible bailouts."[3]

Our Country Deserves Better makes no bones about its long-
term mission, which is explicitly geared toward electoral outcomes: "The Our Country Deserves Better PAC is committed to
defeating the candidates backed by Democrat Senate and House
leaders, Harry Reid and Nancy Pelosi, in the 2010 congressional
elections. We will support conservative challengers in these election campaigns. We will then turn our focus to ensuring that
Barack Obama is defeated should he [choose] to run for re-election
in 2012."[4] On the electoral front, the group has already shown
success. In Massachusetts, it spent over $348,000 in support of
Scott Brown's victorious Senate campaign.

- **Tea Party Nation,** or TPN, identifies itself as "a user-driven
  group of like-minded people who desire our God given Individ-

ual Freedoms which were written out by the Founding Fathers. We believe in Limited Government, Free Speech, the 2nd Amendment, our Military, Secure Borders and our Country!" TPN sponsored the National Tea Party Convention in Nashville, at which Sarah Palin was the keynote speaker. It plans to hold a National Tea Party Unity Convention in Las Vegas in July 2010. TPN's founder, Judson Phillips, started the group in 2009 with his wife Sherry. A Nashville attorney by day, Phillips has come in for harsh criticism for his decision to run TPN as a for-profit group, epitomized by the $549 ticket price to the Nashville convention and the six-figure speaker's fee Palin earned. His detractors claim he funnels proceeds into his wife's PayPal account. But as one reporter wrote: "He can still get Palin on the phone," and the convention came off as he promised it would, attracting enormous media attention.

- **The Tea Party Patriots** is a national organization that provides support and training for "anyone who identifies with the Tea Party movement," according to its national coordinator, Mark Meckler. The organization's website is also the home of the collaborative effort that will produce a twenty-point "Contract From America," a new statement of American principles to be unveiled on Tax Day, April 15, 2010. Tea Party Patriots lists more than four hundred local websites on its website, and organizers estimate there may be a hundred more; it also claims more than fifteen million "associates" through a network of over one thousand affiliated organizations. The group has compiled a massive database of email addresses, which it uses to stay in touch with members. Four national coordinators work with local volunteers to schedule events and meetings. The group has also used social-networking tools to communicate with members and provide links to congressional town hall meetings in their area.

  Tea Party Patriots differs from some of the other large groups in avoiding a strictly partisan agenda and claiming to be a truly grassroots, conservative coalition. As national organizer, Georgia resident, and former GOP consultant Jenny Beth Martin explains: "We can't be involved with PACs. We want to make sure the organizations we align with are in-line with our core values—that they're not just supporting one party over the other."

- **Americans For Prosperity,** founded in 2004 by David H. Koch of Koch Industries, an oil and gas concern. Unlike many of the other Tea Party organizations, AFP came along well before the financial crisis. But a group spokesman was proud to identify the organization as "part of the tea party—little 't,' little 'p.'" Koch sits on the group's Board of Directors and helped fund a number of Tea Party causes. His group was identified as one of the key groups (along with FreedomWorks) behind the April 15, 2009, national Tea Party events. The organization's Hands Off My Health Care bus tour made stops at town-hall events in August 2009. Its Hot Air Tour, organized to fight against taxes on carbon use and institution of a cap-and-trade program, attracted Tea Party activists. The group spent just over $15 million on both campaigns. In addition, its twenty-five state chapters across the country have made alliances with local Tea Party groups.

Individual Organizers

The Tea Party movement relies in the end on the energies and commitment of key individuals. Without their tireless efforts, no amount of donations would keep afloat a movement that requires constant organizing and rallying efforts to keep its members focused and involved. Just as there are too many local and state Tea Party organizations to document, there are too many important individuals. But here's a look at some of the most prominent and influential, whose impact on the national movement has already been felt.

Upon seeing Keli Carender at a Tea Party protest, someone who buys into the caricature of Tea Party protesters as middle-aged, bible touting Revolutionary War impersonators would wonder what this nose-ring sporting 30-year-old actress is doing there.

Looks can be deceiving. Carender may look like someone who got lost on the way to an Obama rally, yet she has been recognized as the founder and the future of the Tea Party movement.

On February 16, 2009, three days before Santelli's infamous rant, Carender organized her very first rally, protesting President Obama's stimulus package, which she dubbed "the porkulus." She used her blog, Liberty Belle, to reach out to other concerned fiscal conservatives, and her first rally drew a modest crowd of 120.

But Carender, who has been praised by the likes of Jenny Beth Martin as "an unlikely avatar of the movement but an ideal one," was just getting started.

As the *New York Times* noted in a profile on Carender: In her activism, "Carender has also drawn on her theatrical experience. Discovering that advocates of a health care overhaul were marching in the city last summer, she staged a 'funeral for health care,' with protesters wearing black and bagpipers playing. For her first Tea Party event, she dressed as Liberty Belle (newspaper accounts mistook her for Little Bo Peep). In a video viewed 68,000 times on YouTube, she confronted Representative Norm Dicks, Democrat of Washington, at a town-hall-style meeting on health care. 'If you believe that it is absolutely moral to take my money and give it to someone else based on their supposed needs,' she said, waving a $20 bill to boos and cheers, 'then you come and take this $20 and use it as a down payment on this health care plan.'"[5]

In January 2010, FreedomWorks honored Carender, flying her to Washington, D.C., along with sixty other Tea Party leaders flown to Washington for training in election activism.

"If the tea party movement has an architect," a CNN reporter wrote in September 2009, "it is Joe Wierzbicki. Unassuming in wrinkled khakis and a polo shirt, he is in near perpetual motion."[6] The national coordinator for Our Country Deserves Better, Wierzbicki told CNN that fall that the Tea Party movement's first and foremost objective was to stop the healthcare reform bill—and then moving on from there to take control of Congress from Democrats. Wierzbicki has referred to himself as a "grass roots coordinator," but he's also a sophisticated and experienced PR professional, a principal in the Republican-associated public relations firm Russo Marsh & Rogers, founded by Sal Russo, another OCDB senior leader and important figure behind the Tea Party movement. During the 2008 presidential campaign, when OCDB ran a political ad questioning Obama's statements on religion, Wierzbicki defended the group's ad, asking: "Is Barack Obama's faith the Muslim registration listed by his family when he was a student growing up in Indonesia?" Wierzbicki asked in defense. "Or is it the black liberation theology espoused by Reverend Jeremiah Wright? Or is it the mainstream Christianity he identified with in the forum hosted by Pastor Rick Warren?"[7]

Wierzbicki believes that the movement should not be in a rush to anoint a leader, which might be "a divisive factor" if decided upon too early. Somewhere between now and 2012, he suggests, "is probably the period of time when you'll find a big national leader that will emerge that the majority of the people in this movement will feel comfortable following." But he warns mainstream Republicans: "Those politicians that aren't responsive to this message are going to face a lot of trouble in their re-election bids in 2010." That's a message that already seems to be getting through.

Vice Chairman and organizer for Our Country Deserves Better, Mark Williams, hosted a political talk show in San Diego for a few years and now pinch-hits for other hosts while also appearing frequently on Fox and MSNBC. He writes a widely read newsletter, used by many talk-radio hosts. In past years, he has led rallies of listeners for border enforcement, for supporting U.S. troops in Iraq and Afghanistan, and on behalf of the nomination of John Bolton as U.S. ambassador to the UN. Williams led rallies in multiple cities during the Tea Party Express Tour of summer 2009, often speaking with his fellow activist and Marine mother, Deborah Johns, who liked to tell crowds: "The men and women in our military didn't fight and die for this country for a communist in the White House." Williams would go her one better, telling crowds: "You can have our country when you pry it from our . . . cold . . . dead . . . fingers!" He also has the capacity for the most incendiary of rhetoric, as in September 2009, when he wrote on his blog that President Obama was an "Indonesian Muslim turned welfare thug" and a "racist in chief"—and then defended his remarks in a CNN interview with Anderson Cooper.

Eric Odom is the kind of figure that typifies the Tea Party grassroots leadership: energetic, impassioned, and, perhaps most of all, unpredictable. He's a 29-year-old libertarian Web developer living in Chicago who is apparently the mastermind of the Patriot Caucus, which he describes as "a peer-powered entity being put in place to facilitate an environment of mass collaboration and communication within the liberty movement." Odom is also the founder of the American Liberty Alliance and perhaps dozens of other organizations and websites that are not easily tracked. He was the chief organizer of the Chicago Tea Party in April 2009, at which RNC National Chairman Michael Steele tried to speak. But Odom rebuffed him, telling him if he was interested, to come listen, and not speak. In November 2009, he formed a new PAC, Liberty First, to raise money from Tea Party activists to donate to congressional challengers whose views uphold movement principles. And he showed his independent streak again in February 2010, when he pulled out of the National Tea Party Convention in Nashville due to his concerns over its financing.

Symbolic Leaders

Many have asked: who are the leaders of the Tea Party movement? The answer is simple: there are no leaders. To be sure, some Republican politicians have tried to co-opt the Tea Party message—some successfully, others unsuccessfully—which we will discuss at length in the next chapter; however, as Sarah Palin put it during her speech at the National Tea Party Convention, "This is about the people, and it's bigger than any one king or queen of a tea party."

There are, of course, symbolic leaders.

If you were to say "Tea Party" to a stranger on the street, they would likely reply "Sarah Palin." Palin is Exhibit Number One for the increasing influence and popularity of the Tea Party. She is the symbolic leader of the movement, and more than anyone else has helped to shape it.

No wonder Palin was tapped to give the keynote address at the first National Tea Party Convention held in Nashville, TN, a gathering that brought hundreds of activists to the country music capital in February 2010. To chants of "run Sarah, run," she offered what some observers described as the rudiments of a potential presidential platform. "America is ready for another revolution," Palin said, criticizing Obama's bailouts as having "replaced private irresponsibility with public irresponsibility."[8]

It's easy to see how Palin took on this role. While she drew harsh criticism from policymakers in both parties during the 2008 presidential election, not to mention those within the McCain campaign itself, Palin was in many ways the first political leader in the nation to appeal directly and overwhelmingly to the emerging right-wing populist sentiment that had no champion among the political elite in Washington. Indeed, some would credit Palin for the emergence of the movement itself. To the contrary, as we have explored in depth, we believe Palin simply echoed the sentiments that were on the ascent throughout 2008 and 2009.

Indeed, Palin wasted no time sounding populist themes during her stint as the Republican vice presidential nominee. Her memorable Republican National Convention speech included shout-outs to "hockey moms" and "Joe six-packs," praised small town mayors, and mocked urban community organizers—a not so veiled attack against Barack Obama and Big Labor. Not since James Stockdale, Ross Perot's running mate in 1992, had Americans seen a figure on the national stage so clearly outside the mainstream power establishment.

However, unlike the unfortunate Stockdale, Palin made the difference work for her. As she told her convention audience in Minneapolis: "Here's a little news flash: I'm not a member of the permanent political establishment. And I've learned quickly these past few days that if you're not a member in good standing of the Washington elite then some in the media consider a candidate unqualified for that reason alone. . . . I'm not going to Washington to seek their good opinion."

Palin had perfected that pitch from the very beginning of her political career a decade earlier, when she'd ran for mayor of Wasilla, Alaska. Even then, her campaign pamphlet proclaimed "I'm tired of 'business as usual' in this town, and of the 'Good Ol' Boys' network that runs the show here." Though a savvy politician in truth, she quickly became styled on the populist right as Everywoman fighting against the Elites.

Palin became the Republican ticket's leading draw on the stump, attracting crowds far larger than John McCain's. Her run-ins with the media only made her right-wing supporters defend her more fiercely; her unique, sometimes surreal syntax only made her fans identify with her more closely. And even in July 2009, when she stunningly stepped down as governor of Alaska, her popularity didn't suffer in the least. She simply used her new status as a free agent to channel populist discontent by lobbing verbal grenades at the president ("we need a commander-in-chief, not a professor of law," she said in Nashville) and his policies. In a shrewd deployment of the new social media that echoed around the world, Palin took to her Facebook page in August 2009 to criticize the Democrats' healthcare reform legislation, saying it would authorize government "death panels" that would make end-of-life decisions for seniors.[9] Although her assertion was widely debunked, it only enhanced her credibility among the growing right-wing populist movement and helped make her a *New York Times* bestselling author. Her memoir of the 2008 campaign, *Going Rogue*, debuted at No. 1 on Nielsen's Book-Scan chart with 1.6 million hardcover copies in print at this writing.[10]

The people are ahead of the pundits: In a mid-July Public Policy Polling survey, she polled equally to Obama in an individual horserace, at 46–46.

As much as Palin has become the champion of the Tea Party movement, she is far from the only national figure leading the right's populist charge. As we explored in the previous chapter, over the course of 2009, a number of figures championed the right-wing populist movement. And many will be on the ballot in 2010.

One of the few Tea Party heroes on Capitol Hill is Representative Michele Bachmann, a Republican who has represented Minnesota's sixth congressional district since 2006. On November 3, 2009, Bachmann appeared on Fox News to call upon fellow conservatives to join her in protesting the healthcare reform bill, at a rally to be held on the steps of the capital on the fifth, which she dubbed the "Super Bowl of freedom." "Nothing scares members of Congress more than freedom-loving Americans," she said during a conference call with bloggers and activists on the evening of November 4.

Bachmann was one of two keynote speakers scheduled to address the National Tea Party Convention in February 2010, but dropped out in late January citing the $500 fee that convention organizer Tea Party Nation was charging each attendee. Bachmann's communications director, David Dziok, issued the following statement: ". . . Some will want to portray her withdrawal as a repudiation of the Tea Party Movement, but that couldn't be further from the truth. Congresswoman Bachmann remains encouraged by all Americans, regardless of political party, who are concerned about this nation's future and dwindling prosperity, and continues to be inspired their passion."[11]

The Base

Who are these Tea Party supporters? They are, by and large, a cross section of America. A February 2010 CNN poll identified the demographic composition of those who have been involved in the Tea Party movement.

- Gender: The majority of Tea Party activists are male: 60% male, 40% female.
- Race: They are predominantly white: 80% white, 12% minorities.

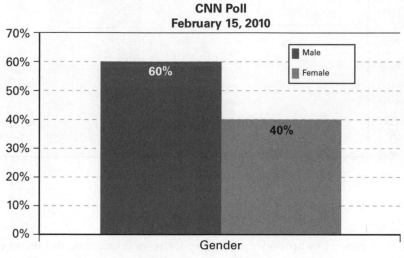

Source: CNN Poll, February 15, 2010.

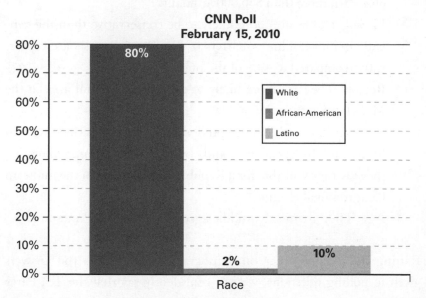

Source: CNN Poll, February 15, 2010.

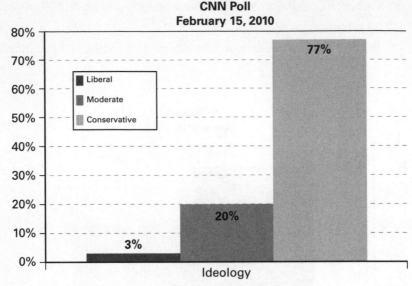

Source: CNN Poll, February 15, 2010.

- Class: They are above average in terms of education, and income: 40% are college graduates. They are above average in income, 66% earn more than $50,000 annually.

- Ideology: They are more likely to be conservative than the general electorate. Three-quarters of Tea Party activists are conservative compared to 40% of the public.

- Region: They are more likely to come from a rural area in the Midwest, South, or West.

- Party Affiliation: They are predominantly self-described Republicans and Independents, and, by an overwhelming majority, they say they will vote for a Republican candidate in the midterm Congressional election.

- Age: They are mostly middle aged (30 to 64) and Protestant.[12]

Putting the data together on demographics as well as the answers given to polling questions, we can confidently say that the Tea Party movement, at present, represents a solid one-third of the electorate, if

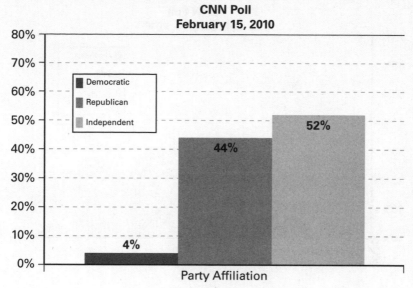

CNN Poll
February 15, 2010

Party Affiliation

Source: CNN Poll, February 15, 2010.

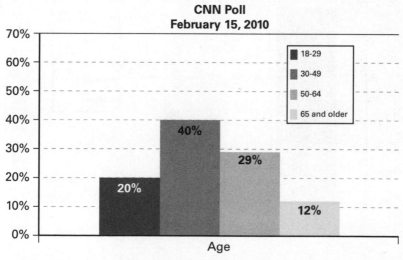

CNN Poll
February 15, 2010

Age

Source: CNN Poll, February 15, 2010.

not considerably more, perhaps right up to 50 percent. These levels of support clearly demonstrate how far the movement has come and how broad its support now is.

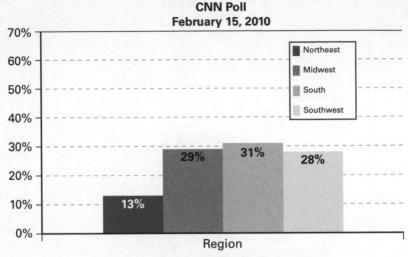

Source: CNN Poll, February 15, 2010.

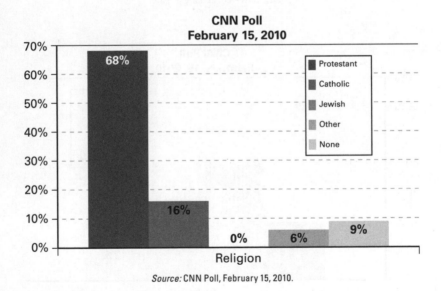

Source: CNN Poll, February 15, 2010.

EXPLAINING THE TEA PARTY "BASE"

The Tea Party base is an unexplained phenomenon. In 2008, we wit-nessed extremely decisive national elections in which the Democratic

Party won the presidency and captured overwhelming majorities in the House and the Senate. Some six months later, a populist movement was afoot that in 2010 threatens the Democrats' congressional majorities, and portends ominously for their chances at retaining the presidency in 2012.

What happened?

In addition to the historic trends described in Chapter 2, two major shifts in American society have conspired to elevate right-wing populism to a national movement: an economic shift and a political shift. We have studied and cataloged these changes through in-person interviews with right-wing populists, as well as surprising new poll data.

Economic Shift

In Chapter 3, we described in detail the economic forces that caused incredible pain and hardship for millions of American families. Recession, globalization, and outsourcing: these forces have converged in a devastating way, resulting in a historic and unprecedented percentage of Americans who are today unemployed and underemployed. The result has been not only the upending of countless lives, but also a near-universal decline in our national outlook.

To put it bluntly, from an economic perspective, Americans feel that things might never be the same again.

We have spoken with dozens of people at right-wing populist events across the country, and our in-depth interviews show this economic dislocation as a major factor in grassroots recruiting for the Tea Party movement.

At a Tea Party Express event in California, for instance, we spoke to a middle-class couple in their fifties who chose not to give us their names. The husband, an independent voter and entrepreneur who works in the real estate industry, explained why he became active in the Tea Party movement: "To be honest with you, I feel like the government and big business have cooked the books. That it's all a big spin.

And the little guys are losing our pensions. My mom? Her pension is shot. She worked her whole life and has lost so much money. The senior citizens and the veterans are getting raw deals. And the bureaucratic spin is so complex that the lawyers can't even figure it out. That's the game. It seems like a game of musical chairs. And all of the insiders have a chair, and the mom-and-pops are kept out. The middle class gets stuck paying for the lower class, while the upper class uses their connections to beat the system. If you're not on the side of the haves or the have-nots, you're *done*."

But it's deeper than solely economic dislocation, as the gentleman quoted above demonstrates. The position of ordinary Americans has declined precipitously and at the same moment that the government came to the rescue of Wall Street and businesses that were, in the opinion of some, "too big to fail." Throughout the course of 2009, Americans were presented with the confounding and enraging fact that Wall Street had rebounded significantly while unemployment continued to mount. Corporate America, with the help of the federal government, seemed well on its way to recovery. Meanwhile, working America struggled with ever-mounting job losses, wage cuts, and home foreclosures.

Indeed, our independent polling on the motivations of Tea Party supporters shows just how significant the Great Recession and economic dislocation have been in driving the right-wing populist movement. In fact, our research clearly identifies economic factors as the number one motivating factor among Americans who now identify with the Tea Party movement.

Political Shift

Since the historic 2008 elections, the American political landscape has simply been transformed. The fundamentals that existed in 2008 have been replaced by new realities.

What has happened is perfectly clear. Across the political spectrum and particularly among Independent voters, a dramatic shift occurred in 2009. As recently as President Obama's election in 2008, Independent voters decisively backed the Democratic Party. According to nationwide exit polling, Independents represented 29 percent of the electorate in 2008. And this extremely large and important bloc of voters supported Barack Obama by a sizable 52 to 44 percent margin.[13]

There is no question that Independents decided the 2008 presidential election. In decisive swing states in particular, Obama's support among Independents was absolutely critical. Obama won 52 percent of the Independent vote in Florida in 2008, compared to 45 percent of independent voters who supported McCain.[14] In Iowa, Independents broke for Obama by a whopping 56 to 41 percent. Similarly, in Nevada, Obama received 56 percent of the Independent vote, compared to 41 percent for McCain.[15] Across the country, Independent voters tipped the scales in favor of the Democratic Party and handed Barack Obama the White House on November 4, 2008.

Independent voters, the largest voting bloc in American politics today, are precisely the mainstream Americans we described in the Chapter 4. They are working people, whose lives have been turned upside down by the convergence of economic, political, and social forces that have resulted in massive unemployment, an unresponsive government, an economic system stacked against them, and a sense that the nation is in a tailspin. They are furious at the political elite for being out of touch, and for ignoring their needs and their plight.

We heard this sentiment expressed countless times in interviews with right-wing populists at events across the country. On the road with the Tea Party Express, we met David, a 19-year-old from Los Angeles, and a student at the University of Southern California. David told us that he is "upset with the direction it's going." He explained that he is completely fed up with both major parties, and sought out the Tea Party movement as an alternative to the usual rhetoric and the failed leadership of the Democratic and Republican parties: "State and national legislators are out of touch. They're prima donnas up there and unfortunately a certain segment of the population keeps voting them back into office year after year. Especially in LA, where it's so liberal, we're just a tiny segment of the audience and we can't get a word in. Arnold's doing a terrible job. California's in a crisis right now."

Support for the Democratic Party among Independent voters was decisive not only in 2008, but also in the critical 2006 midterm Congressional elections, which gave Democrats control of both the House and the Senate. As the *Washington Post* noted, "Most important were independents, the quintessential swing voters: They favored Democrats by a huge 57–39 percent, the Democrats' largest margin among independents in 20 years."[16]

Compared to the 2006 and 2008 election cycles, there has since been a sudden and dramatic change among Independent voters. This all-important segment of the electorate votes just as easily for Democrats or Republicans based on the issues of the day and the political climate of the nation. And as 2009 came to a close, Scott's polling showed that Independents were more inclined to vote for the Tea Party than any other political party.

This rapid turnaround is simply unprecedented in modern American politics. And it shows that right-wing populism is being fueled not merely by conservative Republicans, but also and to a greater extent by mainstream Independents. The Tea Party movement has attracted supporters from each of the three right-wing strands in American politics. The economic, social, and political convergence of forces described in Chapter 2 has also enabled the unification of the economic, libertarian, and social strands of the conservative movement.

This is an unprecedented occurrence in American politics. And it has gone largely unnoticed. There is a simple and obvious explanation for the lack of attention paid and analysis given to this unification of the conservative movement under the banner of right-wing populism. The media and political pundits have ignored this more significant development because they have been distracted by the radical voices that have inevitably crept into the Tea Party movement.

Over the course of 2009, a disproportionate amount of media attention was devoted to those in the Tea Party movement who hold outlandish social and political views. During the healthcare town-hall forums, for instance, a number of right-wing protesters across the country made disgusting comparisons between the president's agenda on health care and National Socialism in Nazi Germany. Indeed, some protesters even brought homemade signs to town-hall meetings depicting Barack Obama as Hitler. Others produced ugly and racists posters of the President as a witch doctor, a brainless attempt to critique the administration's healthcare proposal.

There is no question that despicable acts of protest such as the above were widespread. There is also no question that they were encouraged by right-wing media figures Glenn Beck and Rush Limbaugh, in blatant acts of sensationalism to drive their ratings. Furthermore, the racist views of a minority of right-wing protestors were seized upon by the political elite as a reason to dismiss the Tea Party movement entirely.

The disrespectful and inappropriate actions and statements of numerous Tea Party activists were no doubt unfortunate and counterproductive. And they caused the majority of political observers to miss the dramatic change under way in the electorate. Most were quick to dismiss *all* Tea Party protesters as racist and irrelevant. They failed to *listen* to the underlying concerns of the tens of thousands of activists who attended rallies and town halls.

The result is that the most profound change in American politics in a generation or more has gone underreported and nearly unnoticed. The three strands of the conservative tradition have, for the moment, united. The question remains: can the Tea Party movement maintain unity among these disparate elements?

A DIFFUSE, GRASS-ROOTS MOVEMENT

Clearly, the Tea Party movement's achievements in just over a year's time have been impressive: it has become the most potent popular force in American politics. It has already shaped electoral outcomes and promises to play a major role in elections to come. But for all this—and for all its sometimes well-connected sponsors, like a Dick Armey or a David Koch—it is important to remember that at its core, the movement remains a diffuse, grass-roots phenomenon. As we've pointed out earlier, the people powering the Tea Party movement are in many cases first-time activists from all walks of life, motivated not by political ideology but by their concerns about the future of the country.

Organizationally, the Tea Party movement is a loose collection of dozens, even hundreds of groups. Some, like those profiled above, are well funded, but many more are not; some are national in prominence, while many others operate only locally. There are so many national, state, local, and county organizations using "Tea Party" in their name that it's all but impossible to keep track of them all, and they cannot keep track of one another. As talk-radio host Phil Valentine put it: "The tea-party movement has no leader, and . . . neither did the American Revolution."

Adding to the complexity, the movement is affiliated with many conservative special-interest groups that have only marginal ties to the broader Tea Party movement—especially those groups working on traditional social-conservative issues like abortion or school prayer, which have rarely been the focus of Tea Party political activity. These groups are only loosely aligned with the Republican Party and take pains to define themselves as nonpartisan, though they have worked for the election of certain favored GOP candidates and will continue to do so.

At the same time, the movement's diffusion, and its on-again, off-again tension with the GOP present some long-term challenges. There is some risk of dissension and splintering, and evidence of that has already been seen in some of the grumbling about the National Tea Party Convention in Nashville. Some feel it's time the movement found a national leader. Eric Odom's Patriot Caucus plans to hold a conference at Valley Forge in April to elect national delegates and build consensus within the movement, but it's not clear which groups will participate or what form such a consensus would take.

Tea Party organizers have struggled in recent months to clamp down on fringe elements that have sprung up around—and sometimes within—the movement, including white supremacists and conspiracy theorists who believe that the government played a role in the September 11, 2001, terrorist attacks ("truthers") or that President Barack Obama was not born in the United States and is therefore ineligible to be president ("birthers").[17]

CHALLENGES THE TEA PARTIES FACE

The challenges that the Tea Parties face include extremism on the one hand and racism on the other.

While it may very well have been isolated people who were engaged in racial epithets, nevertheless three Democratic congressmen said something happened, while there were no identified culprits who did this, it's not like anyone denies the occurrence.

On "Meet the Press" Sunday morning, Boehner called the episodes "isolated incidents" but condemned them nonetheless.

And RNC Chairman Michael Steele referred to the protesters as "some stupid people out there saying some very stupid things."

What this does is it isolates the Tea Parties. It means that they are less of a mainstream movement, and less likely to gain mainstream acceptability.

And in the aftermath of the healthcare vote, we are seeing the balance of power between the GOP and the Tea Party movement undergoing a considerable shift from where it had been in February 2010.

Over the course of the week following the House vote, the very same Tea Party leaders who had insisted that they would not be co-opted or manipulated by the Republican Party, were looking to align themselves with the GOP.

Look no further than Dick Armey's rhetorical transformation. Let us not forget that in early February 2010, Armey described Republican lawmakers as "the ones that broke your heart."[18]

Yet, less than two months later, in the aftermath of the House vote, Armey could be found publicly praising GOP lawmakers who, he decreed, "spoke up for liberty unabashedly.

"We were pretty proud of 'em. I watched and said, 'By Jove, I think they've got it.'"

Our view is that the movement's decentralized nature is more a strength than a weakness. Its leaders may comes and go, but the movement is entrenched for the long haul—in whatever forms it may eventually take. It has steadily grown in organization, in capacity, and in impact, not by becoming one giant, merged PAC or the property of one political party, but by maintaining its independence and variety. It has forced the parties, especially the GOP, to move in its direction, not the other way around. While some organizational streamlining may be inevitable in the future, the Tea Party movement's power lies in the way it mirrors the diversity, nonconformity, and individuality of the American people. This "disorganized" quality has put the political class on the run and changed American politics.

THE DYNAMICS, TACTICS, AND FUTURE OF THE TEA PARTY MOVEMENT

People are coming out because they've finally realized that they can't just sit there and hope that the Republicans will take care of everything or that we'll be able to just stay a constitutional republic. They're changing it in Washington, and we want to keep our American values.

—Neil, small business owner Bakersfield, California

For as much coverage as its rallies and events have gotten, the Tea Party movement's tactics and dynamics have gone unanalyzed and unreported. Most commentators have been more interested in covering outlandish personalities or reporting on major political stories in which the Tea Party movement has had an impact, such as Scott Brown's election to the Senate in Massachusetts.

That was the political event of early 2010, to be sure, but most people still don't understand how it happened.

How did the Tea Parties manage to elect the previously unknown Brown to the old Kennedy Seat in Massachusetts, which resembled a legacy fiefdom as close as anything could in American politics? And beyond Massachusetts, how has the Tea Party influenced the Republican Party, and in what ways?

We will answer these fundamental questions in this chapter. And, in doing so, we'll provide a window into the future of the Tea Party movement.

In 2008, a plurality of Americans identified with the Democratic Party and Barack Obama's liberal agenda. Just after the 2008 elections, a Gallup survey conducted from November 13–16, 2008, found that 39 percent of the nation identified themselves as Democratic, 35 percent as Independent, and a meager 26 percent as Republican. America, which has traditionally been a center-right nation, was listing left.

One year later, the electorate looks completely different. Today, 20 percent of America is liberal, 40 percent is conservative, and 40 percent is independent. A Gallup survey conducted from December 11–13, 2009, found that today, 33 percent identify as Democrats, 29 percent as Republicans, and 36 percent as Independents.[1]

In December 2009, Scott conducted a series of polls that captured the dramatic change that has occurred in Americans politics, and the unprecedented nature of insurgent right-wing populism. In short, Scott has found that right-wing conservatives represent a tremendous and growing segment of the American electorate. It is a bloc of voters that are furious with the political elite and the direction of the nation, and this burgeoning group has the potential to transform our politics in the 2010-midterm elections and beyond.

The big take-away of Scott's polling was that for the first time since 1992, a demonstrable segment of the American electorate identified with an independent third party. Scott's poll asked respondents to state which party they would support in Congressional elections if the Tea Party were a national political party. The results were astonishing. About a third of respondents—36 percent—said they would vote Democratic. Coming in a strong second, at 23 percent, were voters who would support a Tea Party candidate. Republican respondents trailed badly at 18 percent, and a sizable 22 percent of voters were unsure in December 2009 whom they would support in 2010 Congressional elections.

Even more astonishing were the responses of critical independent voters, who represent the largest segment of the American electorate and who have decided every presidential contest in modern political history. A solid 33 percent of Independents supported the Tea Party in Scott's poll, while only 25 percent supported the Democrats, and a meager 12 percent supported the Republicans.

Even Republican voters were evenly split on whether they would support their party or a new Tea Party. Only 39 percent of respondents said that they would vote Republican, while 33 percent of Republican voters said they would defect and vote for a Tea Party candidate.

But another question was perhaps the most telling in Scott's poll. When asked whether "Republicans and Democrats are so much alike that an entirely new party needed to represent the American people," a resounding 41 percent of respondents said "yes."

This is a stunning turnaround, barely a year after a highly partisan election in which the difference between the two major parties couldn't have been starker.

The right-wing populist movement has fundamentally changed the Republican Party, too, both in terms of its policy initiatives and its leadership. Sarah Palin sold 700,000 copies of her memoir in less than a week and embarked on a national book tour that drew overflowing, adoring crowds, sparking intense speculation about her 2012 presidential ambitions. Right-wing populism has accelerated a tendency toward ideological purity that had already begun during the Bush years and strained the Republican Party's old reputation as a "big tent" of diverse constituencies. A January 2009 Rasmussen poll, for example, found that "the plurality of GOP voters (43%) say their party has been too moderate over the past eight years, and 55% think it should become more like Alaska Governor Sarah Palin in the future." These numbers reflect a party driven by a populist core increasingly uninterested in compromise.

Conservative activists are putting pressure on Republicans in Congress to vote their way, and even once-proud members of the Right have come under suspicion. A perfect example is Mark Souder of Indiana, one of Newt Gingrich's foot soldiers in 1994, when he won his House seat. By 2010, he faced the prospect of a primary challenge from an even

purer right-wing candidate. "On the big issues, I don't think you're going to see much bipartisanship because our right wing has dug in so
hard," Souder said. The chairmen of the national Republican House
and Senatorial election committees have counseled incumbents on how
to avoid primary challenges: namely, avoid bipartisan compromises
with Obama and the Democrats.

But this advice, while it may save their existing seats, puts Republicans in a difficult bind. How can they broaden their appeal if they don't
reach out?

As Senator Lindsey Graham of South Carolina put it, "We are not
losing blue states and shrinking as a party because we are not conservative enough. If we pursue a party that has no place for someone who
agrees with me 70 percent of the time, that is based on an ideological
purity test rather than a coalition test, then we are going to keep losing." But Graham does not speak for the "base." Like his friend and
colleague John McCain, he is a figure of deep suspicion on the right for
his willingness to work across the aisle.

And Graham misses one key point about the upcoming 2010 Congressional election, which is that it is an energy election. What the Tea
Parties have done is given enthusiasm and a raison d'être to the cause
of the Republican Party.

There is little, if any energy left in the Republican Party. In his Sunday column in late February 2010, *New York Times* columnist Frank
Rich reiterated this point, writing: "The distinction between the Tea
Party movement and the official G.O.P. is real, and we ignore it at our
peril. While Washington is fixated on the natterings of Mitch McConnell, John Boehner, Michael Steele and the presumed 2012 Republican
presidential front-runner, Mitt Romney, these and the other leaders of
the Party of No are anathema or irrelevant to most Tea Partiers. Indeed, McConnell, Romney and company may prove largely irrelevant
to the overall political dynamic taking hold in America right now. The
old G.O.P. guard has no discernible national constituency beyond the
scattered, often impotent remnants of aging country club Republican-

ism. The passion on the right has migrated almost entirely to the Tea Party's counterconservatism."[2]

PARTY HOPPING: THE IMPACT OF THE TEA PARTY MOVEMENT ON THE GOP

In just over a year, the Tea Party movement has gone from being considered a fringe protest movement to becoming the primary driving force in the Republican Party. The evidence is available across the country, in campaign strategies, in gestures small and large, and in political tactics. To roll it up in the most succinct way: the movement has pushed the GOP mainstream further right, so much so that moderate Republican candidates in 2010 are all busily polishing their conservative credentials, even if they have few to show.

In early 2009, when the first Tea Parties were held, it seemed like the latest in a long line of American political protest movements, and its harsh criticism of both Republicans and Democrats made it seem likely that the Tea Parties might try to field candidates outside the two-party structure. But a year later, that's all changed: the Tea Party label has become synonymous with electoral success, and it does not need to form a third party to achieve results—though that's still a possibility, We're seeing even the most moderate of Republicans embracing Tea Party values. It's the Republican Party, wrote Kate Zernike in the *New York Times,* that is "trying to harness the Tea Party energy" and "make nice with Tea Party groups" in states all across the country.[3]

As Valerie Richardson noted in a February 11, 2010, piece for the *Washington Times*: "When moderate Republicans do well, it's often because they're running to the right. Colorado's [Jane] Norton has tried to win conservative support by calling for a balanced-budget amendment, a two-thirds vote in Congress to raise taxes, and a moratorium on 'earmarks.'. . . . 'I think conservatives see a different picture out there with all the candidates trying to wrap themselves in tea party and limited-government principles,' said a senior aide to a top conservative senator. 'If moderates have succeeded, it's because they've . . . come our way and embraced less spending, less debt, less government control. When everyone is trying to out-conservative each other, that's a sign of success.'"[4]

In Massachusetts, Scott Brown's victory has sent a slew of gubernatorial candidates in search of Tea Party approval. "People across Massachusetts are trying to step in and take advantage of our movement," said Christen Varley, an organizer for the Tea Party of Greater Boston. Republican candidates Christy Mihos and Charles Baker have already reached out to Tea Party groups in advance of the state's November election. Independent candidate Timothy Cahill, and even sitting Governor Deval Patrick, a Democrat, have expressed interest in winning support from grass-roots groups.[5] In South Carolina, the state Republican Party has announced that it would unite with and share resources with Tea Party groups in the state, an alliance that both groups concede will "push the GOP in a more conservative direction."[6]

Not even the Republican Party's 2008 standard-bearer, John McCain, is immune to this trend.

McCain is facing a tough primary challenge from former Congressman J. D. Hayworth, who has pilloried him for his moderate stands on issues like global warming and taxes. Now he's moving rightwards in his campaign for another term, mocking global-warming science on the Sean Hannity show and speaking out against "Don't Ask, Don't Tell," an issue on which he had expressed an open mind previously and repeatedly. But McCain's longtime service to the GOP has put him in good position to call in favors, and he's wasted no time in doing so: Sarah Palin has announced that she'll campaign for him, and Tea Party hero Scott Brown has made robo-calls on his behalf. Right-wing blogger Michelle Malkin, bemused, calls it McCain Regression Syndrome: "After a career bashing the right flank of the party, Sen. McCain is now clinging to its coattails to save his incumbent hide."

The Illinois Senate seat vacated by the man who beat McCain for the presidency in 2008 is open in November 2010, and Congressman Mark Kirk will be the GOP's candidate in that race. Over five terms in the House, Kirk has built up a solid moderate voting record: he voted for cap-and-trade legislation and led a small group of GOP congressmen in opposition to the Iraq Surge. The NRA gives him an "F," while NARAL gives him a 100 percent pro-choice rating. But that was then, and this is now. As Reid Wilson of HotlineOnCall put it: "Kirk has tacked to the right lately, going back on his cap and trade vote, voting in favor of the pro-life Stupak Amendment two weeks ago and vociferously supporting a troop surge in Afghanistan." But mere words may not be enough for Kirk to stave off right-wing criticism of his candidacy—a new resolution within the GOP targets the voting records of Republican office holders and holds them up to harsh scrutiny.

The defection of Arlen Specter to the Democratic Party was a perfect example of what can happen to Republicans who do not court the populist base. For years, the centrist, moderate Specter was detested on the Right's talk-show circuit for not being a true conservative. Facing a primary challenge in 2010 from a conservative candidate, the Club for Growth's Pat Toomey, Specter saw the handwriting on the wall and crossed the aisle to become a Democrat. He was no longer willing, he said, to be "judged by the Pennsylvania Republican primary electorate."

You might think losing one of the party's most powerful senators would count as a setback, but on the populist right, the sentiment was "good riddance." Specter was "deadly for the Republican brand," said South Carolina governor Mark Sanford (not long before becoming rather deadly himself, due to a sex scandal). Rush Limbaugh cheered Specter's defection for "weeding out people who aren't really Republicans."

And what constitutes a "real Republican" has far more to do with commitment to core economic and social conservative values than political experience or position in the traditional Republican Party hierarchy.

A May 2009 USA Today/Gallup poll asked voters who they believe is the main person who speaks for the Republican Party. Among Re-

publicans and Republican leaners, talk radio host Rush Limbaugh was
tied for first place with former Speaker of the House and contemporary
Tea Party ally, Newt Gingrich, while John McCain trailed with 6 percent and George W. Bush came dead least with 0 percent.

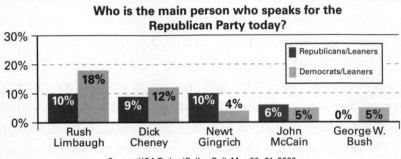

Source: USA Today/Gallup Poll, May 29–31, 2009.

In November 2009, the Republican National Committee considered
a resolution, a so-called "Purity Test," that would deny funding and
endorsements to candidates who didn't uphold a set of core conservative
principles. Members failing to make the cut on eight out of the ten principles would be cut off from funding. The measure didn't get through
in its original form, but a few months later the GOP adopted a similar
version of the purity test without the binding penalties. Candidates
would merely have to express "support" for that platform.

Presidential hopefuls from "big P" Populist William Jennings
Bryan to the plutocratic populist Ross Perot have attempted to reach out
to mainstream Americans by defining their candidacy as "populist." As
writer and philosopher, Larrey Anderson noted in a February 7, 2010,
piece for *American Thinker*: "There have been populist (and wannabe
populist) political movements, on the left, on the right, and even in the
middle (wherever that is), in the history of American politics. None of
the movements were particularly successful—and many of them were
outright scams."[7]

In the months leading up to the 2010 midterm elections, various

THE DYNAMICS, TACTICS, AND FUTURE OF THE TEA PARTY MOVEMENT   177

politicians have jumped on board the Tea Party bandwagon as strategic means for electoral success. We will profile a number of these candidates later in this chapter.

However, a warning for all Tea Partiers in Name Only:

> We Declare ourselves INDEPENDENT of the Republican Party, which has in the past manipulated its Conservative Base to win election after election and which then betrays everything that Base fought for and believed.

So reads Article III in the "Tea Party Declaration of Independence," which can be found on the website Saveourmovement.com, created by the Tea Party Patriots in response to Michael Steele's attempt to "hijack" their movement.

The GOP has been trying to tap into Tea Party sentiment and corral it for party momentum in multiple ways. As the *Washington Post*'s Phillip Rucker noted: "Steele, House Republican leader John A. Boehner (Ohio) and other party leaders have said recently that winning over tea party activists is critical to the GOP's hopes of regaining congressional majorities in November."[8]

RNC Chairman Michael Steele has been vocal in his praise for the Tea Party movement, even suggesting at one point that if he didn't have his current job, he'd be a Tea Party organizer. In December 2009, Steele's RNC organized a Capitol Hill Tea Party Rally, and Steele hit the road with FreedomWorks' Dick Armey to campaign against the Obama administration's healthcare reform bill. When you have a national party chairman taking stands indistinguishable from those of a protest movement, you know that the movement has broken through.

Still, fissures remain. So long as Obama and the Democrats remain in charge, the Tea Party and the GOP will likely maintain an uneasy alliance. If the GOP regains power, however, the relationship is bound to become more contentious and complicated.

For now, Steele and other party leaders seem eager to follow the advice—at least superficially—of two of the Tea Party's most revered political figures, Michele Bachmann and Sarah Palin. In January 2010, Bachmann was blunt in saying that "if the Republican Party is wise, they will allow themselves to be re-defined by the tea party movement."

But Steele and the RNC crossed the line when they launched a Tea Party–themed website, www.teaparty.gop.com, to try to draw on the political energies of Tea Party supporters. The site encourages visitors to send a teabag-imprinted electronic "postcard" to Obama, Harry Reid, or Nancy Pelosi protesting the Democrats' tax-and-spend policies.

Tea Party activists have no interest in being used as a marketing tool by the old Republican Guard. As the Tea Party Patriots Florida coordinator, Everett Wilkinson, explained in an interview with Newsmax: "I think Michael Steele has shown a pattern of arrogance with his own party by having speaking tours, by having a book come out, where he should be focusing on the issues of his party. He's not, he wants to run a publicity campaign. . . . In this case, he wants to hijack the tea-party movement to promote his own name, rather than focus on the issues facing his party. . . . We feel Michael Steele is intentionally trying to hijack the movement, because he's been aware of the national tea party leaders . . . he's been advised of our stance regarding the GOP and the tea-party movement, that our intentions are not to be involved with a specific party—specifically the GOP—but rather to influence public policy in order to secure our mission."[9]

The controversy proved to be humiliating for the RNC and Steele, who learned the hard way that, as we detailed in Chapters 5 and 6, the Tea Party movement is a bottom-up movement with no interest in being commandeered by ruling elites.

The only way that the Republican Party can harness the Tea Party energy is if they demonstratively embrace the core values that lie at the heart of the movement. As Fox News host and Tea Party figurehead Glenn Beck's closing remarks at the 2010 Conservative Political Action Committee Convention: "I have not heard people in the Republican Party admit yet that they have a problem. I haven't seen the Come-

To-Jesus moment from Republicans yet. One party will tax and spend. One party won't tax and will spend. It is both of them together. Dick Cheney a couple days ago . . . says it is going to be a good year for conservative ideas. It is going to be a very good year. But it is not enough just to not suck as much as the other side."

At the National Tea Party Convention in Nashville, Palin had similar advice, urging a course of action that would push the Republican Party further rightwards. She urged the Tea Party movement and the GOP to work together toward common goals, but she suggested that the GOP needed to become more like the Tea Party, not the other way around. "The Republican Party would be really smart to try and absorb as much of the Tea Party movement as possible," she said. And she urged Tea Party candidates to take on RINOs (Republicans in Name Only) in 2010 and 2012 primary contests. She pledged to campaign for these candidates, according to a *Washington Post* report, "in contested Republican primaries, even if doing so might split the GOP electorate."[10]

This has already begun happening in a number of states, as we have documented. Tea Party candidates from Alabama and Missouri to California and Illinois are stepping forward in races for Congress, the Senate, and governorships, often joining a primary field that includes approved GOP candidates.

How these races play out, of course, remains to be seen. But Tea Party candidates already have a template from which to build their campaigns: the shocking, transformative victory of Scott Brown in Massachusetts.

ELECTING SCOTT BROWN

Holding on to the old Kennedy Senate seat in Massachusetts should have been a no-brainer for Democrats, or so held the conventional wisdom. But Brown's victory illustrated how far the Tea Party movement has come in just a year from a diffuse protest movement to a formidable electoral player. The Democrats certainly contributed to their own demise: they ran an uninspired, aloof candidate, state attorney general Martha Coakley; the national party viewed the seat as a shoo-in and was late to recognize the trouble she was in; and Coakley's own campaigning was lackluster and failed to connect with voters, who began identifying her more and more with President Obama and ruling elites. Yet the story in Massachusetts was not how the Democratic candidate lost, but how the Republican candidate—who was also, crucially, the Tea Party candidate—won.

Part of achieving electoral success is making compromises and being pragmatic, and many seasoned political observers were surprised that Tea Party groups would get behind the socially moderate Brown, who was a bit of a RINO himself by national GOP standards. Brown was savvy in casting himself as a candidate who was independent and beholden to no one, downplaying his Republican Party affiliation by saying that he was a "Scott Brown Republican" battling the Democratic Party establishment. He tapped into public anger about the Wall Street and banking bailouts and the spiraling federal deficit. And he appealed to Tea Party supporters everywhere and their disdain for entrenched Washington elites when he said, "It's not the Kennedy seat. It's the people's seat."

Tea Party support for Brown began building long before the national media noticed that his race with Coakley had become close. Early on, his campaign focused on winning over conservative media leaders, first in Massachusetts, then out of state, and finally branching out to national political leaders. This began to pay dividends gradually. Brown's online strategist, Rob Willington, emphasized the importance of getting local and even out-of-state activists involved in the campaign.

In October 2009, Bob Lashua, a member of the FreedomWorks Tea Party Group in Leominster, Massachusetts, posted a message on the FreedomWorks website's discussion board. He urged visitors to join the "Brown Brigade" and pointed them toward a social-networking site that the candidate had set up to spread the word and solicit donations. FreedomWorks' national organization was drawn into the campaign in December, when it received repeated email appeals from Brown supporters in Massachusetts. FreedomWorks saw that a victory in Massachusetts—which would give the GOP forty-one senators, enough for a filibuster—could be the silver bullet against Obama's healthcare reform legislation.

The decision by FreedomWorks to commit to the Brown campaign illustrates an important truth about the Tea Party movement: it is far more pragmatic than its critics want to admit. If electing Scott Brown could stop Obama's healthcare plan, then there was no point in worrying about his being perfect on every issue. "He's the kind of Republican who will give conservatives heartburn, but it's better than the other side," said RedState.com editor Erick Erickson, who normally doesn't endorse pro-choice candidates. He began posting frequent appeals on his blog directing readers to Brown's website to contribute.

Once FreedomWorks climbed aboard, momentum began to accelerate. Brown's campaign was able to generate a massive surge in energy, support, national attention, and money. Many of the activists working for his campaign were fresh from the failed campaign of Doug Hoffman in New York District 23, and they had learned a lot from that experience. What the Brown campaigned had that the earlier Hoffman effort lacked was a well-organized, get-out-the-vote effort: from door-to-door efforts to phone banks to online fund-raising and Web campaigns to raise awareness of the approaching January 19 election.

The campaign's conservative media outreach paid off in late December, when Patrick Ruffini, a GOP strategist and blogger, posted a widely circulated commentary arguing what still seemed far-fetched: that Brown could win the election. And Ruffini boiled down the stakes of the race in terms that anyone could understand: "If Brown wins, Obamacare is dead."

Still, the candidate was short of cash and behind in polls. Coakley reported having $937,383.31 in cash on hand, while Brown had just $367,150.88. That's when the Tea Party movement showed how much

they had learned from left-wing groups like MoveOn.org. They organized a "money bomb"—an intense online fund-raising effort over a
brief, fixed time to bring in campaign cash quickly. Money bombs use
all the viral techniques that make the Internet such a potent campaign
tool: email blasts, blogger postings and links, social-networking pages
that accept donations, YouTube video appeals, and so on.

Calling it the "Red Invades Blue" fund-raiser, *the Brown money-
bomb campaign raised $1.3 million in one day*—January 11, 2010. Perhaps
even more impressive, its one-day haul came from over sixteen thousand contributors whose average donation was just $77.89. Less than a
week later, the Our Country Deserves Better PAC launched a $100,000
follow-up money bomb for Brown.

Being an Internet tool, money bombs know no state boundaries;
and sure enough, Tea Party activists in other states participated. This is
a remarkable fact to consider. The Arizona Tea Party Network helped
solicit online donations for a Massachusetts Senate race. But out-of-state
participation wasn't confined to the Web: Tea Party campaign volunteers from New York, Connecticut, and Rhode Island flooded Massachusetts. Members of Tea Parties in Montana, Texas, and Georgia
called in with donations, and the Tea Party Express, based in California, purchased political ads for Brown.

It showed how well the Tea Party movement understood the stakes
of the Massachusetts race, which were indeed national in scope, as well
as how successfully they had begun to pool their efforts.

In addition, the Republican Party, for once, showed that it had
learned something, too. Seeing that Brown's momentum was building
more from his appeal to the Tea Party than his identity as a GOP candidate, the Republican National Senatorial Committee kept its support
low key. In part, they didn't want to tip off sleepwalking Democrats
that they now believed the race was winnable. But their reticence also
showed a new pragmatism in not getting in the way of the Tea Party
message, as well as a new respect for the movement's legitimacy.

Brown's election, says Eric Odom of the American Liberty Alliance, "is not so much about Scott Brown as it is about the idea that if we really collaborate as a mass movement, we can take any seat in the country."

And that movement, though by nature more hospitable to the GOP than to the Democrats, is broad-based and not definable in simple party terms. "In spite of being viewed as conservative," noted Anthony G. Martin in a February 2010 piece for the *Washington Examiner*, "the Tea Party as a movement has not introduced any litmus tests for candidates. The movement, being grassroots, has tended more to focus on the broad issues that unite conservatives of all stripes, such as lower taxes and smaller government, maximum individual liberty, the Constitution as THE ultimate rule of law in the land, free market capitalism, and a strong national defense."[11]

At Brown's victory party on January 19, triumphant activists like Mark Meckler and Jenny Beth Martin of Tea Party Patriots had good reason to exult. Meckler pointed out that Democrats had tried to tar Brown with his Tea Party association; instead, that association had carried him to victory. "What you're seeing here in Massachusetts is a reflection of what's happening all across the country," Meckler said. That remains to be seen. But the importance of the Massachusetts Senate race can't be overstated. As Tea Party activist Jeffrey McQueen, founder of USRevolution2.com, said simply: "If we can win a Senate seat in Massachusetts, there's no place we can't win."

And even before he was sworn in, a Gallup survey found Scott Brown ranking fourth among eleven possible presidential candidates for 2012 among Republicans and Independents. "Brown placed on a statistical par with former Arkansas Gov. Mike Huckabee and former Speaker of the House Newt Gingrich, each with years of national politics behind them," wrote the *Chicago Tribune*'s Michael Muskal. "They pulled 3 percent support in this survey."[12]

THE FUTURE OF THE TEA PARTY MOVEMENT

Scott Brown's election was the beginning, not the end, of the Tea Party's impact on state, local, and national politics. In a number of states, such as Connecticut, Texas, Nevada, Florida, and Pennsylvania, right-wing populism is impacting local and statewide politics. Tea Party, Club for Growth—a conservative, free-market group that promotes lower taxes and less regulation—or unaffiliated right-wing candidates are appealing to the growing number of Independents that are aligned with the Tea Party. The Tea Party movement is having a major impact on some of the year's most important political races.

Tea Party–Affiliated and Supported Candidates

Over the course of 2009, several additional symbolic leaders emerged in the Tea Party movement who are candidates for office in 2010. It is notable that many of these candidates are challenging more moderate Republicans in primary elections.

One of the marquee races of 2010 will be former Republican Congressman Pat Toomey's challenge of former Republican and now Democratic Senator Arlen Specter in Pennsylvania. Toomey is the former President and CEO of the Club for Growth, a PAC that raises money for candidates who support lower taxes and smaller government. A staunch fiscal conservative who has been vehemently opposed to the bank bailouts, Toomey decided to challenge then-Republican incumbent Senator Arlen Specter in the 2010 GOP primary after Specter supported President Obama's stimulus bill. He resigned from Club for Growth and officially declared his candidacy on Tax Day, April 15, 2009.

In a video posted on his website, Toomey noted, "Even though Arlen Specter and I are both Republicans, we differ on these issues, and many others. . . . You see what I see: A nation heading in the wrong direction. . . . Unfortunately, the Washington politicians who helped get us into this mess are making things worse." It was a decidedly populist message meant to portray Specter as a member of the political elite.

Interestingly enough, Specter could levy (and indeed has levied) the same charge against Toomey. After graduating from Harvard, Toomey worked as an investment banker and derivatives trader—for which he has come under fire from the Specter campaign, which accused him of trying to downplay his Wall Street background. He has also opened and owned four restaurants in Allentown and Lancaster, Pennsylvania, along with his brothers. Despite his elite credentials, Toomey has stuck to his populist message, which continues to resonate with voters in recent polling.

In Pennsylvania, according to a February 2010 Franklin & Marshall College poll, two-thirds of Pennsylvania voters have heard of the Tea Party movement, while 35 percent had not. Forty-five percent said that they would vote for candidates who support Tea Party goals, 34 percent said they would not, and 21 percent said that they did not know. One-quarter of the Democrats in the Franklin & Marshall poll said they'd likely vote for a Tea Party-aligned candidate, 68 percent of Republicans and 52 percent of Independent voters said they probably would vote for such a candidate.

Toomey ran for Congress in Pennsylvania's 15th district in 1998, serving until 2004, at which time he resigned in accordance with a pledge he had signed during his first campaign that he would only

Franklin & Marshall Poll

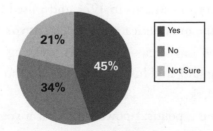

Support Tea Party Candidate

Source: Franklin & Marshall College Poll, February 2010.

serve three terms. Interestingly, Toomey served on the House Budget Committee, the Financial Services Committee, and the Small Business Committee, during a time in which the federal budget ballooned and the lack of regulation of financial services contributed to the financial collapse of 2008.

But Toomey wasn't done with politics: In 2004, aided by Club for Growth publicity, he unsuccessfully challenged Specter in the Republican Primary, coming within two points of denying Specter the nomination even though the GOP establishment, including President Bush, endorsed Specter. Specter was then one of the most powerful Republican Senators, in line to become chairman of the Senate Judiciary Committee.

The experience soured Specter on the GOP. Eventually, in the spring of 2009, he decided to change parties, complaining that the Republican base had grown so conservative as to be incompatible with his personal politics. Many attributed his defection to the fact that polling showed Toomey leading Specter by a wide margin.

Another highly anticipated election is the Republican primary for Florida's U.S. Senate seat, a race that is likely to be decided by precisely those same Independents who elected Barack Obama, and who are not swinging in ever-larger numbers to the right wing. This 2010 race pits moderate Governor Charlie Crist, who has embraced President Obama both literally and figuratively, against Marco Rubio, a 38-year-old charismatic Cuban American former Speaker of the Florida House of Representatives.

Rubio was born in Miami in 1971 and raised by his Cuban-born parents who came to America after Fidel Castro's takeover. He grew up in Miami and Las Vegas—his father working as a bartender and later a crossing guard, and his mother as a hotel housekeeper and later a Kmart stock clerk.

Rubio became a political powerbroker at a young age, serving as a city commissioner for the West Miami community before running for the Florida House in 2000. He served as a Representative from 2000–2008, where he promoted a decidedly conservative legislative agenda, including lower taxes, a leaner and more efficient government, and free market empowerment.

Rubio was appointed Speaker in 2006. He had spent the two years prior to assuming the speakership traveling around the state of Florida, hosting meetings with Florida residents, which he called "Idearaisers," during which he asked them to share their ideas to improve the state. He turned a hundred best ideas into a book entitled *100 Innovative Ideas for Florida's Future*, which was hailed by former Speaker Newt Gingrich as "a work of genius." The Florida House passed every one of the ideas, and fifty-seven became law, including "measures to crack down on gangs and sexual predators, promote energy efficient buildings, appliances and vehicles, and help small businesses obtain affordable health coverage."

Additionally, "Rubio championed a major overhaul of the Florida tax system that would have eliminated all property taxes on primary residences in favor of a flat consumption tax. The effort garnered national attention, with Grover Norquist, president of the fiscally conservative Americans for Tax Reform, praising Rubio as 'the most pro-taxpayer legislative leader in the country.'" [13]

Rubio retired from the Florida House in 2008 due to state term-limit restrictions, and he has been steadily accumulating national support from conservatives since the beginning of his Senate campaign. It is notable here that Crist has angered many conservative Republicans for his support of President Obama's stimulus package. Crist has presided as Florida's chief executive during the economic crisis and housing crash, which hit the state particularly hard.

The strength of a Tea Party candidacy is evident in the results from Doug Schoen's January 2010 survey of Florida voters. In a generic ballot test, 37 percent of respondents said they would vote for a Tea Party candidate (33 percent said they would vote for a Democratic candidate, and 30 percent Republican) and, specifically, among Republican Primary voters, Rubio was the frontrunner, leading Crist 40 percent to 32 percent.

The Tea Party movement also scored an important Florida victory in January 2010 by forcing out Florida Republican Party Chairman Jim Greer for being too moderate, installing right-wing ally John Thrasher. Noted Democratic National Committee Chairman Tim Kaine: "By deposing the top party official in a state that is virtually unmatched in electoral importance, and that has perhaps the most contested GOP Senate primary race of 2010, the tea party movement has landed a powerful blow squarely on the chin of the Republican Party."

It's not surprising then that mounting populist anger at government spending and persisting economic pain in Florida has given momentum to Rubio and his right-wing populist message and credentials. Rubio has received endorsements from RedState blogger Erick Erickson, Senator Jim DeMint, and the Club for Growth, formerly headed by Pat Toomey. He has become the hottest ticket on Florida's Tea Party circuit, and is the favored candidate for disaffected, disillusioned, and generally fed-up conservative Tea Party voters.

Like the Rubio-Crist matchup in Florida, the GOP primary for governor of California is a showdown between the political establishment and right-wing populists. Chuck DeVore has been a member of the California State Assembly since 2004, representing the state's 70th District. He is challenging former Hewlett-Packard CEO Carly Fiorina, who has been endorsed by nearly every member of the Republican political elite, including Senators Tom Coburn (Okla.), Susan Collins (Maine), Lindsey Graham (SC), Jon Kyl (Ariz.), John McCain (Ariz.), Mitch McConnell (Ky.), Lisa Murkowski (Alaska), and Olympia Snowe (Maine).

While DeVore doesn't have the backing of the Washington establishment, he does have solid conservative credentials that make him a favorite among right-wing populists who are furious with politicians in Sacramento as well as with California's declining quality of life.

DeVore attended college on a ROTC scholarship, graduated in 1985 as an officer with a degree in Strategic Studies, and served in the National Guard for twenty-four years, retiring as Lieutenant Colonel. In the eighties, he served as a Special Assistant for Foreign Affairs in the Reagan administration. DeVore was the City Commissioner of Irvine from 1991–1996 and co-authored a novel, *China Attacks*, about a future military conflagration between the U.S. and China over Taiwan.

Since 2004, DeVore has served in the California Assembly, and he launched his gubernatorial campaign in November 2008 on a small government, anti-tax platform. DeVore is pro-life, anti-stimulus, anti-bailout, anti-healthcare reform, anti-cap and trade, anti-amnesty for illegal immigrants, and, not surprising, pro-tax cut. In fact, he retired from his former position as Chief Republican Whip out of protest over a tax increase agreed to by California's Republican leadership. His campaign has emphasized the fact that he is among the few politicians who have been allowed to speak at Tea Parties. He has been endorsed by the Senate Conservative Fund and Senator Jim DeMint. DeVore also has ties to Floyd Brown, the creator of the 1988 Willie Horton ad, who is a known member of the "Birther Movement," which launched a failed effort to impeach President Obama based on the continually debunked assertion that Obama was not born in the United States.

On Thursday, January 14, 2010, following the devastating earthquake in Haiti, DeVore's communications director, Josh Trevino, controversially Tweeted: "[T]he best thing the int'l community can do is tend the wounded, bury the dead, and then LEAVE. That includes all UN and charity."

DeVore is clearly outside the conservative political mainstream and thus has tremendous appeal to disaffected voters in California, making his primary contest against Fiorina one of the most widely anticipated Tea Party elections of 2010.

Indeed, in 2010, there was already discussion under way of fielding a Tea Party affiliated candidate in the 2012 presidential election. Not knowing the outcome of the anticipated contests profiled above, it is premature to consider the prospects of a Tea Party message on the biggest national political stage. However, Gary Johnson, the libertarian-leaning Republican former governor of New Mexico, is rumored to be a contender in the 2012 presidential election, and possibly the preferred presidential candidate of the Tea Party movement.

While Johnson, who has attended several Tea Party rallies, diverges from the Tea Party movement on certain issues such as immigration and support for the Iraq war, he has been praised by Tea Party groups for his support for personal liberty and smaller government. As governor, Johnson vetoed 750 bills, more than all the vetoes of the country's forty-nine other governors combined, and he gained national notoriety for his support of legalizing drugs. Despite his Libertarian beliefs, Johnson turned down a solicitation to run in the 2000 presidential race on the Libertarian Party ticket and, despite his vehement opposition to the Republican Party's record during the Bush administration, he has maintained: "I am still a Republican."

The Tea Party movement is also making itself felt in the Midwest, like the south a region with a long populist tradition. In Ohio, a state, like Michigan, hit hard economically by the shuttering of major manufacturing industries, Democratic Governor Ted Strickland is struggling. In polls, he is consistently running some eight points behind the leading Republican candidate, former Congressman John Kasich, even before the GOP had settled its nominee. The strongly conservative Kasich, a confederate of the Gingrich-led revolution that took over the house in 1994, has significant small-government credentials. As chairman of the House Budget Committee in the mid 1990s, Kasich engineered the Balanced Budget Act of 1997, which paved the way for the government surpluses of the later Clinton years.

He also has middle-American populist appeal: for several years in the mid 2000s, he hosted the Fox News television talk show "From the Heartland," based in Columbus, Ohio. Kasich has tried to harness the power of the Tea Party movement for his candidacy by speaking at local Ohio Tea Party gatherings.[14]

"I've been all over the state, including with our friends in the Tea Party movement," Kasich told one such crowd. He added: "I think I was in the Tea Party before there was a Tea Party."[15]

Finally, the small government populists have gained a first-rate ideas man in the form of a handsome, wonky, young Republican congressman from Wisconsin, Paul Ryan.

Born in 1970, Ryan in the 1990s worked for a top social conservative (as legislative director for Senator Sam Brownback of Kansas) and for one of the nation's foremost economic conservatives (as speechwriter for Jack Kemp during his vice presidential run). Something of a wunderkind, Ryan has served in congress since 1998, representing a swing district that went for George Bush in 2004 and Obama in 2008.

As the ranking member of the House Budget Committee, Ryan in 2008 introduced legislation that he called "a roadmap for America's future" that he updated in January 2010 in response to President Obama's healthcare reforms and budget.[16] Democrats sat up and took notice: President Obama and his budget director Peter Orszag singled it out as a "serious proposal," while House Speaker Nancy Pelosi scored it as "rehashing the same old failed Bush policies."[17]

Others, however, cheered aspects of the proposal, including the non-partisan Congressional Budget Office, often described as the neutral scorekeeper in Washington fiscal debates. "The lower budget deficits under your proposal would result in much less federal debt than under the alternative fiscal scenario and thereby a much more favorable macro-economic outlook," CBO director Douglas Elmendorf wrote in a letter to Ryan. Elmendorf added, "The Roadmap would put the federal budget on a sustainable path, generating an annual budget surplus of about 5 percent of GDP by 2080."[18]

Exhorting Americans to abjure the path of government dependency and economic stagnation for that of personal liberty and economic growth, Ryan's road map offers a plan for radically simplifying the tax code, expanding health insurance coverage, ensuring the solvency of Social Security and Medicare, and paying off the national debt.

As Ryan describes it, he'd keep Medicare and Social Security as is for individuals over age 55, but would establish means testing and a voucher system for younger Americans. He'd expand health insurance through tax credits and by letting people buy insurance across state lines. Social security would be means tested and offer an opt-in for private accounts. Ryan would enact two tax rates: 10 percent on income for joint filers up to $100,000 and for single filers up to $50,000, and 25 percent on income above that, with a big personal exemption and no loopholes. He wants to eliminate taxes on capital gains, interest, dividends and estates, and replace the corporate tax with a business consumption tax to make America more competitive internationally.[19]

Rhetorically, Ryan cultivates a populist aura. In a Forbes.com opinion column, "Down with Big Business," he castigated the administration's bailouts of the financial giants as "crony capitalism."

"Since bringing us back from the precipice however, the Troubled Asset Relief Program [TARP] has morphed into crony capitalism at its worst," he wrote. "Abandoning its original purpose providing targeted assistance to unlock credit markets, TARP has evolved into an ad hoc, opaque slush fund for large institutions that are able to influence the Treasury Department's investment decisions behind-the-scenes."[20]

Given the publicity surrounding Ryan's proposals, some Republicans have predicted a bright political future for him, perhaps even a run for the presidency. Ryan, for his part, has ruled out any such run in 2012, saying his children are too young. Even so, he's garnered praise from the Tea Parties' symbolic leadership. Sarah Palin told a Fox interviewer, "I'm very impressed with Paul Ryan. . . . He's good. Man, he is sharp. He is smart, articulate. And he is passionate about these commonsense solutions that America has got to adopt to get us on the right road."[21]

Some have even described the national movement's structure as "deliberately disorganized."[22] As Lynn Brannon, who leads a Delaware Tea Party group, told *USA Today*, the diffusion allows individual groups to focus on what they care about. "We decided as a group that we wanted to focus on immigration. We don't want another organization to say, 'You can't get in on doing that.'"

As of February 2010, poll to poll, 35 percent of respondents self-identified as Tea Party supporters. This consistent benchmark of a one-third, or greater, percentage of support for the Tea Party movement simply did not exist a year ago.

This national trend of greater support for the Tea Parties is also evident at the state level. We polled two crucial battleground states—Iowa and Florida—and found similar trends. In Florida, 47 percent of respondents expressed a "Very Positive" view of the Tea Party movement. Another 13 percent said their view was "Somewhat Positive." That's 60 percent on the positive, plus another 19 percent expressing a "Neutral" view. And when asked whether they'd prefer a Tea Party candidate, a Republican candidate, or a Democratic candidate in the state's Senate race, 37 percent said Tea Party—higher than either of the two major parties.

In Iowa, one-third of voters, drawn from all political persuasions, said they are "supporters" of the Tea Parties. Independents, at 49 percent, were the largest group.

In terms of voters' electoral preferences in 2010, our polling suggests great inroads of support for the idea of official "Tea Party" candidates, should there be such a thing. Our "horse race" table below charts overall congressional vote preferences and a number of hypothetical three-way races in which Democratic and Republican candidates face off against a separate Tea Party candidate. It clearly shows that, while Democrats and President Obama retain a fairly strong hold on their supporters, among right-leaning voters it is essentially a toss-up between Republican candidates and Tea Party candidates. Sarah Palin and Mike Huckabee, running on our hypothetical Tea Party ballot line, ran neck-and-neck with an establishment Republican like Mitt Romney.

Polling consistently in the range of 20 to 25 percent, it's clear that the Tea Parties have already attained the political viability of a third party.

Still, despite this national momentum for the movement, some commentators have pointed to fractures and fissures in the Tea Party that suggest this trend is bound to be short-lived. They believe the Tea Party, like every third-party movement in American history, will eventually subside. The Perot movement, after all, garnered close to 20 percent in the 1992 presidential election, and ultimately led to the election of Independent Minnesota Governor Jesse Ventura among others. However, the movement fractured thereafter and, in retrospect, had little impact on our long-term national politics.

There is a sense among the vast majority of analysts in the political elite that the Tea Party movement will similarly fizzle as economic conditions improve. In our view, this is a dangerous and wrong assumption, not supported by our proprietary polling or facts on the ground.

The tendencies and trends that have developed and that we have explored in these chapters have not fallen along necessarily traditional cleavages, confounding political observers and political leaders alike. Put another way, when one looks at the confluence of events, initiatives, and activities from Tea Party groups and the responses from Tea Party constituencies, one can see a hidden force in American politics that has not been properly documented, understood, or chronicled.

We believe this force will be one that the major parties will have to contend with for years to come. The reason is simple: Insurgent right-wing populism is a broad-based movement, driven by angry independent and conservative voters, who no longer have a home in either major political party. And the Tea Party is uniquely positioned as a "non party" to capture the support of disillusioned and angry voters—particularly independents—who, as we have shown, turned increasingly and demonstrably conservative over the course of 2009.

Still, there are two significant hurdles for the Tea Party movement.

First, it must deal with the small faction of right-wing populists who hold radical and offensive views and thus threaten to discredit and derail the movement. It was a serious mistake that national Tea Party leaders did not do more to distance themselves from those who hold unrepresentative and controversial views, and who have used the Tea Party movement as a vehicle for those views.

One such person is Andrew Beacham, a young man who was quoted as calling President Obama a "fascist tyrant" at an anti-healthcare rally held outside the capital in Washington, D.C.: "Mr. Beacham, his hair in a ponytail, said in an interview that he believed Mr. Obama was a fascist because, he asserted, the bill would force Americans to pay for abortions and for government-provided health care. Reminded that Americans have long contributed to Medicare and Medicaid, Mr. Beacham replied, 'I would favor getting rid of both of them, and Social Security, too. They're all going broke anyway.' A freelance producer of film documentaries, Mr. Beacham said he did not have health insurance. 'When I need health care, I pay for it out of pocket,' he said, adding that he did not fear the possibility that an accident or illness would leave him with unaffordable bills. 'I'm a Christian, so I'm not afraid of death,' he said. The young man said he was one of about a dozen members of an anti-abortion group called Insurrecta Nex, which he described as a local chapter of followers of Randall Terry, the anti-abortion activist." [23]

Much ink has been devoted to people like Mr. Beacham who have been drawn to Tea Party movement activities. But these individuals are not the norm. In the course of our many interviews at Tea Party events, we encountered a number of individuals who expressed anti-Semitic, racist, and paranoid views about government and public figures such as the president. However, these individuals were the exception, not the rule. As we have demonstrated, the majority of people we met had valid concerns about the direction of the nation. They were angry, and sometimes disrespectful, but they deserve to be heard. To that end, the Tea Party movement will have to distance itself from those who obscure the message that the vast majority of its activists are hoping to deliver.

Recently, the Tea Party leadership itself has begun publicly to denounce extremists in its ranks.

"I don't believe we should be giving [extremists] a platform or empowering them to do anything based off their conspiracy theories . . . because they give the left ammunition to try to define the tea party movement as crazy and fringy," explained Ned Ryun, president of American Majority to *Politico* correspondent Kenneth P. Vogel. The American Majority website no longer allows those who self-identify as being part of the birther, truther, or militia movements or the John Birch Society to engage in discussions on its website.[24]

This tactic, explains RedState's Erick Erickson, is a necessary attempt "to clean up our own house . . . because traditional press outlets have decided to spotlight these fringe elements that get attracted to the movement, and focus on them as if they're a large part of this tea party movement. And I don't think they are."

A second challenge for the Tea Party movement is that it must pull off the difficult feat of coalescing around a unifying platform and set of principles. In other words, it must contend with the organizational issues that have bogged down the major parties, while maintaining its identity as a "non party."

In meeting this challenge, the Tea Party movement must be careful not to forfeit or dilute the advantages that come with its being a decentralized, diffuse force. Conservative writer and activist Richard Viguerie argued that the movement's strength is best captured in the analogy drawn by Ori Brafman and Rod Beckstrom's book, *The Starfish and the Spider: The Unstoppable Power of Leaderless Organizations*. The authors describe successful, "leaderless" organizations as starfish, because when you cut off one tentacle, it just grows a new one. By contrast, when you cut off the head of a spider—or the head of a top-down, hierarchical organization—you kill it with one stroke. As Viguerie writes: "We are seeing the 'starfish' Tea Party Movement, with candidates running in both Democratic and Republican primaries. . . . 'Starfish' tea partiers are learning how to organize, raise money, and utilize the alternative media in record numbers. They are voicing their opposition to unaccountable Big Government and promoting productive policy alternatives through the Founders' guiding principles, "From the tea parties, the grassroots, and the alternative media, we are seeing new leaders emerge. Like our Founders, they understand that their strength of leadership does not come from a political party, but from consent of the governed. That is why they don't hitch their wagons to one person or one party." [25]

Should the Tea Party become an actual political party? What does it stand for? What does it stand against? What would a Tea Party governor, senator, or member of Congress advocate?

Today, the movement draws strength from being on the outside and looking in. Its numbers and the political change it is at the center of suggests that in the future—perhaps the near future—it may be on the inside looking out. Given everything we have witnessed and reported, not to mention the data we have analyzed, we certainly don't discount that possibility. If the unification of the three conservative strands is to be a lasting and impactful force, the Tea Party movement will need to shed its outsider status, and begin the difficult work of articulating what it is for, in addition to what it is against.

THE ORIGIN, COMPOSITION, AND FUTURE OF POPULISM ON THE LEFT

On October 8, 2009, seven members of the Chicago Single Payer Action Network laid siege to Cigna's glass-domed reception hall at the Midwest sales office at 52 Monroe Street in downtown Chicago.

Outside, forty to fifty liberal activists could be seen waving signs reading "CIGNA profits, people die, Medicare for all" and chanting slogans such as "Health care is a human right!" as they held a single payer/Medicare for all protest.

Amid the crowd, a white middle-class woman waved a sign featuring the photograph of a young woman. Underneath it said: JENNY, 1984–2009. "SHE COULD NOT WAIT!" Jenny Fritts died while seven and a half months pregnant.

"Jenny our 24 year old daughter in-law and unborn baby died because she could not afford health insurance. In the richest country in the world our Jenny died."

The members of the "Cigna 7" were no longer willing to sit silently and wait for the House and the Senate to pass a mutilated health-care bill and demanded to speak with CIGNA executives, calling on CIGNA to approve all doctor-recommended treatments. When they were denied, they sat down on the lobby floor, and began to chant. They were arrested.

The Chicago Single Payer Action Network (ChiSPAN) is a Chicago-based grassroots group whose mission is to achieve guaranteed health care for all. They believe that private insurance companies are the number one barrier to universal health insurance and that they should be eliminated.

"I think a lot of us came in here without a lot of faith in elected politicians to introduce truly progressive legislation. We're here to push for what we think is the right thing, which is nothing less than single payer, Medicare for all, so that's our position and it's not up to be politicians and its not up to us to compromise. And I think that most politicians spin it off, and compromise, and lie to themselves about what the right thing to do is. You know, Obama always spoke about keeping companies honest, well we're here to keep politicians honest. We're basically here to make Obama live up to his rhetoric," insists Edward, press liaison for ChiSPAN.

"I knew getting arrested was going to be scary, but I was willing to risk it because I'm so sick of health care being treated like a pair of Air Jordans. It's not a commodity. It's something all people need. Shortly after the group of us seven activists entered Cigna and demanded that the corporation immediately approve all doctor-recommended treatment, my fear subsided.

"Chanting in solidarity with my fellow activists in the marble, castle-like atrium of Cigna headquarters gave me courage. I remember looking in the eyes of police who expressed support for our claims and lamented having to drag us out of the building as we resisted arrest nonviolently by letting our bodies go limp, stating that we refused to leave voluntarily until Cigna met our demand. The time spent at the booking station and the soreness in my shoulders and upper back were worthy sacrifices to make to give people a glimpse of the virility of the movement to make health care a human right. I am grateful to have had the resources and ability to participate in the action, and hope it inspires people to get involved in the fight—because it ain't over yet!"[1] said Marilena Marchesas, one of the Cigna 7.

Since the inauguration of Barack Obama in 2009, we have witnessed a level of government intervention in America's public sector that has been rarely seen in the history of the union. From the historic stimulus bill, to the bank bailouts, to the auto industry takeovers, to the proposed revamping of the nation's health care system, these interventions and actions would have been nearly unfathomable even three years ago.

It's fair to say the economic collapse changed everything. It radicalized the left to pursue their goal of an even more activist government than President Obama campaigned on in 2008. And as we have explored, the right has been equally radicalized in response.

At the core of this incredible political drama are the same underlying issues and forces that are driving right-wing populists. Indeed, left-wing populists have the same analysis as right-wing populists. They see the world in shockingly similar terms. Progressive populists are equally cynical about government, equally alienated from the elites, and equally angry at Wall Street and the bailouts received by the mega banks. Left-wing populists have in fact come to the same analysis as the right: that the system is rigged against ordinary Americans. Left-wing populists, like right-wing populists, are incensed about the way the federal government works. They worry as much as the right about the out-of-touch nature of Washington elites and the fact that interest groups in Washington are, in large part, controlling the debate, the initiatives, and the nation's purse strings to the detriment of the American mainstream.

However, where the left and right populists part—and they part dramatically—is in their prescription for change. Progressive populists have reached a far different conclusion: that we need more government intervention to correct the inequities; that instead of distributing bailouts to the banks, we need unprecedented government spending to bailout the lives of the middle and lower class; that we need to redistribute private sector wealth for public sector gain.

In short, on the right, skepticism of and anger at Washington and Wall Street have led the Tea Party supporters to rally against government and for the private sector. On the left, this same skepticism has led progressive populists to a call for more government, more regulation, and redistribution of wealth as a means of alleviating societal ails.

While we have focused the vast majority of our attention thus far on the origins and dynamics of right-wing populism in the form of the Tea Party movement and related organizations, there has been a no less active, albeit certainly smaller, degree of populist agitation and organization on the left.

Indeed, while right-wing populism has been the primary focus on the mainstream media as well, Scott Brown's election to the Senate in early 2010 brought the vocal left-wing populist movement into stark relief. The left was incensed that the very seat once held by the Liberal Lion of the Senate, Teddy Kennedy, would be occupied by an arch-conservative. While left-wing populism had been overshadowed by the Tea Party movement for most of 2009, at the outset of 2010, left-wing populists began to raise their collective voice.

Thus began President Obama's left-wing populist offensive of his second year in office. After Brown's election, the *New York Times* dubbed President Obama the "First Populist." While Obama had championed a number of liberal policy initiatives during his first year in office, from the massive stimulus package to the "public option" that enraged the right, he and his administration had come under fire from the populist left for putting the interests of Wall Street first and foremost. In an attempt to regain the loyalty of the left-populist base, Obama began to champion financial regulation and reform with gusto, and proposed a new bank tax to recapture fully the funds lent to Wall Street to prevent a second Great Depression.

In truth, it's not as simple as the *Times* would have us believe.

Obama isn't the first populist, or the second or the third. Populism on the left, while not as politically dominant as populism on the right, is just as complex. The events of 2008 and 2009 exposed a fascinating tension on the left, between hard-core progressives, interest group liberalism and Big Labor, and the more traditional liberal centrists who flocked to support Obama during the 2008 campaign. Indeed, much as there are three converging strands of right-wing populism that we identified and dissected in Chapters 5 through 7, we believe there are two competing strands of progressive populism: elite left-wing populism and mainstream left-wing populism.

In this chapter, we will untangle the complicated knot of left-wing populism, where it comes from and where it is going. While far from a dominating political force, left-wing populism exerts tremendous influence over the Democratic Party and the Obama administration, perhaps unlike any other moment in history. And progressive populism will certainly play an important role in the direction and outcome of the 2010 midterm elections, as well as the 2012 presidential contest.

LEFT-WING POPULISM DEFINED

From the late 19th century up until the mid 20th century, populism was the sole property, the birthright, of the left—and to see it reawakening now in the 21st century America naturally arouses the imagination of historians.

Many felt that a tough-minded, confrontational brand of economic populism had passed from history. In the Clinton years, it was easy to believe this, with a booming stock market, income gains across all socioeconomic levels, and a robust, soaring economy with low unemployment. Hard-core, left-wing populism was confined to the fringes. Just a decade later, though, progressive populism is front and center. And since the election of the nation's most liberal president since FDR, it has made its presence known every day that Barack Obama has been in office.

Like conservative populism, liberal populism targets government failures to protect the people's interests. But where conservative populists see government as the enemy of free enterprise and personal autonomy, liberal populists traditionally believe that government has facilitated the interests of a small group of elites on Wall Street, helping them to become obscenely wealthy.

In short, when this ideology is translated into policy, it manifests itself in three broad goals:

1. Protect the safety net
2. Redistribute wealth
3. Restrain corporate power and abuse

The left-wing populists believe that ordinary people need government to step in and protect them from any number of external actors and forces. Indeed, in their view, government has a *moral responsibility* and an *obligation* to fill this function in our democracy.

Put simply, left-wing populists want to alter traditional capitalist arrangements in America and give the government unprecedented influence and control over the financial markets and private sector industries in ways that were virtually unimaginable years ago. They are coming together in a coordinated effort to achieve their mutual goals.

The practical applications of this worldview are straightforward. Rather than bailing out the AIG's of the world, rather than bailing out the big banks, rather than providing assistance to Wall Street, left-wing populists believe there needs to be a systematic reordering of priorities. They hold that the government ought fundamentally to assist ordinary people through mortgage relief, through access to credit, and even through public sector jobs.

Moreover, the role of government from the perspective of progressive populists is broad and expansive. They believe that government should guarantee retirement security, health care, education, and employment opportunities. Their anger in the wake of the economic crisis stems from the fact that they believe the government has failed to do this and needs to take action.

THE TWO STRANDS OF LEFT-WING POPULISM

In the previous three chapters, we discussed the strands of right-wing populism that converged in an unprecedented way: fiscal conservatives, libertarians, and social conservatives. As we noted, this historic convergences of three very different aspects of conservatism has driven the right-wing populist revolt and the Tea Party movement to unpredicted and never-before-seen heights, a trend that has serious implications for the 2010 election cycle and beyond.

A different dynamic is playing out among left-wing populists. Two strands in this movement are at odds, if not clashing, and the Obama administration is being forced to referee this fight. The extent to which it succeeds or fails also has major implications for the upcoming mid-term elections and the future of the Democratic Party.

Simply put, on the left, there are two dominant strands of thinking and organization: a mainstream strand and an elite strand.

The mainstream strand is comprised of union workers, liberal interest groups, and hard left Democratic hoi polloi who are outraged at the economic crisis and the administration's response to it.

Labor unions are a major component of the populist left. They drive Obama administration's agenda. When the White House released its visitor log in October 2009, the most frequent visitor was SEIU leader Andy Stern. The labor unions are seeking more government intervention, regulation, ownership, and control. It is instructive that in March 2010 the unions' reaction to lagging economic recovery was to take on the banks directly by launching a two-week long national protest movement "Good Jobs Now, Make Wall Street Pay."

The elite strand is comprised of two distinct wings. The first is comprised of what was once the traditional liberal wing of the Democratic Party, which has morphed into a left-populist caucus advocating the affirmative role of government: more government, less business, more re-distribution, less growth. Key players include the most liberal members of the Democratic Party, particularly in the House of Representatives, such as Charles Rangel, Nancy Pelosi, and Barney Frank.

The other wing of the elite strand of the populist left is comprised of liberal activist groups. Such groups include MoveOn.org, a nonprofit, progressive advocacy group and political action committee launched in response to the Clinton impeachment trial in 1998 and now function-ing as a left-wing pressure group with over 5 million members; Daily Kos, a liberal/progressive discussion forum and blog seeking to influ-ence and empower the Democratic Party, as well as a variety of issue-based activist groups such as the Sierra Club and the Chicago Single Payer Action Network.

Straddling the stark battle lines between these two strands is Presi-dent Obama, who must appease both or risk political turmoil. Thus, Obama in his first year in office has been forced to repeatedly tack back and forth between these two poles.

HISTORICAL LEFT-WING POPULISM

Left-wing populists didn't just show up out of the blue in 2008 and elect Barack Obama president. Strong historical antecedents for the left-wing populist movement drive the agenda of the Obama administration, and much of the Democratic Party. Redistribution of wealth, pro-safety net, and pro-intervention in the private sector were key components in late 19th- to mid 20th-century political movements from William Jennings Bryan and the People's Party in the 1890s, to Teddy Roosevelt's progres-sivism, to FDR and Huey Long in the Depression/New Deal era.

The People's Party

Average Americans were furious when the federal government failed to recognize the silver dollar—the currency of the masses—in 1873.

Thus began the Free Silver Movement, which found common cause with the growing agrarian movement of farmers upset with economic conditions and the political and business elite.

This populist uprising culminated in the creation of the People's Party, also known as the Populist Party, in the 1890s. In July 1892, the People's Party made its formal political debut during a convention in Omaha, Nebraska. On July 4, 1892, the Omaha Platform was officially adopted, providing the framework upon which the populist movement was based. The Omaha Platform called for the expansion of the federal government's authority to act on behalf of the marginalized workers—both rural and urban—and protect them from "oppression, injustice, and poverty": "The fruits of the toil of millions are boldly stolen to build up colossal fortunes for a few, unprecedented in the history of mankind; and the possessors of those, in turn, despise the republic and endanger liberty."

The Panic of 1893—caused by a reduction in gold reserves in the U.S. Treasury—led to an economic downturn that drove up debt and unemployment for American workers. The People's Party rose in popularity as a result, winning the Kansas and Colorado governorships in the 1894 midterm elections, as well as seven seats in the House and six in the Senate.

William Jennings Bryan, the great populist crusader, was nominated as the People's Party candidate for president in 1896. The Democratic Party, seeing the populist writing on the wall, nominated Bryan as well. Bryan lost the election of 1896 to Republican William McKinley. However, as Michael Federici notes, "While the Populist Party eventually split in 1900, leading to its decline, its influence resonated for decades and many of its reforms were adopted by the Roosevelt and Wilson administrations."[2]

Teddy Roosevelt

Like the contemporary populist left, Teddy Roosevelt believed that government had a responsibility to be the "steward of the people." As president, Roosevelt expanded government's role in various areas of the private sector in the attempt to benefit working Americans. In 1902, he expanded government regulation creating the Bureau of Corporations and laws to regulate interstate commerce, monitor safety of food and drugs, and land conservation. He was an ally of the labor unions and took on Wall Street, filing public "trust busting" suits against firms such as J.P Morgan.

FDR

During the Great Depression, with widespread anger and fear over large-scale economic dislocation, FDR became the warrior of the working class. He championed the empowerment of ordinary Americans, and railed against the corporate and government co-conspirators who derailed the U.S. economy and the lives of millions.

FDR and his big Democratic majority in Congress were the founding fathers of the elite strand of contemporary left-wing populism "enacted legislation that helped dry up support for his populist opponents. Some of these bills remain the bedrock of our limited welfare state: Social Security abated the misery of the elderly and the unemployed, the Fair Labor Standards Act established a minimum wage and prohibited the hiring of children on most jobs, and the National Labor Relations Act made it illegal to fire a worker for trying to organize a union. By the time the U.S. entered World War II, more of the feed was making its way into the stall where most Americans lived."[3]

His speeches were equally anti-elite and pro-populist. As Alan Brinkley summarized in the *Wall Street Journal*: "[FDR] made a series of speeches in 1936 excoriating the selfishness and greed of the 'economic royalists.' He had struggled, he said, 'with the old enemies of peace, business and financial monopoly, speculation, reckless banking, class antagonism, sectionalism, war profiteering. . . . Never before in all our history have these forces been so united against one candidate as they stand today. They are unanimous in their hate for me, and I welcome their hatred.' This polarizing rhetoric was greeted with some of the most enthusiastic responses of any of his speeches."[4]

If FDR captured the support of the vast populist center of the American electorate, two other Depression-era leaders came to typify the far right- and left-wing populist fringes.

Huey Long

Profiled in Chapter 2, Father Coughlin's radical counterpart on the left was Huey Long, governor of Louisiana from 1928 to 1932, and Louisiana's U.S. Senator from 1933 to 1935. Just as Coughlin espoused the fringe populist views of the right, Long espoused the fringe views of the populist left. Like Coughlin and FDR, Long railed against the failings and greed of Wall Street. And while he was an elected Democrat, his ideas were markedly socialist.

Long, whose motto was "Every Man a King," sought to redistribute income through his the Share Our Wealth Society. He promoted an enormous tax on the wealthy, in order to provide every single American with a secure income and an upper-middle-class lifestyle. He also advocated massive government spending on public works projects and social programs.

Long, like Couglin, was controversial and popular. And, like Coughlin, his left-wing populist movement was relatively short-lived. In 1935, Long was shot and killed in Louisiana; the assassin was never identified.

TWO DECADES OF LIBERAL FRUSTRATION

In previous chapters, we explored why populism in general has seen resurgence in recent years. We discussed the impact of economic devastation, socio-political realignment, and historic factors. Each of these played a role in the burgeoning left-wing populist movement. However, to understand fully why progressive populism has arrived on the scene with such force in recent years, we must look at the events of recent decades.

It is more accurate to say that a resurgent left-wing populism had been building for years—if not decades—and needed the right blend of circumstances to gain momentum. In 2008 and 2009, both the economic circumstances and the political circumstances resulted in an explosion of left-wing populism.

Left-wing populists take a harsh view of the policies of the last twenty years—particularly those of the George W. Bush years—which, they argue, enriched only a few, while insulating the political from criticism and driving governmental and business elites into an even tighter embrace.

Liberal populists believe that the ordinary American worker lost ground and bore the brunt of economic pain over the last few decades. And they increasingly fear that working people no longer have a voice in Washington. They believe that the central role of a Democratic Congress and a Democratic President is to address this imbalance and promote fundamental economic and social change.

It is important to remember that the last Democratic president, Bill Clinton, was a centrist in disposition, in politics, and in governing. President Clinton pushed free trade in the form of the North American Free Trade Agreement (NAFTA) and pledged that it would create jobs. He defended pro-Wall Street policies by saying they would help lower interest rates and benefit the broader economy. The economic trends of the George W. Bush years put those assumptions under harsher scrutiny, reopening the economic debate in the Democratic Party.

A decade and a half after the passage of NAFTA, many on the left felt vindicated in opposing the bill, as manufacturing jobs fled the United States in staggering numbers. While free trade had certainly brought increased economic prosperity on a macro level, improving corporate bottom lines and enriching the coffers of Wall Street firms and investors, its record in the broader economic sector was much more uneven. The manufacturing economy, already on the run since the 1960s, hastened its job losses. Displaced blue-collar workers struggled to learn new skills. The concerns of anti-free trade populists didn't get much of a hearing until the economic pain became more widespread in recent years.

After eight years of being marginalized during the Clinton presidency, the left had to suffer through the indignation of the Bush years as well, from his tax cuts in 2001 and 2003 to his hawkish foreign policy after 9/11. The left stayed on the president's case throughout his two terms, reacting to the Abu Ghraib scandal, to the ongoing bloodshed in Iraq, to the administration's failure in New Orleans after Hurricane Katrina, and to Bush's Supreme Court nominations.

However, during this time, liberals gained little traction against Bush's economic and foreign policies. The stock market performed well and the economy seemed strong, though manufacturing jobs continued to leave the United States in alarming numbers. It wasn't until 2007, just before the sub-prime mortgage bubble burst, inaugurating the downturn, that large-scale economic dissatisfaction was starting to take hold. To this point, liberals had been beaten back, as recently (and as overwhelmingly) as the utter failure of John Kerry's campaign in 2004.

In short, for two decades or more, liberals had been sidelined, first by their own party and then by the Bush presidency.

All this changed, of course, in 2008. As the economic bubble burst, so too did the pent-up frustration of left-leaning Americans who had been marginalized. As the presidential election approached, Democrats began speaking out on tax policy, health care, energy, and education.

Senate Democrats held hearings to debate proposals that would raise taxes on top-level executives at private equity and hedge fund firms.

This momentum continued as the financial crisis escalated. During the fall of 2008, as the presidential campaign unfolded during a time of nearly unprecedented fiscal distress, Americans consistently opposed the Bush bailouts offered to firms like Citigroup and AIG. Many of these people would never consider themselves left-wing populists, either, but left-wing populists were clearly emboldened by the public mood, which meshed well with their ideology. Their arguments that corporate executives, who were responsible for so much of the corruption and irresponsibility, had not been adequately punished took hold in the political culture at large.

Left-wing populism was on the ascent, and, as we know, that ascent helped it capture both Congress and the White House. How this populist ideology translated into governance, however, is a more complicated matter.

LEFT-WING GOALS

As we stated at the beginning of the chapter, left-wing populists are driven by three core goals:

1. Protect the safety net
2. Redistribute wealth
3. Restrain corporate power and abuse

The healthcare debate is one in which the views of left-wing populists are quite transparent. Health care is not a commodity. It is a fundamental right in which all Americans deserve equal access. We heard this trope sounded again and again during dozens of interviews with left-wing populists across the country. Georgia Bond, a musician from Chicago, told us movingly of her best friend's husband's struggle against brain cancer. "His health insurance rates went up to about three thousand dollars a month, and they couldn't afford to pay for both his health insurance and his life insurance," she told us. "So they chose health insurance so he could get the necessary care. Well, he was just given a maximum of eighteen months to live and now he has no life insurance. And they have three little boys. I just can't understand why people are giving the president such a hard time. Finally, someone in Washington is looking out for us first. And they call that socialism? Well, I'd rather take that then keep being taken advantage of."

Consider AFL-CIO president John Sweeney's opening remarks at the 2009 AFL-CIO Convention in Pittsburgh, Pennsylvania, on September 13, 2009: "We elected a champion of working families as the first African American president in the history of our country—and what a thrill it was to watch him last week as he took on the ugly forces that are ripping at the right of every American family to have health care—health care as a right, not a privilege. With him out front, we're restoring government as a force for ensuring individual opportunity, eliminating special privilege, and promoting the common good. Those are his values, those are our values and they are America's values. . . ."

At the 2009 AFL-CIO Convention in Pittsburgh, Henry, a 63-year-old cancer survivor and member of the Alliance for Retired Americans from Ohio, argued that not only are private insurance companies profiting off customers, they are also denying them care.

"I'm sixty three years old right now. I'm doing well in terms of my health right now; at fifty-five, I had cancer. Some of my friends are still paying their insurance premiums of eight or nine hundred dollars a month, but they don't have any coverage. Would you buy auto insurance—would you be allowed to buy auto insurance like that? Or a car that stops and starts every couple of blocks?

"In Ohio where I come from, I can't get an individual policy, I have to get it through being employed. That is because of my 'preexisting condition.' Mind you, the kind of cancer that I had never will come back. I'm perfectly healthy. So it's that kind of thing. Those of us who have preexisting conditions and those whose age makes us unable to afford it. My friend who just walked by, his cousin pays forty-eight thousand dollars a year, four thousand a month to purchase health insurance for himself and his wife. Because of heart conditions that they both had."

The only way to fix our unjust healthcare system, Henry says, is for the government to enact healthcare reform that would include a government-run insurance entity to compete directly with the big private insurance companies, the whipping boys of the populist left.

Henry would not support a healthcare reform bill that did not include a public option, which he believes would not only increase access to affordable health care, but help small businesses, stimulate job creation, and jump-start the rebuilding of American industry.

Henry adds, "A public option would help our *employers* become more competitive. It would help us bring American jobs back into America. Bring back the steel for instance. We're in the steel city . . . yet we don't make steel in this country anymore."

This idea that the government should take care of its citizens, to shield them from being taken advantage of, is the core of the left-wing populist ideology. It applies equally to health care, in their view, as it does to jobs and the economy.

This was perhaps most candidly enunciated by left-wing populist filmmaker Michael Moore, in his film, in *Capitalism: a Love Story.* According to Moore, government has an obligation to "assure us equality in the pursuit of happiness." It is the role of government, he argues, to ensure that every single American citizen has "the right to a useful and remunerative job. . . . The right to earn enough to provide adequate food and clothing and recreation. . . . The right of every family to a decent home. . . . The right to adequate medical care. . . . The right to adequate protection from the economic fears of old age, sickness, accident, and unemployment. . . . The right to a good education."

This, of course, is the underlying rationale of left-wing policies that seek to redistribute wealth. From taxing the income of the super rich and those who receive or purchase expensive "Cadillac" healthcare plans, to taxing the bonuses of those who work on Wall Street, to implementing a new bank tax that will be redirected to federal job creation programs—these policies are championed by progressive populists who believe in an activist government.

It also follows that an activist government will restrain corporate power and abuse. And, indeed, left-wing populists across the country echoed this sentiment. Jordan Bonomo, a young man who works for a nonprofit called Learn NY, disputed the idea that the left was championing so-called socialist policies. "The right throws around the word socialism," he said. "It's just a talking point that's been in use for a hundred years. The government's role should be to check corporations and make sure that they're not profiting off the maltreatment of citizens!"

At a healthcare rally in New York City, a similar idea was expressed somewhat differently by Josh Starcher, an activist with the liberal group Healthcare-NOW!. "I think that the Wall Street debacle shows that we can't trust [corporations] with money, [so] why should we trust them with care," Josh said in explaining his support of healthcare reform. "They've shown that they're irresponsible, why should we let them continue to profit off of health care. They're not going to stop; they're not going to change without the government stepping in."

These legislative initiatives typify the left-wing populist response. They are the result of the same logic that has informed the right-wing populist mentality. Both the left and right populists believe the elite and moneyed interests in government and the private sector are holding the average American hostage. To the right, the solution is less regulation, less spending, and less government—the contraction of the state. To the left, the solution is more regulation, more spending, and more government—the expansion of the state.

This view of America—that the government needs to "step in"—is held by a vocal segment of the populist left, and echoed by many of the Democratic members of the House, particularly from urban districts. And as we have shown, this view is deeply held, fervent, and drives much of the action in Washington. Indeed, it was the rationale for a number of legislative proposals on Capitol Hill in 2009 to facilitate government intervention in the private sector:

- Senator Chris Dodd (D-CT) proposed legislation to create a consolidated bank regulator, limit the fallout if a bank deemed "too big to fail" collapses, and set up a consumer-protection agency to oversee mortgages and credit cards.

- Representative Barney Frank (D-MA) championed more oversight and stronger capital cushions for the largest banks and Wall Street firms. His proposed legislation would force these banks to pay a total of as much as $150 billion into an emergency fund that could be tapped when a troubled company needs to be taken over and broken up.

- The Democratic leadership in the House proposed a new Consumer Financial Protection Agency to regulate products such as credit cards and mortgages. Travis Plunkett, legislative director of the Consumer Federation of America argued, "We need an independent regulator because the existing regulators have shown themselves to be incapable and unwilling of protecting consumers from abusive financial products."[5]

- In support of these and other measures, Nancy Pelosi summed up the liberal populist argument: "We are sending a clear message to Wall Street, the party is over. Never again will reckless behavior on the part of the few threaten the fiscal stability of our people. . . . The legislation will finally protect Main Street from the worst of Wall Street."[6]

And the unfolding of the healthcare debate has made abundantly clear how powerful the populist left has become and the influence it is having on the administration. Even Senate Majority Leader Harry Reid argued against compromise on healthcare reform legislation, telling healthcare committee chairman Max Baucus that making a deal too eagerly with Republicans on healthcare legislation would lose too many Democratic votes. Essentially, Reid was arguing for a party-line vote, if necessary—which is precisely what he got.

This argument to reject bipartisanship echoes throughout the left-wing commentaries as well. In *The New Republic*, Jonathan Cohn urged the Obama administration to forgo bipartisanship in order to fulfill the left-populist policy agenda for health care. He wrote: "Don't give the Republicans anything more. If we have to pass this on a purely party-line vote, we will. Which, as far as I'm concerned, is just fine. Bipartisanship is good but a sound health reform bill is better. If winning over just one or even a handful of Republicans means gutting the bill, it's not worth it." Citing arguments made by his colleague Matthew Yglesias, Cohn wrote, "[I]t's not clear a bipartisan bill would actually be more representative of the country's sentiments than a partisan one."[7]

As North Dakota Senator Kent Conrad explained during a March 2, 2010, interview on *Countdown with Keith Olbermann:* " . . . we see this happening on the right and the left. Republicans are afraid they're going to get challenged on the right. That's their only meaningful competition. Democrats in certain states afraid they're going to get challenged on the left . . . what it means is the ability to actually get things done is being reduced, because what's happening is you've got a push to the extremes. The left and the right. The result is it's much more difficult to have people who are centrist still survive and play a role in actually getting results."

We see firsthand what happens to centrist Democrats who fail to appease the left-populist base. Like their Republican counterparts, moderate Democratic lawmakers are facing opposition from the populist left.

In March 2010, MoveOn.org launched a national campaign called the Health Care Accountability Pledge, a pledge to support primary challengers to any member of the House of Representatives who fails to vote for the final healthcare reform package.

In a March 15, 2010, email to all MoveOn members, they wrote: "So we're asking every MoveOn member: will you pledge to support progressive primary challengers to House Democrats who side with Republicans to kill health care reform? With the big vote happening as early as this Friday, Conservative Democrats need to know the stakes if they choose to side with Big Insurance over the voters on health care reform. Our pledge will send that message loud and clear. We'll publicize the amount pledged, and make sure the media and every wavering representative know about it."

Nothing emphasizes left-populist clout better than when Arkansas Lieutenant Governor Bill Halter suddenly announced that he would challenge Senator Blanche Lincoln in the 2010 Democratic primary for U.S. Senator, and was quickly able to mobilize a constituency in the populist left. A coalition of left-wing populist groups including MoveOn.org, and four major labor unions (AFL-CIO, AFSCME, Communications Workers of America, and United Steelworkers of America), raised over $5 million and launched an aggressive advertising campaign to support Halter's candidacy. In return, Halter publicly endorsed the healthcare reform bill, the "public option," while denouncing Wall Street and the private insurance industry.

BARACK OBAMA AND THE PROGRESSIVE SHOWDOWN

Obama's agenda in 2009 has represented the most breathtaking acts of federal intervention in the private sector since Franklin Roosevelt: the stimulus package; the budget deal; government takeovers of the auto industry, where so many blue-collar, Democratic-voting constituents work; and a massive and super-ambitious "green jobs" environmental initiative. And, to cap it all off, the president spent the second part of 2009 fighting for nothing less than a complete reorganization of the American healthcare system, hearing the cries from right-wing protesters and left-wing advocates every inch of the way.

By way of fleshing out this political drama on the left, it's important to remember that Obama ran for president as a conciliator, a post-partisan, sensible centrist whose appealing manner, lack of ideological passion, and absence from the red-hot political fights of the last two decades would allow him to bridge the political divide in Washington. Every poll showed that Americans found this prospect appealing, and they saw Obama as the most likely candidate to bring it off. (Hillary Clinton was too heavily associated with the battles of the Clinton presidency, and John McCain, while admirably bipartisan, had simply been in Washington too long.)

After Obama's stunning victory, it seemed like such lofty promises just might be fulfilled. Consider Obama's Inaugural Address, an eloquent and understated call for national renewal, cooperation, and responsibility. "Obama's speech," conservative commentator Bill Kristol wrote "was unabashedly pro-American and implicitly conservative."[8] Obama paid tribute to the Founders, praised the American way of life, and stressed not the expansion of government—the calling card of left-wing populism—but personal responsibility, a trademark of the conservative movement. It seemed very much the speech of a conciliator, a man whose leanings were liberal but whose inclinations were toward consensus.

One of the first things that Obama did after taking the oath of office was to meet with the Republican congressional caucus. Several Republicans praised him for his willingness to listen and for the respect he showed them and their ideas and concerns. But the net result of these efforts was not one Republican vote for either his stimulus package or his budget deal. The Republicans were feeling the tug of their own populist pressures. They couldn't meet Obama halfway, or any way. And all the while, Obama's left-wing populists were howling that the president was giving away the store.

At this point in 2009, Obama tacked hard to his left. The result was a staggering $787 billion stimulus package and $3.6 trillion budget that worried even some Democrats. On the budget, the vote was 233–196, with 20 conservative Democrats dissenting. As if to underscore the harsh partisan voting lines, House Speaker Nancy Pelosi announced the results herself. And even the president seemed to draw those lines when, in a message accompanying the budget, he said: "For the better part of three decades, a disproportionate share of the nation's wealth has been accumulated by the very wealthy. Yet, instead of using the tax code to lessen these increasing wage disparities, changes in the tax code over the past eight years exacerbated them." That sounded like redistribution to many. The president's words simultaneously appeased mainstream populists on the left, while providing a spark to the Tea Party movement.

Both the stimulus and budget deals, passed without a single Republican vote, reflected the wishes of the progressive left: lots of spending on government initiatives, few if any checks on how the money was spent, and little in the way of political compromise. For all we know, neither the stimulus nor the budget reflected the president's true wishes; he seemed eager to find a way to work with Republicans from the get-go, but those wishes were thwarted by the hard currents pushing on both right and left. Obama, being a smart politician, simply adapted. He saw where the winds were blowing. He hedged his bets with the left-wing populists, on the basis that their support would be more influential in helping him achieve his policy goals than those from the other side of the partisan divide. In doing so, he largely rejected centrism, except for rhetorical flourishes.

While Obama has consistently tacked to the left in response to progressive mainstream pressures, he has also had to appease the liberal elite. In several instances, doing so has infuriated the hard left populists.

Perhaps the first instance of Obama's populist tendencies being checked by the establishment was with respect to AIG. For millions of Americans, and not just left-wing populists, Washington's decision to bail out the giant insurer represented a clear sign that the government was more committed to assisting corporate interests than those of the American taxpayer. AIG thus became one of the principal rallying cries for left-wing populists in the waning days of the Bush era and at the outset of the Obama administration.

On March 13, 2009, AIG announced that it had used federal bailout money to distribute $165 million in retention bonuses to employees in the Financial Products Unit. The initial reaction of the Obama administration and congressional leaders was to "clawback" the bonuses by any means possible through confiscatory legislation. President Obama publicly chastised AIG for "recklessness and greed," vowing to "pursue every single legal avenue" to block the bonuses.

However, the liberal elite balked at this populist tactic, and the administration was divided on the issue internally. Obama eventually backed down amid arguments from liberal Washington insiders that this "clawback" could have a cataclysmic impact on our nation's financial system.

This was the first in a series of skirmishes between the elite and mainstream on the left. And the contentious debate over healthcare reform exposed additional fault lines between the liberal elite and left-leaning mainstream populists.

As the House prepared to wrap up months of deliberation and negotiation on healthcare overhaul, conservative Democrat Bart Stupak (D-MI) led a coalition of anti-abortion advocates to force an amendment that would place restrictions on reproductive services for women who receive health insurance through new government-managed health exchanges. To this point, the White House urged Congress that the only unacceptable outcome on health care was to do nothing. Heeding that advice, Nancy Pelosi allowed the amendment to go to a floor vote, where it passed easily with Republican support and Stupak's conservative Democratic coalition over the objections of most Democrats.

The left was furious, but the Democratic leadership—read: the liberal elite—opted to save health care rather than take a stand on a signature issue of progressives.

Yet another showdown related to the healthcare reform efforts occurred between the administration and labor unions. Indeed, the

Obama administration and the liberal elite have felt the heat from unions perhaps more than any other constituency.

Barack Obama's election energized and emboldened the unions. Take for example, the remarks made by Rose Tucker, Treasurer of Council 1707 local 215—the Service Employees of the Community and Social Agency Employees Union. Rose is a 40-year-old African American woman from New York City who we met during a Break-out Session at the 2009 AFL-CIO Convention called "Politics as Usual? Political Mobilization and Accountability in the Age of Obama." Rose never thought that she would one day become a political activist.

"For as long as I can remember, government seemed so far away from us, it was like 'oh they don't care about us,' so we didn't get involved. But now it's more down to where regular people like me can understand. And it motivates you to want to be involved. I think that since Obama has become president, my voice has had more impact than it did before."

For years, Rose felt that her concerns and those of her fellow union members had been systematically ignored by leaders of both parties in Washington. Tucker now believes that she can have an impact on government decisions: "More and more, people like me want to know and want to get more involved in how government is influencing their life."

Rose Tucker is a left-wing populist. She believes that the government has a moral obligation to provide public assistance to struggling citizens. She believes in redistribution of wealth to take care of those in need and that health care is a fundamental human right. And she seemed confident that under President Obama, the left-wing populist agenda would be realized.

"He's changing the system. I think he's really going to be committed. He knows that there are people that need help from the government. And he will make sure they get the public assistance they need. Already, I hear they're starting a program where you can get food stamps and cash assistance online—before you had to go through the bureaucracy. It's getting more human."

The September 2009 AFL-CIO Convention in Pittsburgh gave a good indication of where union members' sympathies lie: healthcare reform, the protection of American jobs, and support for the Employee Free Choice Act—a bill that, if passed, would make it easier to unionize workplaces.

Why is the Employee Free Choice Act such a fundamental component of the left-wing populist platform? The Employee Free Choice Act movement is driven by the very same public sector versus private sector pro-regulation, anti-corporatism, and pro-safety net driving the other major left-wing populist initiatives.

Sue, a middle-aged African American woman from Connecticut, who we met during the "Politics as Usual?" breakout session at the Convention, felt that workers needed to be protected from being marginalized and abused by powerful corporations.

"You need to understand the reason why you have an eight-hour workday, that you have sick leave and all of that, was because people fought and died for that. You could be in a sweatshop working for like twenty hours a day getting three dollars an hour," Sue explained.

Many of the resolutions proposed and adopted over the course of the Convention reflected the proposals being debated in Washington, including whether to enact a single-payer universal healthcare system, and how to achieve retirement security for working families. Speakers lashed out at the corruption of Bear Stearns and Lehman Brothers, banks that spent years rewarding those whose shortsighted risk-taking decimated our country's financial system, causing countless public sector workers to be laid off and denied their pensions. Another speaker called for better working conditions, telling the story of a woman in Milwaukee who worked at a factory and went into labor while at work, yet was forced to wait until the end of the workday to go to the hospital.

When President Obama arrived at the Convention, Delegates and guests leapt to their feet, cheering at the top of their lungs while waving their signs proudly, and it took about ten minutes for the audience to quiet down enough so that he could begin, something that occurred time and again throughout the duration of his forty-five-minute speech, during which he voiced his commitment to the passage of the Employee Free Choice Act, his plans to grow the middle class, and protect and create American jobs from being outsourced. And, of course, his health-care reform plan to provide coverage for the uninsured and create a public option to drive private insurance costs down, which prompted the audience to break into a chant of "We can't wait! We can't wait!"

Clearly Democrats are deeply committed to their union support and fear running afoul of the unions on various aspects of the health-care package. In fact, Obama was forced to tack once more when he voiced his support for a "Cadillac Tax" on high-cost, high-end health insurance policies. It turns out that unions have, over the years, negotiated generous healthcare packages for their members—packages that would be subject to the Cadillac Tax. Thus, language was inserted into House legislation that would exempt union contracts from the tax until 2018, five years beyond the start date for other workers.

Such conflicts illustrate the stubborn realities of ironing out health-care reform. But more than that, they illustrate the kinds of tensions that Obama must somehow balance if he is to be successful.

Indeed, there is an undeniable tension within the Democratic Party between the liberal elite and the mainstream populists. To date, the Obama administration has balanced delicately (and sometimes not so delicately) the conflicting positions and competing pressures of these groups. Going forward, the challenge will only grow more complex, and will involve higher stakes.

The president's ability to navigate this liberal minefield will determine in many ways the course of the 2010 election cycle. If he can successfully appease both elements of the Democratic Party—and speak to disaffected Independents at the same time—he will stem the losses than many predict for the upcoming midterm elections. If he can't bridge the widening divide between the elite and mainstream left, look to the Republican Party and Tea Party allies to drive an electoral truck through this gaping political hole.

THE MEDIA

I'm Upton Sinclair 2.0 . . . except instead of attacking rotten meatpacking houses, I'm attacking the rotten political establishment and the main-stream media that discourage dissent in this country.

—Andrew Breitbart, conservative media personality

The media. I think that they've become lapdogs for the administration, after being attack dogs for the last one. And I just don't like their bias. They're supposed to be the *watchdogs* for the public. And when you spend three and a half weeks on Michael Jackson's death, and you watch them put through a bill, virtually in the middle of the night. By one vote on cap-and-trade, and it's not even *mentioned*. Cap-and-trade is going to totally change this country, and people aren't even *aware* of it.

—Ralph Sproveer, former employee at a health insurance agency, "Can You Hear Us Now?" March on the Media, ABC Studios, Chicago

The Tea Party movement seemingly came from nowhere. There was no organized media support. Nor was there any particular unorganized media support. It grew spontaneously and virally.

To be sure, Rick Santelli on the floor of the Chicago Mercantile Exchange helped stimulate its initial formation. But it was by no means the case that the people who were watching CNBC midday on February 19, 2009, got up and organized the Tea Party movement—for no other reason than the fact that CNBC's primary daytime audience is Wall Street elites and business executives.

So to assume that it was Rick Santelli's rant when there were at most a couple thousand people watching (CNBC had a total day rating of 268,000 viewers), most of whom were business executives, and virtually none of whom have had any connection with the Tea Party movement.

Rather, the answer—as we documented at length in Chapter 5—is much more subtle and arguably more sophisticated. Because what grew from that rant was a spontaneous outpouring of support across the country, motivated not only by a desire to core constitutional principles, but to reduce the size of government.

Where new technologies like the Internet and blogs opened up political commentary to other professionals who often didn't get heard in traditional media, social networking opens up political commentary and activism on a much broader scale—namely, to anyone and everyone with something to say. The potential implications are profound.

Put simply, there would be no Tea Party movement had there not been a fundamental transformation of America's media landscape. The birth and growth of the grassroots, bottom-up Tea Party movement is a perfect example of how everyday citizens can use the new technologies to shape political events.

Even before the term "Tea Party" became a household name—thanks to Youtube.com, which helped the video recording of Rick Santelli's rant go viral—conservative bloggers such as Keli Carender and Michele Malkin were already using the Internet to organize and mobilize frustrated citizens.

And within hours of Santelli's February 19 rant, as the *Weekly Standard*'s John Last noted, Santelli-inspired Tea Party organizing websites sprouted up across the Web, and "on Facebook, dozens of Santelli groups formed, ranging from fan clubs to draft-president movements to tea party plans for Chicago, Texas, New York, and Los Angeles."[1]

As Last reported: "ChicagoTeaParty.com bills itself as the official home of Santelli's tea party. The site belongs to Zack Christenson, a Chicago radio producer. Christenson had bought the domain last August, thinking it might be a good name for a group. Within 12 hours of Santelli's rant, Christenson had retooled the site, and 4,000 people quickly signed up."[2]

As the movement picked up steam, conservative opponents of the Obama administration's initiatives used Facebook and Twitter, and websites such as TeaPartyPatriots.org to organize protest rallies, "meet-ups" and events.

The Internet provided an ideal medium for local and national Tea Party groups, as well as individual members, activists, and supporters to come together to organize events such as the 912 Project, the August 2009 town-hall protests, and the first annual National Tea Party Convention. Online grassroots campaigning and fund-raising facilitated the election of Tea Party endorsed candidates like Scott Brown. And now, the Tea Party movement is using new media tools as it drafts its official agenda—the Contract From America—Wiki-style, online.

In essence, the Tea Party movement was as much of a reaction against the presidency of George W. Bush and the growth in the size of the deficit as it was to the potential overreaching of the Obama administration.

And make no mistake, we are not arguing that George W. Bush created the Tea Party movement, but rather that when analysts point to the strong nonpartisan nature of the Tea Party movement, it stems from the fact that both Parties have been and are responsible for what Tea Party movement supporters and advocates quite rightly see as over-reaching of big government.

The almost spontaneous organization of the Tea Party movement had as much to do with the nature and extent of the way the new media operates as it does with anything else.

Very few analysts to date have put the Tea Party movement in the context of how the new media operate and exist—particularly in the context of traditional right-wing talk radio and cable TV, principally Fox News.

What we are seeing now in the mainstream media—more than one year after the start of the Tea Party movement—is the marry-ing of the mainstream and online worlds. At the time of this writing, ABC had just announced that its Sunday morning public affairs program, "This Week," would be starting an online fact-checking feature called the "Truth-o-Meter"—in conjunction with fact-checking website PolitiFact.com. And Propublica.com became the first online service to win a Pulitzer Prize, when Sheri Fink of ProPublica was honored for her investigative reporting about controversial deaths at a New Orleans medical center following Hurricane Katrina, done in collaboration with the *New York Times Magazine*.

These recent developments merely ratify what has been going on, which is that the engine of news dissemination and creation and political organization is done principally online. Indeed, the Tea Party movement is as much a successor of the 2004 Dean campaign and the more successful and lasting Obama 2008, which grew to include close to two million supporters online.

By our reckoning, the Tea Party movement itself has reached well over two million supporters, members, and advocates as well— although the precise numbers are hard to fathom given the decentralized nature of the movement.

What this chapter is designed to do is describe how the new media has developed in the last couple of years, with specific emphasis on the most recent past, to provide a context to understand how a movement that the mainstream media grew and has come to thrive in an environment most analysts and most media critics simply don't understand.

To be sure, it is a story that is not entirely straightforward. In some instances it is even bizarre. But what is most extraordinary is that disparate interests, operating separately, have changed fundamentally and irrevocably the media landscape in America. And in so doing, created a movement whose impact is still being felt, recognized, and understood.

Perhaps the single best recent example of how everyday citizens can use the new technologies to shape political events is a young conservative journalist, James O'Keefe III.

In September 2009, the world of media, politics, and government was sent into a state of chaos by a homemade series of videos by a young conservative journalist, James O'Keefe III. O'Keefe and his friend, a young woman named Hannah Giles, decided to visit several offices of the left-wing poverty advocacy group, ACORN, presenting themselves as a couple looking for help getting a mortgage.

But they had a novel kind of mortgage in mind: he and Giles claimed they needed the house for prostitution purposes—O'Keefe was Giles's pimp, in the ruse—and they wanted advice on how to obtain the mortgage and disguise their business so they didn't run into legal trouble. Filming the discussions with a hidden camera, O'Keefe caught ACORN officials in three different cities happily offering advice on how to run their criminal enterprise, which, he said, would eventually include importing underage girls from Central America for prostitution. The ACORN officials blinked at none of this. O'Keefe gave them multiple opportunities to object to his plans; they never did.

O'Keefe's ACORN film became a media sensation in the by-now familiar, "viral" fashion: bloggers passed it around and posted it on their sites, and Fox News (especially on Glenn Beck's program) rolled the video again and again. Traditional media like the *New York Times*, showing that it had learned nothing from its misjudgment of the Tea Parties, ignored the ACORN scandal until criticism eventually forced it to cover the story. O'Keefe's film sparked a public outcry about ACORN's ethics and practices, and the group, which had past ties to President Obama and received taxpayer funding, became Capitol Hill's newest villain. The House voted overwhelmingly to halt all federal money to the organization.

This new kind of attacking, insurgent-style media, employed by unknowns, conducted on shoestring budgets, and disseminated through social-networking technologies, is something we will see much more of in the future. (And we'll see excess, too: O'Keefe was later arrested on his follow-up project, in which he entered a federal building in an effort to monitor the phones of Senator Mary Landrieu.) It completes the arc of the media revolution that began with the collapse of the traditional media. The role of the media in American political culture has changed, in just a generation, from gatekeepers to guerrillas. The media's transformation from a hierarchical, elitist institution that mediated political-class debates to a bottom-up, ever-changing, and deeply partisan force that threatens the political class, presents major challenges—and opportunities—for our political life. And the only thing certain is that more change is coming.

In the old days, the established media—the only media there was— spoke for a presumptive ruling class on behalf of the public interest. Fast forward to the first decade of the 21st century. Today's new media is driven by a bottom-up, anti-establishment, populist spirit. It empowers individual bloggers and media insurgents of all kinds— independent filmmakers, YouTube video-makers, guerrilla reporters, website entrepreneurs—who have changed the way the right and the left disseminate political information. And it has changed the way political groups organize, mobilize, and connect with one another.

Meanwhile, the mainstream media is going down as the big news giants begin to implode.

Since the election of Barack Obama to the presidency, the ratings of Fox News have skyrocketed. During the same period, the ratings of CNN, MSNBC, and CNBC have plummeted.

In March 2010, ABC News announced that it is cutting its news correspondent staff by half and that it will close all its "brick and mortar" news bureaus, except for its Washington hub; and mainstream newspapers, such as the *New York Times*, continue to operate under heavy financial pressure as subscriptions tank and advertising revenues fall to historic lows.

Meanwhile, CNN, whose President Jon Klein has "consistently defended its down-the-middle news strategy, despite the increasingly large ratings leads opened up by MSNBC and particularly Fox, with their ideological slants and big personalities,"[3] experienced a 40 percent drop in prime-time viewers since 2009.

To get a sense of how much has changed, consider the summer 2009 passing of Walter Cronkite, the most iconic figure of the broadcast network era. Figures of Cronkite's stature are gone forever, and network television is suffering as a result, with ratings showing an increasing exodus from broadcast to cable television. At his peak, Cronkite drew from twenty-seven million to twenty-nine million viewers each night for his CBS News evening broadcast. Today, the *combined* audience of the evening news programs on CBS, NBC, and ABC is smaller than the one that watched just Cronkite alone. In a 2008 Pew survey, just 8 percent of respondents said they watched Katie Couric on the CBS Evening News broadcast.

In 2008, the Pew Organization recorded for the first time that less than half the public reported reading a daily newspaper—46 percent, down from 52 percent in 2006 and 71 percent in 1992. The drop-off occurred across the board: among men and women, whites and blacks, college graduates, and those who never attended college. Not surprising, the decline was particularly sharp among the young, who were the least likely to read a daily newspaper. Just 15 percent told Pew they had read a paper "yesterday."

Online Newspaper More Popular, While Print Declines

	Total	18-24	25-34	35-49	50-64	65+
			—AGE—			
2008	%	%	%	%	%	%
Newspaper Yesterday*	39	21	31	37	44	56
Print only	25	12	12	20	30	50
Web only	9	7	16	11	7	3
Both	5	2	3	6	7	3
NET: Web version	**14**	**9**	**19**	**17**	**14**	**6**
2006						
Newspaper Yesterday*	43	27	31	43	50	58
Print only	34	18	22	30	41	55
Web only	5	7	7	7	4	1
Both	4	2	2	6	5	2
NET: Web version	**9**	**9**	**9**	**13**	**9**	**3**
Change in web version	*+5*	*0*	*+10*	*+4*	*+5*	*+3*

*Figure includes people who said they got news online yesterday and, when prompted, said they visited the websites of one or more newspapers when online yesterday.

Recent Falloff In Newspaper Readership

	2006	2008	Change
Read a newspaper yesterday:	%	%	%
Total	**40**	**34**	**−6**
Age			
18–24	22	15	−7
25–34	28	24	−4
35–49	39	31	−8
50–64	47	40	−7
65+	58	55	−3

Trend in Regular News Consumption: TV News Sources

	1998	2000	2002	2004	2006	2008
	%	%	%	%	%	%
General categories:						
Local TV news	64	56	57	59	54	52
Cable TV news	—	—	33	38	34	39
Nightly network news	38	30	32	34	28	29
Network morning shows	23	20	22	22	23	22
Sunday morning shows	—	—	—	12	12	13
Cable Networks:						
CNN	23	21	25	22	22	24
Fox News Channel	17	17	22	25	23	23
MSNBC	8	11	15	11	11	15
CNBC	12	13	13	10	11	12
Evening News Programs:						
NBC Nightly News	—	—	20	17	15	14
ABC World News Tonight	—	—	18	16	14	14
CBS Evening News	—	—	18	16	13	8
NewsHour	4	5	5	5	5	5

Source: Pew Organization Poll, 2008.

The traditional, mainstream media, has not only lost audience share, it has also, more damaging, lost authority and credibility.

As the 2010 Edelman Trust Barometer Executive Summary notes, in 2010: "trust in traditional media continues to wane. Among older informed publics, over the past two years the credibility of television news dropped 20-plus points in the U.S."[4]

Part of this trend was inevitable: Changes in Americans' media consumption, demographic shifts, and the explosion of new technologies were all destined to put traditional media in a bind.

As Zogby Interactive's John Zogby notes, in a June 2009 survey: "We asked which of the four primary information sources was most reliable. The Internet was way out front with 37%, with the others closely bunched as follows: television 17%, newspapers 16% and radio 13%. On which media source is most reliable, only 6% of Republicans chose newspapers, compared with 25% of Democrats and 14% of Independents."[5]

But the old-line media has also explicitly undermined its own standing due to a long series of episodes and habits that show its resistance to independent thinking, as well as, increasingly, its affiliation and identification with the political class.

The mainstream media, in short, has a built-in bias to the political class that renders it unable to report accurately on the most important political stories of our time, including the Tea Party, which the mainstream media ignored, belittled, and reviled at every turn. This combination of technological displacement and loss of integrity has made the traditional media a bystander, a player of diminishing influence in the national political debate.

Today, more than two-thirds (68 percent) believe that reporters favor their preferred political candidates in their coverage. In early 2009, only 8 percent of Americans told an NBC/*Wall Street Journal* poll that they had a "great deal" of confidence in the national news media, while 18 percent said they had "no confidence at all."

And a majority of Americans believes that media bias is slanted to the left. An April 2010 Rasmussen Reports survey found that 51 percent of voters say the average reporter is more liberal than they are. Eighteen percent say that the average reporter is more conservative, and 20 percent think their views are about the same ideologically as the average reporter.

And the Rasmussen Reports Media Meter shows that media coverage in Texas is far more favorable for Democratic gubernatorial candi-

Trend in Print Credibility*

Believe all of most of what organization says	1996 %	1998 %	2000 %	2002 %	2004 %
U.S. News	—	—	—	26	24
Wall St. Journal	36	41	41	33	24
Time	—	27	29	23	22
New York Times	—	—	—	—	21
Newsweek	—	24	24	20	19
USA Today	24	23	23	19	19
Your daily paper	25	29	25	21	19
Associated Press	16	18	21	17	18
People	—	10	10	9	7
National Enquirer	—	3	4	3	5

*Percentages based on those who could rate each.

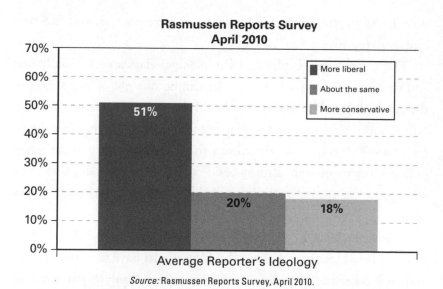

Source: Rasmussen Reports Survey, April 2010.

date Bill White than for incumbent Republican Governor Rick Perry. For the week ending Sunday, March 28, 2010, 79.5 percent of the media mentions for White were positive, and only 20.5 percent were negative. For Perry, during the same time frame, the coverage was far more

Downward Trend in Credibility*

	1996	1998	2000	2002	2004
Believe all or most of what organization says	%	%	%	%	%
60 Minutes	—	35	34	34	33
CNN	38	42	39	37	32
C-SPAN	30	32	33	30	27
Fox News Channel	—	—	26	24	25
Local TV News	—	34	33	27	25
NBC News	29	30	29	25	24
ABC News	31	30	30	24	24
CBS News	32	28	29	26	24
NewsHour	—	29	24	26	23
NPR	—	19	25	23	23
MSNBC	—	—	28	28	22

*Percentages based on those who could rate each.

mixed: 45.6 percent of the media mentions were positive, and 54.4 percent were negative.

The mainstream media and the political class are essentially one and the same; the mainstream media can be thought of as a subset of the political class. The kinds of political disputes that exercise ordinary Americans—the issues that tend to get them calling their political representatives or talk radio, the things they say they worry about when pollsters ask them—are almost beside the point. Policy disputes arise among the political class, to be sure, but a broader worldview unites them.

A January 14, 2010, Rasmussen Reports survey found that 67 percent of likely U.S. voters believe the news media have too much power and influence over government decisions, while only 8 percent said that the media has too little power, and 19 percent said that their level of power is just about right. Moreover, only 20 percent of all voters say most reporters try to offer unbiased coverage of a political campaign. Seventy-two percent say most reporters try to help the candidate they want to win.

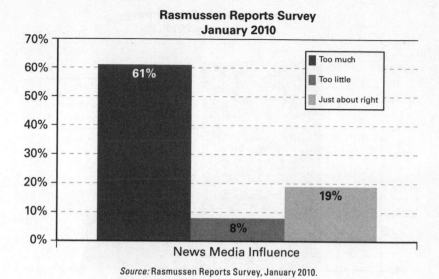

Source: Rasmussen Reports Survey, January 2010.

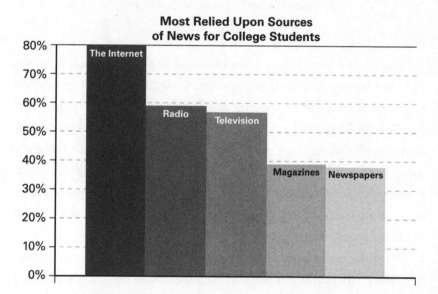

These findings are consistent with a March 2007 Institute for Politics, Democracy, and the Internet/Zogby Poll in which 83 percent of likely voters said the media is biased in one direction or another, while just 11 percent believe the media doesn't take political sides.[6]

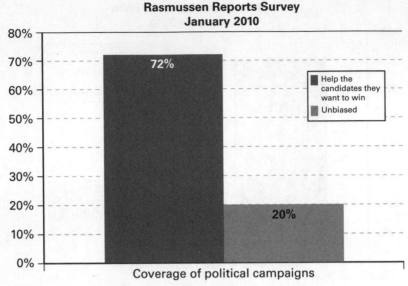

Rasmussen Reports Survey
January 2010

Coverage of political campaigns

Source: Rasmussen Reports Survey, January 2010.

The mainstream media's loss of credibility with ordinary Americans has been a long-running narrative, playing out over several decades but heightened and accelerated by the times we live in, in which people have access to empowering media tools that allow them to hear alternative views and even provide their own critiques. What more and more Americans see when they look at the traditional media is an apparatus that has, continually, missed the big political stories altogether, or misunderstood them, or attempted to dismiss them until events made ignoring them impossible.

"I think they're lapdogs for this current administration. I think the only place where you can get anything legitimate on TV is Fox News. And I don't really even trust them that much. But they have a tendency to talk about stories that are far more pertinent than the boy in the hot air balloon. . . . Why don't instead they talk about the two trillion dollars we're going to spend to wreck our healthcare system. Just to let the government take control. They don't *belong* in the healthcare system," said Ralph Sproveer, protesting outside of ABC Studios in down-

Partisanship and Credibility*

Believe all or most of what organization says	Rep. %	Dem. %	Gap
Broadcast & Cable Outlets:			
CNN	26	45	+19
CBS News	15	34	+19
NPR	15	33	+18
NewsHour	12	29	+17
60 Minutes	25	42	+17
ABC News	17	34	+17
MSNBC	14	29	+15
C-SPAN	22	36	+14
NBC News	16	30	+14
Local TV News	21	29	+8
Fox News Channel	29	24	−5
Print Outlets:			
Associated Press	12	29	+17
New York Times	14	31	+17
Time	15	30	+15
Newsweek	12	26	+14
USA Today	14	25	+11
Daily newspaper	16	23	+7
Wall St. Journal	23	29	+6

*Percentages based on those who could rate each.

town Chicago during an October 2009 "Can You Hear Us Now?" protest.

In fact, a majority of Americans, 55 percent, believe that media bias is a bigger problem in politics today than big campaign contributions.

A number of issues in recent history have illustrated the traditional media's unwillingness to ask tough questions or poke underneath the official version of the story told by elites. The traditional media served the public very poorly during the housing bubble, for example. "They relied almost entirely," Dean Baker, co-director of the Center for Economic and Policy Research in Washington, D.C., wrote in late 2008, "on sources who either had an interest in not calling attention to an $8 trillion housing bubble or somehow were unable to see it. As a re-

Most Believable News Sources*

Republicans	Democrats	Independents
Fox News (29)	CNN (45)	60 Minutes (29)
CNN (26)	60 Minutes (42)	CNN (28)
60 Minutes (25)	C-SPAN (36)	C-SPAN (26)
Wall St. Journal (23)	ABC News (34)	U.S. News (26)
C-SPAN (22)	CBS News (34)	NBC News (24)
Local TV News (21)	NPR (33)	NewsHour (24)

* Percent who believe all or most of what the organization reports, based on those able to rate the organization.

sult they did not warn the public that their house prices were likely to plunge in the future."[7]

Voices like Pacific Capital's Peter Schiff, who warned for years about the unsustainable nature of the housing boom, were given short shrift, or were laughed at by panels full of stock market bulls on financial programs. Instead, the media served as cheerleaders, encouraging the public to believe the old saw that housing values never go down, and that what all Americans needed to do was buy a home, however much debt they had to accrue to get it. The media served the interests of the political class, which did not want to hear from "doomsayers" like Schiff or others who questioned whether the bubble was sustainable. Only when the bubble collapsed did the mainstream media show the ability to do the kind of reporting it should have been doing all along.

In the fall of 2008, when the entire U.S. economy teetered on financial collapse, the traditional media became staunch advocates for government intervention and a $700 billion "rescue package"—the Troubled Assets Relief Program, or TARP—despite intense opposition from the general public. The media portrayed the bailouts not only as necessary and unavoidable but as popular, which was demonstrably not the case. According to the coverage on four major networks— ABC, CBS, CNN, and NBC—the economic situation would be worse without a bailout. Network anchors like Katie Couric described those in Washington who opposed the package as blocking it for "political" reasons. Couric's interview with House Minority Leader John Boehner was typical:

"Congressman Boehner, Warren Buffett warned if Congress doesn't act, quote, 'there would be the biggest financial meltdown in American history.' What in the world are you people doing?"

The rescue package initially failed to pass; after intense criticism, a revised version did win congressional approval and presidential signature. But the first-round defeat stunned most mainstream commentators. ABC's Jake Tapper called it "an historic legislative disaster," while an equally befuddled Carol Costello of CNN, citing polling showed that the public opposed the measure 47 percent to 45 percent, said simply: "I talked to our own polling experts and they are perplexed by the numbers." If she or her mainstream media colleagues had looked at more polling numbers, they would have been less perplexed, as the surveys showed nearly unanimous public opposition to the bailout:[8]

- A September 25, 2008, poll from Rasmussen found that only 30 percent of voters agreed with the federal government stepping in to rescue financial markets, while 63 percent of people were worried the government would do too much.
- After the failure of the first bailout bill, a Gallup survey showed 57 percent favored starting over and coming up with a new plan.
- A CNN poll found that after the bailout bill passed, 53 percent of respondents still opposed it and didn't think it would prevent a "deep and long recession," according to the *Boston Globe*.
- Time.com reported on September 29, 2008, that phone calls to congressional offices were running 100 to 1 against the bailout.

You have to be pretty locked into your worldview to miss that kind of trend, and to express on the air that you're "perplexed" by the opposition. The numbers were clear to anyone who could read them. But the mainstream media, adjunct to the political class, was unable to absorb facts that didn't fit its narrative.

Finally, consider the traditional media's treatment of the Tea Party movement.

From the beginning, critics questioned the extent to which the Tea Parties truly represented grievances shared by a majority of the American public. As we've noted earlier, the mainstream media's initial take on the Tea Party was identical to that of Nancy Pelosi, who initially branded Tea Partiers "Astroturf." In response to the April 15 Tea Party protests, the *New York Times* suggested that perhaps the critics were correct: "Although organizers insisted they had created a nonpartisan grass-roots movement, others argued that these parties were more of the Astroturf variety: an occasion largely created by the clamor of cable news and fueled by the financial and political support of current and former Republican leaders. . . . The Web site TaxDayTeaParty.com listed its sponsors, including FreedomWorks, a group founded by Dick Armey, the former House majority leader; Top Conservatives on Twitter; and RFCRadio.com."[9]

Times columnist Paul Krugman quipped: These parties— antitaxation demonstrations that are supposed to evoke the memory of the Boston Tea Party and the American Revolution—have been the subject of considerable mockery, and rightly so . . . it turns out that the tea parties don't represent a spontaneous outpouring of public sentiment. They're AstroTurf (fake grass roots) events, manufactured by the usual suspects.[10]

The reality was far different. In fact, Tea Party participants tend to believe that the Republican Party has strayed far from its ideological roots, and that Republican policymakers in Washington are no different than the Democrats. As we discussed at length in Chapter 7, far from being the driving force behind the Tea Parties, the GOP is trying desperately to hitch its wagon to this growing protest movement. When the two forces have a common interest—as they did in Massachusetts, where Scott Brown won both Tea Party and GOP endorsement on his way to winning Ted Kennedy's old Senate Seat—they work together. But the Tea Party movement has consistently advertised its anti-establishment orientation, and it puts the GOP on notice regularly that it is not an arm of the party.

The January 2010 Massachusetts Senate special election, Republican Scott Brown won the seat that had belonged to Democrats for nearly sixty years. Brown's victory shocked not just the Democrats, but also the traditional media, which had maintained for nearly a year that the Tea Party movement wouldn't be able to influence electoral outcomes. But Brown's victory would not have been possible without the strong support he received from Tea Party groups.

Few voices from outside the elite political and media centers have a national voice in the mainstream media. Within the traditional organs of media power today, the range of backgrounds and of opinion is vanishingly small. No wonder polls show that ordinary Americans tend to have little or no faith left in mainstream media outlets; the pundits who put forth in columns and Sunday morning panels are often describing a world that these Americans don't recognize.

Fortunately, while the traditional broadcast and print media have failed repeatedly in their roles as critics and investigators, the American people now have access to a universe of alternative media sources scarcely imaginable even a decade ago.

There would be no Tea Party movement had there not been a fundamental transformation of America's media landscape. The conservative bloggers and activists who are responsible for the birth and growth of the grassroots, bottom-up Tea Party movement are a perfect example of how everyday citizens can use the new technologies to shape political events.

The right has used the Web and blogs to drive its political agenda, both in the media and in Washington. Conservative bloggers like Michelle Malkin and media entrepreneurs like Matt Drudge and Andrew Breitbart are some of the most influential media figures working today: all have broken or pushed stories that the mainstream media were ignoring to the forefront of the news cycle. Conservative multimedia sites like Pajamas Media and Big Hollywood, which offer video as well as text, have become hugely popular alternative destinations for conservatives hungry for perspective and opinion. Erik Erickson, who runs the conservative RedState blog, writes a "Morning Briefing" email that ricochets around the conservative universe, from websites to blogs to talk radio, often shaping the conservative message. Conservative opinion portals like Townhall.com serve not just as platforms for writers and columnists but as organizing centers for political activity: "It's through this venue that state and local political assembly and vital discourse occurs; it's an example of the First Amendment in action," said Gayle Plato-Besley, an Arizona-based blogger and columnist.

One would be hard pressed to find a more vocal critic of the mainstream media than Andrew Breitbart.

"If they think that ACORN or the Democratic Party or the NEA or the Office of Public Engagement is the primary target, they couldn't be more wrong. It is the Democrat-media complex. It is the mainstream media," says Breitbart,[11] whose website, bigjournalism.com, was designed specifically to "fight the mainstream media . . . who have repeatedly, and under the guise of objectivity and political neutrality, promoted a blatantly left-of-center, pro-Democratic party agenda."[12]

Breitbart adds, "We are Tea Party-esque, with outraged Americans who have had it up to here with mainstream media. Our audience is comprised of normal, mainstream people: blue-collar workers, actors, students—black, white, straight, Gay, Jewish, Hispanic. They are at wit's end and want to go to war with the Democratic-media complex."[13]

Meanwhile, RedState.com's Erick Erickson has emerged as "One of the most important and prescient new voices and opinion-shapers in the Republican Party. And he is an increasingly influential headache for party leaders seen as straying from conservative principles."

Pity the party leaders Erickson thinks are selling out conservatism, because they can quickly become a target among grass roots activists, and conservative giants like Rush Limbaugh, who often cites Erickson's posts on his radio show. RedState can mobilize activists to overwhelm congressional phone lines or—in the case of Charlie Crist—help drive mainstream media coverage about endangered centrist Republicans.[14]

Erickson's influence has not gone unnoticed by media and political elites. CNN announced on March 16, 2010, that Erickson would join as a political contributor for their new seven p.m., ET program, *John King, USA.*

CNN political director Sam Feist said: "Erick's a perfect fit for *John King, USA,* because not only is he an agenda-setter whose words are closely watched in Washington, but as a person who still lives in small-town America, Erick is in touch with the very people John hopes to reach."[15]

As Robert Bluey, director of online strategy for the Heritage Foundation explains: "It is the blog that's read by Capitol Hill staffers and Capital Hill lawmakers. It's the place in the Republican Party you can go to get a pulse of what's happening in the heartland . . . And if you're working at the (National Republican Congressional Committee or National Republican Senatorial Committee), you're always on edge about what Erick Erickson is going to do because he can either be your biggest advocate or a huge thorn in your side."[16]

And at a time where trust in elites are at record lows, Erickson's reputation as a trusted agenda-setter puts him in a very good position for achieving his goals for 2010, which include:

- Beating Governor Charlie Crist and electing Marco Rubio as Florida's junior senator.
- "Taking out" Republican Senator Bob Bennett of Utah because he's a centrist.
- Ensuring the Republican establishment receives no credit for whatever success the GOP has in November.[17]

Today, the engine that really powers political interest is the *insurgent media*, from the Internet to talk radio to cable news. It shapes politics on both the right (blogs, websites, talk radio, and Fox News) and on the left (blogs, websites, and MSNBC). It is no coincidence that the Tea Party movement and the populist resurgence in America has been on the ascent at precisely the moment that the traditional media has been on the decline.

THE COLLAPSE OF TRADITIONAL MEDIA

In the old media order, newspapers and network television were the only games in town, and news was delivered and interpreted by the most exclusive of clubs: reporters, editors, and anchors working for a few select newspapers; and the broadcast networks, CBS, NBC, and ABC, which together had 90 percent of the viewing audience. They set the agenda for the national conversation and exerted enormous influence on political campaigns. These individuals were the gatekeepers, the middlemen between breaking news and the American public. News content relied on what the editors of the *New York Times* deemed "fit to print," and on the judgment of TV anchors like Walter Cronkite, in whom Americans placed immense trust to frame the most important issues and events of their time.

In the old system, it was difficult to get content visible and distributed. A writer, for example, had to get his or her piece through producers at the broadcast networks or through the editors' desk at a major newspaper. Once a writer did that, though, he or she had a built-in audience: an article on the op-ed page of the *New York Times* or *Washington Post*, a report filed on ABC's World News Tonight. Anyone interested in news watched those programs or read those publications; it was understood that they *were* the news.

Cronkite's power was not just that he was the most watched network journalist; it was that millions of Americans put stock in what he said and looked to him with confidence that what he told them was true. Lyndon Johnson, watching the famous newscast where Cronkite came out against the Vietnam War, is said to have turned to an aide and exclaimed: "If I've lost Cronkite, I've lost Middle America." In 1973, a famous poll revealed that Cronkite was "the most trusted man in America." When he retired, 81 percent still had a positive opinion of him. By contrast, shortly before his successor, Dan Rather, delivered his last broadcast in the CBS anchor's chair in 2006, just 21 percent of respondents in a Gallup poll said that they believed in him all or even most of the time.

One reason why trust declined so much in Rather—and by extension his colleagues in anchor's chairs at the major networks—was because traditional media had, over several decades, gradually but inexorably lost its moral authority.

Americans, through new media like blogs and websites, wanted to examine and critique for themselves the claims that the mainstream media were making. What they found, all too often, was that the traditional media was an emperor with no clothes: his facts were wrong, his conclusions way off, and, worst of all, his attitude was arrogant, condescending, and dismissive.

The broadcast networks lost the central role they once had in delivering and interpreting news because, quite simply, people have more viewing choices. In 1985, the average home got eighteen cable channels; by 2007, that total had climbed to more than 118. New networks—most important, Fox News—created powerful alternatives, as did the increasing importance of news satirists like Jon Stewart, comedians like Bill Maher, and documentarians like Michael Moore, all of whom had the impact, especially among the young, of undermining confidence in established mainstream narratives. Thirty-two percent of Americans under the age of 40 say satirical, news-oriented television programs like *The Colbert Report* and *The Daily Show* are taking the place of traditional news outlets. The choices of what to read, watch, or listen to are almost beyond number.

But the new forms of media represent more than new distribution channels. They fundamentally offer a different kind of content: hard-edged, deeply partisan reporting and commentary that makes no secret of its ideological positions. This is the stark opposite of the standard that ruled in the age of Cronkite: even when reporters had political leanings, they generally kept them to themselves, and the mission of the news was, however imperfect, to present a broad and fair-minded picture of the world. When Cronkite famously editorialized against the Vietnam War, he was breaking character to offer an opinion, something he normally did not do. His editorial statement was memorable for that very reason.

Today, cable news and the blogosphere is awash in opinion; programming is driven by opinion, and the top-rated news shows all involve highly opinionated hosts like Bill O'Reilly, Sean Hannity, or Keith Olbermann, along with their guests, who also voice strongly held partisan views. This change has both driven, and been driven by, changes in the U.S. political climate. The political power within the Republican Party, and the party's voting base, has moved steadily rightwards since the presidency of Ronald Reagan. The party has few moderates left. Conversely, the Democratic Party has moved leftwards in recent years. Redistricting has gerrymandered voting areas into Democratic or Republican strongholds, making it harder for moderates on either side. Partisanship holds the keys to power in Washington on both sides of the aisle; it also drives television ratings. And the intensity of partisanship in both sectors has the effect of drawing the two environments closer together, so that the media reflects the polarization between the two parties.

The result is what Rem Rieder, writing in the *American Journalism Review*, calls "separate megaphones for separate audiences. As in the blogosphere, with its pugnacious mix of conservative and liberal Web sites, there is political TV for the left and political TV for the right. Increasingly, we are a nation of partisans talking only to themselves." [18] Rieder has a point: media today thrives on the extreme. They do not seek to build a consensus—in the manner of a Cronkite—but to generate compelling programming from the passions and divisions that roil American politics.

CNN's fall from grace demonstrates that when the majority of the American public believes that the media is biased, it is best for a network to be open about it and the neutral view-from-nowhere. "CNN needs to find an identity and own that identity," explains former editorial director of MSNBC, David Goldin.

Bill Press thinks CNN "is going to have to bite the bullet and do some advocacy programming . . . there ain't no room in the middle." Viewers are "looking for opinion in prime time . . . anchors with an edge."

Bill O'Reilly's ratings are higher than all the top programs on CNN, MSNBC, and CNBC combined. And when the big three at Fox—O'Reilly, Glenn Beck, and Sean Hannity—are counted together, the network rivals the combination of the three network news broadcasts at CBS, NBC, and ABC, an unprecedented coup for a cable news network.

All indications point to a continuation of the decline of the liberal, mainstream media as conservative and alternative news sources enjoy their best days in history.

INSURGENT MEDIA, RIGHT AND LEFT

Cable

On the right, Fox News is the dominant news source for Americans whose political leanings are Republican or conservative. From its emergence in 1995, Fox's success has long since made clear how strong a market demand there was for highly partisan and, in this case conservative, political content. In such a competitive media market, this political slant allowed Fox to create a powerful niche for itself immediately, setting it off from its more "objective" network competitors. The network became more and more embedded in political affiliation: clearly taking a pro-Bush tone during President George W. Bush's terms in office and, just as adamantly, taking an anti-Obama tone starting in January 2009. The network's viewership shot up even higher after Obama took

Network vs. Cable: Distinct Audiences

Regularly watch...	Nightly Network News %	Cable News Channels %
Total	29	39
Male	27	**44**
Female	31	35
18–29	21	36
30–49	22	38
50–64	34	42
65+	46	44
College Grad	28	**45**
Some College	27	42
High School Grad	33	36
Less than H.S. Grad	25	32
Political knowledge		
High	28	**55**
Medium	32	43
Low	26	27

Source: Pew Research Center, June 2004

office, and has seen their influence grow to unprecedented heights as they position themselves as the headquarters of the Obama opposition. By March 2010, while Fox News continues to see record ratings, their cable news competitors are dropping off even more year-to-year. In the 25 to 54 demographic during prime time, FNC was up 16 percent while CNN dropped 42 percent, MSNBC was down 22 percent and HLN was down 40 percent. In total viewers during prime time, FNC was up 3 percent while the rest declined as well (CNN to 39 percent, MSNBC to 15 percent, and HLN to 24 percent).

As Mediaite.com's Steve Karakauer observed:

"While CNN continues to decline in prime time . . . Fox News remains unaffected. In fact, with health care passing, there's no reason to doubt the second quarter of 2010 will be any different. With midterm elections just around the corner, Fox News could conceivably be headed for another year of stronger ratings than the one before." [19]

The Obama administration has unwittingly emboldened conservative media, especially Fox, by attempting to freeze out the network from access: not giving Fox anchors interviews with the president for a time, and not sending administration to talk on *Fox News Sunday*, for example. White House press secretary Robert Gibbs said that in the administration's view, Fox was "not a news organization." What was it, then? Communications director Anita Dunn had the answer, saying that the network "operates almost as either the research arm or the communications arm of the Republican Party."

The Obama White House's ill-advised attacks on the network gave Fox an extra lift and set it up to deliver its best rating year ever in 2009. This year, Fox News has averaged nearly 1.2 million viewers across all its programming, a 16 percent increase over the same period last year, according to Nielsen. If anything, the Obama administration only succeeded in strengthening Fox's credentials on the right, especially the populist right. The network, for all its institutional success, has always maintained an "insurgent" mentality. "We may be number one," said senior political analyst Brit Hume, "but there is sort of an insurgent quality to Fox News. And that's kind of our attitude: 'Hoist a Jolly Roger, pull out our daggers and look for more throats to slit.' This is tremendous fodder for us. My lord, we've been living on it."

Talk Radio

Rush Limbaugh's power was never more in evidence than in the winter of 2009.

First, in the days before Obama was sworn in, Limbaugh ignited a firestorm of controversy by saying that he hoped Obama failed in office, because the president's plan was to impose socialism, and he would not want to see socialism succeed. At a time when most of the hardiest conservative pundits were taking pains to wish the new president well, Limbaugh's words sounded a harsh, discordant note, but a popular one on the right. Not long afterward, Limbaugh addressed the

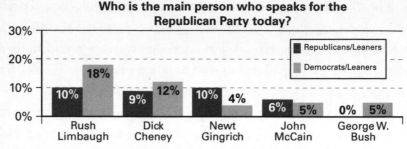

Who is the main person who speaks for the Republican Party today?

Source: USA Today/Gallup Poll, May 29–30, 2009.

faithful at the Conservative Political Action Conference, drawing the largest crowd in the event's thirty-five-year history. His speech, scheduled for less than half an hour, went on for over an hour, to raucous applause. He urged his listeners not to "think like a minority," and to resist Obama's policies: "President Obama," he said, "your agenda is not new, it's not change, and it's not hope," as the crowd applauded wildly. "Spending a nation into generational debt is not an act of compassion." Conservatism itself, preached Limbaugh, was the sole bulwark against the frightening consequences of Obama's policies. "[Conservatism] is what it is and has been forever," he said. "It is not something you can bend or shape."

Shortly after his CPAC speech, Limbaugh got into a dust-up with the Republican Party national chairman, Michael Steele, one that made abundantly clear how much more public influence a radio talk show host has than a Republican Party official. Steele was appearing on CNN's short-lived comedy program, *D.L. Hughley Breaks the News.* Discussing the GOP's image problem with black voters, Hughley mentioned the nation's most-listened to radio talk-show host:

HUGHLEY: Rush Limbaugh, who is the de facto leader of the Republican Party . . .
STEELE: No, he's not.
HUGHLEY: Well, I'll tell you what, I've never . . .
STEELE: I'm the de facto leader of the Republican Party.

HUGHLEY: Then you know what? Then I can appreciate that, but no—no one will—will actually pry down some of the things he says, like when he comes out and says that he wants the president to fail, I understand he wants liberalism to fail.

STEELE: How is that any different than what was said about George Bush during his presidency? Let's put it into context here. Rush Limbaugh is an entertainer. Rush Limbaugh, the whole thing is entertainment. Yes, it's incendiary, yes, it's ugly. . . .

The interview continued, with other controversial moments, such as when Steele let pass unchallenged Hughley's observation that the Republicans' 2008 national convention "looked like Nazi Germany." But it was Steele's Limbaugh comments that set off the firestorm. Conservative bloggers and commentators ripped him for criticizing as "incendiary" and "ugly" a radio host who has a weekly audience of twenty million listeners and who consistently rallies conservative Americans. Limbaugh himself denounced Steele on his program, ridiculing him for being weak and ineffective in his opposition to Obama's policies. With stunning swiftness, Steele retracted his comments. His words were abject, almost Orwellian in their total revision of what he had originally said: "I have enormous respect for Rush Limbaugh. I was maybe a little bit inarticulate. There was no attempt on my part to diminish his voice or his leadership. I went back at that tape and I realized words that I said weren't what I was thinking. It was one of those things where I think I was saying one thing, and it came out differently. What I was trying to say was a lot of people want to make Rush the scapegoat, the bogeyman, and he's not."

Limbaugh, Steele said now, was "a national conservative leader, and in no way do I want to diminish his voice. I truly apologize." As if that were not enough, Steele called Limbaugh privately as well. "We had a nice conversation last night," Steele eagerly told CNN. "We are all good." His penance complete, Steele moved on, careful to avoid mention of Rush Limbaugh ever again.

The Steele-Limbaugh incident followed on the heels of several other Republican political leaders' retracting their public criticisms of the talk-show host. One, Republican Congressman Phil Gingrey, had ripped into Limbaugh and other conservative talk-show hosts, saying it was easy to "throw bricks" but difficult to "do what's best for your people and your party." But a few days later, a chastened and almost panicky Gingrey called Limbaugh on the air to apologize, telling the host: "I clearly ended up putting my foot in my mouth on some of those comments and I just wanted to tell you, Rush . . . that I regret those stupid comments."

No wonder Obama's Chief of Staff, Rahm Emanuel, said of Limbaugh: "Whenever a Republican criticizes him, they have to run back and apologize to him."

And then consider the rise of Glenn Beck, whom some even see as a contender for Limbaugh's throne. Beck hosted a reasonably popular TV program on CNN; but when he switched to Fox in the fall of 2008, his populist credentials zoomed up, his delivery and presentation of material became more impassioned, combative, and apocalyptic, and his viewership skyrocketed. Despite being on at five p.m. in the East Coast, Beck has more cable viewers than anyone except Bill O'Reilly and Sean Hannity, who are on in prime time.

Lampooning himself as a "rodeo clown," Beck nevertheless exhorts and inspires millions of viewers in the most serious way. "The truth is—that you are the defender of liberty," he said on one broadcast. "It's not the government. It's not an army or anybody else. It's you. This is your country." He tapped into a deep vein of American public discontent at just the right time. "What ever happened to the country that loved the underdog and stood up for the little guy?" he asked on one broadcast, speaking for a sentiment that millions of Americans currently share. Beck continually reminds his listeners that "You are not alone." His program regularly suggests that the United States has in effect been taken over by people who don't share ordinary Americans' values, but Beck reassures his listeners on this score, too: "We surround them," he's sometimes said vaguely, in words that some observers take as threatening or suggestive of violence.

But all this would be just sideshow if it weren't for the fact that Beck has had genuine political impact, directly affecting decisions made in Washington. In August and September 2009, it seemed like his was the voice of conservative opposition to the Obama administration. His relentless airing of videos showing Van Jones, the administration's point person for its "green jobs" initiative, helped reveal Jones's radicalism—including his support for the 9/11 "Truthers"—and his reckless way of expressing himself, whether calling Republicans "assholes" in public or engaging in race baiting. Opposition to Jones mushroomed as Beck kept up the drumbeat against him, and Jones stepped aside to spare the administration further embarrassment.

On the left, the long search for a cable answer to Fox bore fruit when MSNBC began framing its news from a decidedly liberal point of view. During the Obama presidency, the network has become the closest thing imaginable to a mirror image of Fox on the left, relentlessly defending President Obama.

For years, MSNBC languished in the ratings, a cable-news afterthought. That all changed when it installed Keith Olbermann in the evening slot directly opposite Fox's *O'Reilly Factor.* Olbermann's brilliantly delivered, if hard-edged and utterly partisan, rants connected with left-wing viewers. Now they had their cable television answer to O'Reilly. In 2008, a reporter quoted an MSNBC executive who said that Olbermann "runs" the network due to his success, using hyperbole, no doubt, but also making the point about the impact the popular host had on the network's fortunes. In the nine o'clock hour, MSNBC eventually found an answer to Fox's hugely popular Sean Hannity when it followed Olbermann with Rachel Maddow, another devoted partisan of liberal causes, though her on-air style is much calmer.

During the 2008 campaign, the network often seemed willing to cross a line of almost openly cheering on Obama's candidacy. Even Democrats objected, like Pennsylvania Governor Ed Rendell, a Hillary Clinton supporter, who criticized the network for its pro-Obama bias. During election week in November 2008, MSNBC even used an on-air slogan that seemed a direct homage to the Obama campaign: "The Power of Change." Conversely, the network was very hard on Republicans and conservatives, particularly Sarah Palin, a trend that did not end with the election. In November 2009, just before the publication of Palin's book, *Going Rogue*, Dylan Ratigan, host of an MSNBC financial program, used Photoshopped pictures to mock Palin on the network's morning program. Ratigan later apologized, but such stunts are a perfect example of the openly partisan nature of today's broadcast media.

But if that were all there was to it—that partisanship gets ratings—this media transformation would not be so important. It's not just that the media climate is so polarized; it's that this polarization is feeding political developments and becoming embedded with political activity itself.

The Internet

And then there's Newsmax, long attacked on the left for its hard-right politics—but there is no arguing with its success. A classic example of how the Internet has enabled alternative news outlets to flourish, Newsmax got its start around the time of the Clinton impeachment, grew enormously during the Florida recount controversy, and has amazingly kept growing another 40 percent in the decade since. Its unapologetic, partisan focus has not changed, proving again how polarization pays. Dick Morris calls Newsmax the "most influential Republican-leaning media outlet in the country" because—tellingly—it conveys "what Republicans in the heartland are really thinking."

The left-wing blogosphere is in many ways the mirror image of the right as well: powerful personalities, entrepreneurs, and reporters have made their impact felt not just on the nation's media landscape but on actual political developments. The leaders are the websites/blogs, Daily

Kos and the Huffington Post, the latter which gets more readers than the *Wall Street Journal*, the *Los Angeles Times*, and the *Washington Post*. The Huffington Post is also the most linked-to blog on the Internet. Daily Kos is essentially the Web headquarters for what has come to be known as the "Netroots," left-wing political activists on the Web. Markos Moulitsas, the site's founder, eventually founded the first blog-gers' convention, Yearly Kos (now called Netroots Nation), at which Democratic Party presidential candidates have often appeared. The Huffington Post is often thought of as the left's answer to the Drudge Report, though the comparison is not quite apt as the two sites are different in what they offer and how they operate. Still, Arianna Huff-ington's vision of creating a left-wing portal that would threaten the supremacy of right-wingers on the Web has proven astute and hugely successful.

Of course, American politics has seen periods of intense partisan-ship before, even in the media. For a long time after the founding of the nation and up to the mid 20th century, the nation had dozens of parti-san newspapers, not unlike what we see today in Europe. But according to media critic Gregg Easterbrook, what's new about today's situation is that communications technologies have made us more efficient at telecasting and broadcasting our own opinions. And if Diana Mutz, a professor of political science and communication at the University of Pennsylvania, is correct, this new partisan media is only delivering what we're genetically hard-wired to want anyway: conflict. She cites evolutionary-psychology research, indicating that human beings prefer conflict over agreement. Think of all the "civil," high-minded pro-grams on both radio and television that have gone by the wayside over the years, and then think of the popularity of partisan shows that wheel out impassioned talking heads, night after night, to argue the issues.

In this sense, the media market respond only to consumer demand and what drive ratings. Indeed television coverage and viewership has become increasingly niche-based. Ratings clearly show that viewership in nonpartisan news stations has dropped, as liberal viewers are increasingly drawn to edgier, more partisan MSNBC while conservatives are loyal to Fox News. Partisan news programs, both right-leaning and left-leaning, have grown since the Bush presidency. The Internet only heightens this tendency, since it increases the ability of all users to seek out only the content that accords with their views, and to ignore the rest. The Internet makes it possible to expose oneself to political information, commentary, and analysis on a highly selective basis. On the Internet, wrote Cass Sunstein, people can "wall themselves off from topics and opinions that they would prefer to avoid." The result, many believe, is an electorate less informed and more polarized, more adamant about their own beliefs while perhaps less knowledgeable about the world they live in.

Since that world is already overloaded with information, news viewers increasingly seek out content that helps them, in media critic Tom Rosenstiel's words, "make sense of the world." Hence the great appeal of new-media "anchors" like O'Reilly on the right and Olbermann on the left: they put a confusing world into order for viewers, reporting a story and then, at great length, "explaining" what it all means. The two most partisan cable networks—Fox and MSNBC—excel at this approach.

BECOME THE MEDIA:
WHAT THE FUTURE HOLDS

Sarah Palin has used social networking tools to stay in touch with supporters, to promote her book, to comment on political developments, and to build and extend her own political "brand." Her Facebook page is heavily trafficked; in summer 2009, she used Facebook to brand the Obama healthcare plan's provisions for the elderly "death panels," putting the administration on the defensive and changing the healthcare debate. Her Facebook entry in February 2010, in which she called for White House chief of staff Rahm Emanuel to resign after making an off-color comment about "retards," also made news, putting heat on

Emanuel to defuse the controversy. (Emanuel didn't resign but did issue a public apology.)

This is the final piece of the New Media puzzle, and the most dynamic and unpredictable: the social networking tools that have allowed individuals—from nationally known politicians like Palin to unknown citizens—to raise their voices, get heard, and often have an impact on the political debate. Social networking makes organizing, campaigning, and communicating an entirely new game for politicians.

Other than Palin, the politician who tapped into this new source of communication and organization most effectively so far was Barack Obama during his presidential campaign. As Netscape founder and Facebook member Marc Andreesen put it: "Other politicians I have met with are always impressed by the Web and surprised by what it could do, but their interest sort of ended in how much money you could raise. [Obama] was the first politician I dealt with who understood that the technology was a given and that it could be used in new ways."

Obama's campaign merged his experience as a community organizer with Web technology to make his campaign workers participants, even semi-autonomous partners, in the campaign. Using the social networking applications like gurus, he and his campaign created an invisible but enormous force over the Internet that didn't just raise money: it organized events locally; it fought back against attacks on the candidate; it conducted its own get-out-the-vote drives; it made homemade videos, some ingenious and memorable.

Obama and his team masterfully used the Web to create a sense of connection and engagement with their supporters. Obama's campaign ran a "meetup"-style section of his website, myBarackObama .com (which supporters called "myBo"), for volunteers to get involved— the first election in which a national campaign made such sophisticated e-tools available to mobilize and engage ordinary voters. Supporters who wanted to participate could find Obama-related events within five miles of their location, get information about the organizer, and register to participate. The campaign then sent the supporter an automatic email confirmation; often a campaign organizer got in touch personally.

Now that he's in the White House, Obama has understandably been less able to build such grass-roots support and energize the mass electorate. The business of governing is very different from the business of campaigning. But others have continued to build on social-networking tools' potential to create political change. The Left got there first, during Howard Dean's 2004 presidential campaign, where supporters used the new tools of MySpace, Meetup, and Facebook to organize campaign events, rallies, and fund-raising.

Since then, the Right has caught up.

The most visible demonstration of this is the extraordinary and explosive growth of the Tea Party movement, as documented herein. What this chapter has shown is that the Tea Party movement, both advertently and inadvertently, has been able to utilize the new media and the Web, as well as social networking sites, in a way that has produced tens of thousands of local chapters, and millions of members. Some of these have been facilitated by national organizations, but the vast majority has been spontaneous and self-generating.

In a certain sense, the traditional media and even cable is playing catch up to keep pace with the vibrancy and dynamism of the Tea Party movement. And it is literally the case now, because of the efforts and energies of many first-time participants, political independents, and frustrated political activists with no particularly strong ties to the mainstream political structure—more people have actually participated in supporting and advocating the Tea Party movement than actively worked on behalf of and supported Barack Obama during the 2008 presidential campaign.

OBAMA AND THE POPULIST SURGE

This is about what our country was founded upon. I would absolutely say that the government has to stay out of the private sector. It has no right in the private sector. The way to get out of this economic downturn is by lowering taxes so people have money to invest and spend. Obama, Pelosi, and Reid want to turn our country into a socialist country, well there's plenty of those out there. Leave our country alone. If you want everything run by your government, go to one of those countries. I think that the president is going to keep slowly moving to the left. And he's going to take an inch at a time. And four years are going to go by. And people are going to look up and say: What happened? How the *hell* did we end up here? That's the way I see it playing out.

—**Freddie Roth, private wealth manager, New Jersey**

Barack Obama is a crucial figure in this book, and not just because, as president, he stands at the epicenter of the populist divide. His political journey to the presidency and what it represented to millions of voters, and then his subsequent actions in office, illustrate the shift the country itself has taken in a few years' time: from a centrist nation hopeful for a fresh bipartisanship approach, to an intense, often angry electorate that is furious with both parties, both houses of Congress, and the administration at large. No figure has charted this downward arc more tellingly than our forty-fourth president, whose policies have enhanced the intensity of both left- and right-wing populism.

President Obama has not only deepened the partisan divide but brought the government itself into a crisis of legitimacy. If the Democrats suffer at the polls in November it will be Obama's doing. More-over, the tendency of Obama to blame George Bush and right-wing media both for the problems he faces and for public opposition to his plans has undermined public trust in his program.

As Jack Rice, an Obama voter who has been subsequently disil-lusioned by the president, explained as we waited for the arrival of the Tea Party Express RVs at the Griffith Park, Los Angeles stop of the Tea Party Express: II tour: "My thing with government is: smaller is better. I've thought that since I was in college. Because the government is very inefficient in the way that they do things because they don't have to answer to shareholders or anyone else. They don't have to toe the line. They're just very inefficient with the way that they do things. And so in that regard, them taking control of health care and health insur-ance is just going to make government bigger. I don't think that they will do a very good job. And it will just mean more taxes."

In contrast to the moderate-seeming figure of the presidential cam-paign who won 52 percent of the independent vote, Obama has em-braced and pushed the most ambitious, expensive, and far-reaching liberal big-government agenda in generations: enacting a massive eco-nomic stimulus plan, pursuing a major makeover of the healthcare system, taking over the management of automakers to protect workers (at the expense of bondholders), pursuing a major New Deal-like jobs program, intervening massively in the housing market, and even at-tempting to rein in the Federal Reserve. These are not minor, custom-ary steps of a new president taking power and subtly shifting policy in a different direction from his predecessor. They suggest a funda-mental transformation of the way Americans will understand the role of government in their lives. Obama's actions have largely been out of necessity (saving the auto industry was a bipartisan effort, for instance), but his interventions in the private economy—building on the massive bailouts and emergency TARP program instituted in the waning days of the Bush administration—represent a level of government involve-ment in the economy not seen since the 1930s.

While Obama has moved in an activist direction, at the same time, it has not been thematically consistent. Obama has veered between classic liberalism and left-wing populism on virtually a day-to-day basis. His overall agenda is overarching and people react negatively to it. But while pursuing this movement, President Obama has vacillated, and he has been criticized by some on the left who have responded to this by urging him to make a strong case for these initiatives.

Obama has made a number of mistakes. He has opted for overreaching versus a smaller government approach. He has yet to frame his policy initiatives and goals within the context of a core message. He has failed to give voters a sense of what he is trying to achieve other than programmatic initiatives. In doing so, he has led people on the right to view his presidency as overreaching, expansionist government; people in the center to see an elaboration of policy without a theme; and people on the left see him as playing footsie with the Republicans because he does not have a set of populist themes.

Political observers disagree about how and why the president has moved in this activist direction. Some believe that it was Obama's design all along; after all, his Senate voting record was among the most liberal of any legislator. In the general election, he was doing what any candidate does: trying to build bridges to moderate voters. Others argue that Obama genuinely did wish to pursue centrism, but was pulled left by the vehemence of his base and by the recalcitrance of the Republicans in making any policy compromises whatsoever. And still others wonder just how left-ward the administration's policy drift really is: they point to Obama's financial team of Clinton holdovers and the administration's deference to Wall Street concerns. Yet that very perception, while valid, has only helped spark further populist initiatives from within the administration.

It could be that Obama's personal instincts—aligned with the Democratic base—led him to believe that voters wanted the government to protect them from the big bad companies and free markets. More precise, he likely thought this was the role of the political class and he wanted to put them in charge of the nation. He never picked up on the fact that people distrust the government at least as much as they distrust big business. So, the president saw his task as making the political class and the government work better. Most Americans wanted the political class sent packing.

Whatever the reason, as a consequence of the Obama administration's decision to advocate a left-leaning populist agenda, the political right has become incensed. A January 2010 *Democracy Corps* report noted: "The upset in Massachusetts was the culmination of yearlong trends that reached their boiling point even before these voters gave Ted Kennedy's Senate seat to a Republican. Voters are increasingly consumed by unemployment and want their leaders to address that priority, yet leaders in Washington seem polarized and gridlocked, pushing a health care bill now defined by special deals rather than its benefits and the reforms that voters want. They are worried about spending and angry about the bailout of Wall Street that has no shame. . . . There is a populist and conservative revolt against Wall Street and financial elites, Congress and government, and it is centered among independents. Democrats and President Obama are seen as more interested in bailing out Wall Street than helping Main Street. Stir in demoralized Democrats and energized Republicans and you reach a boiling point."[1]

AUDACIOUS HOPE

Even by the standards of normal political disappointment, it's been an astonishing comedown. Consider how it all began, and the hopes this one-of-a-kind candidate inspired in millions of Americans.

Barack Obama's 2008 campaign was modeled after another successful presidential campaign from an earlier decade. You might think we are talking about Bill Clinton. In fact, we mean Ronald Reagan.

As Scott penned in the *Wall Street Journal* just after the 2008 elections, the Obama campaign followed the Reagan roadmap at several critical junctures on the winding road to the White House. Obama, like Reagan, offered optimism during a time of great pessimism, ran against the record of an unpopular incumbent (the 2008 campaign was as much about George W. Bush as it was about Obama or McCain), and, most important, Obama followed in Reagan's footsteps by promising tax cuts for 95 percent of Americans. More than anything else, according to Scott's polling, Obama was elected because Americans thought he, more than McCain, would lower their taxes.

Senator Barack Obama announced his candidacy for the presidency in Springfield, Illinois, on February 2007. Describing the frustration of Americans as they watched their legislative leaders fail to put together solutions to the nation's most pressing problems, he told the crowd gathered in single-digit winter temperatures: "What's stopped us from meeting these challenges is not the absence of sound policies and sensible plans. What's stopped us is the failure of leadership, the smallness of our politics—the ease with which we're distracted by the petty and trivial, our chronic avoidance of tough decisions, our preference for scoring cheap political points instead of rolling up our sleeves and building a working consensus to tackle big problems." Obama fashioned himself as a conciliator, a post-partisan, sensible centrist whose appealing manner, lack of ideological passion, and absence from the red-hot political fights of the last two decades would allow him to bridge the political divide in Washington. He spoke to Americans' disgust with politics as usual. And, being an outsider himself, new to Washington, his critique meant something.

At the time, Obama was not expected to overcome Hillary Clinton's seeming lock on the Democratic presidential nomination. In a more tranquil climate, he probably wouldn't have been able to do so. But from the beginning, he appealed to a post-partisan, centrist impulse within an electorate exhausted by the partisan bloodletting of the Bush and Clinton presidencies. Obama went on to run a state-of-the-art presidential campaign, one that relied substantially on the candidate's across-the-aisle appeal—not just to loyal Democrats and especially liberals, but to Independents and even some disaffected Republicans.

Though his voting record in the Senate was staunchly liberal, candidate Obama pledged repeatedly to work in a bipartisan fashion with Republicans and seek commonsense solutions. Throughout the campaign, he urged Americans to break out of the constricting political categories of left and right.

Obama also tried from the beginning of his campaign to appeal to a post-partisan impulse within an electorate exhausted not just by the Bush presidency, but also by the partisan bloodletting that had been so much a part of it, and which really traced back to Bill Clinton's terms in office.

In fact, one of Obama's shrewdest early statements was to make clear that he was not from the Baby Boom generation, suggesting to voters that generational obsessions had sparked much of the furious partisanship of the Clinton-Bush years. As John P. Avlon wrote in early 2008, Obama represented "a new generation of post-partisan politics. While Obama is certainly a center-left politician, he analyzes problems in a way that coolly criticizes the extremes of left and right. He reflects a more pragmatic approach to problem solving and brings an uncommon principled civility to politics. All this translates to unusual crossover appeal."[2]

During the general election campaign, Obama ran on a platform of conciliation and bringing people together, overcoming "partisan bickering," and getting beyond "old labels" like right and left, Red States and Blue States, and forging compromises based on shared values even in areas of substantial disagreement, such as abortion. Obama certainly advocated a number of liberal-sounding policy proposals during the campaign, but he also tacked to the center on things like the death penalty, merit pay for teachers, and putting more troops into Afghanistan.

His very demeanor seemed to exude moderation and centrism: rarely flustered, never angry or raising his voice, he refused to demonize his opponents on the right while arguing for policies that, even at their most liberal, sounded less like ideology and more like common sense when he described them.

And not all his centrist appeal was merely rhetorical or stylistic. In the months leading up to the 2008 election, Obama showed flexibility on his previously rigid withdrawal plan for U.S. troops in Iraq, while supporting more troops for Afghanistan; defended the death penalty and government eavesdropping on terrorism suspects; and voiced support for increasing federal funding for "faith-based" groups providing social services and instituting merit pay for teachers. On November 4, 2008, the night of Obama's historic election victory, he told the enormous crowd gathered in Chicago's Grant Park: "In this country, we rise or fall as one nation, as one people. Let's resist the temptation to fall back on the same partisanship and pettiness and immaturity that has poisoned our politics for so long. . . . As Lincoln said to a nation far more divided than ours, 'we are not enemies but friends. Though passion may have strained, it must not break our bonds of affection.'"

When appointing his Cabinet, noted Jonathan McClory of the *Guardian*, Obama "refused to play to the gallery of his core." Instead, "he built a meritocratic cabinet of intellectual heavyweights, where reason, debate and consensus will govern his administration."[3] He did not discriminate on the basis of Party, ideology, or politics; he even appointed men like the formidable economist Lawrence Summers to chair his Council of Economic Advisors and the New York Fed Chairman Timothy Geithner to lead the Treasury Department, who the *New York Times* dubbed "the Robert Rubin Memorial All-stars," despite the fact that their pro-business, anti-regulatory positions diverged significantly from his own.

At the State Department, he appointed Senator Clinton, whose views had been consistently more hawkish than his own during the campaign, and at the Pentagon he chose to keep on Robert Gates, Bush's defense secretary, who had earned widespread respect on both sides of the aisle after taking over from the radioactive Donald Rumsfeld.

When Obama took office in January 2009, many were hopeful that the long and dispiriting era of party polarization might end.

Those hopes didn't last long.

THE OBAMA ADMINISTRATION VEERS LEFT

As we have previously discussed, the hope of a truly bipartisan administration didn't last long. The historic forces at play across the nation pulled the electorate to the far right and left wings, and Obama has since been forced to oscillate between these two competing poles.

The result is that this impulse has drawn the president away from centrist policies. The administration simply cannot pursue centrism as a political course for the nation. There is no longer a base to support centrism. Former centrists have been pulled to the poles of right- or left-wing populism, constraining the way the administration can effectively govern.

As a further complicating factor, Obama was forced to continue the bailouts that were in fact started under George Bush. The pro–Wall Street element in the White House—notably Tim Geithner and Larry Summers—ensured this. The political effect has been that Obama has needed to be even more supplicant to the left on other issues to prevent a full-scale revolt among Democrats.

Not even one month into his term in office, President Obama began to see his pledges for bipartisanship collapse. He put through a staggeringly expensive economic stimulus package without a single Republican vote. True to his word, he reached out to Republicans, at least early on, but he ran into a two-sided wall: conservative opposition to compromising with his expansionist agenda, and resistance from the left wing of the Democratic Party, shut out for so long from policy power, to making any serious compromises with conservatives and moderates. As a result, the president began to realize that the bipartisan wellspring was drying up.

As longtime Washington observer Fred Barnes wrote in November 2009: "With rare exception and with no objection from the president, Democrats draft bills with no input from Republicans. In return, Republicans vote in lockstep against Democratic legislation. Every House

Republican voted against the stimulus, all but one against liberal health-care reform, and all but eight against cap-and-trade legislation that passed the House earlier this year."[4]

Obama went up to Capitol Hill early on after being sworn in, pledging to meet with Republican leaders to find common ground on the two major initiatives that would dominate his first month in office: passage of the economic stimulus and of the federal budget. One week after being sworn in, he made good on this pledge. He told Republicans that he would address their demands to incorporate some tax cuts into the stimulus bill and suggested that he was open to some limited revisions.

Republicans were initially impressed with his outreach efforts. But when the chips were down, agreement was hard to come by. Perhaps it was best symbolized by Obama's statement to the Republican leadership when the meeting reached an impasse: "I won."

It was a distinctly uncentrist thing to say, but it reflected the reality that compromise could only go so far. When the stimulus bill went to the House of Representatives, it failed to earn a single Republican vote. Three months later, on Obama's one hundredth day in office, House and Senate Democrats approved the president's $3.4 trillion federal budget.

To be fair, this is no different than the dynamic during President George W. Bush's tenure, or Bill Clinton's for that matter. In 1993, Vice President Al Gore had to cast the tiebreaking vote in the Senate for Clinton's economic plan. But because Obama moved away from his centrist campaign rhetoric, he facilitated and emboldened forces on the left (such as labor unions) who wanted to see more government involvement in the economy and in everyday life. And the sharp turn leftward has caused a rupture in our politics that's being exacerbated by economic globalization and new methods of communication, as we explored in Chapter 3. And it's begun driving away the independent voters who helped put Obama in the White House.

While most Democrats stood foursquare behind the president's staggering spending proposals, Obama's moderate supporters began to blanch.

The *National Journal*'s influential columnist, Stuart Taylor, spoke for many when he worried that Obama might be "deepening what looks more and more like a depression and may engineer so much spending, debt, and government control of the economy as to leave most Americans permanently less prosperous and less free."

Beyond the Beltway, ordinary Americans were taking notice, too, as polls reflected growing concern over the administration's new spending, Obama's takeover of the auto and banking industries, and his plan to push for sweeping healthcare reform. In several surveys, Americans still voiced an attitude closer to Ronald Reagan's ideology—that government was more often the problem, not the solution—than Obama's. They expressed support for tax cuts and controlled levels of spending. Moreover, a majority saw Washington under President Obama even *more* partisan than it had been under George W. Bush.

All the while, Democrats raced ahead with more ambitious agenda items, often controversial and driven heavily by liberal interest groups. Many were eager to see Obama advance "card-check" legislation, a bill that would allow labor unions to bypass the traditional secret ballot in workplaces and enroll workers who simply checked off a box on a card. During the stimulus negotiations, they undermined welfare reform—one of the great policy successes of the last generation—by creating a spending formula that rewarded states for having more welfare dependents. During the budget negotiations, they pulled the plug on Washington, D.C.'s school voucher program, showing clearly that any pledge of "post partisan" approaches did not extend to taking on the teachers' unions. Obama did not resist these efforts, whatever he may have thought of them privately.

REVOLT ON THE RIGHT

We are already seeing backlash against Obama's left-populist governing style at the ballots. On Scott Brown's victory in the Massachusetts Special Election for U.S. Senator in 2010, the *Economist* wrote "the result could be remembered as a message more profound than the disparate mutterings of a grumpy electorate that has lost faith in its leader—as a growl of hostility to the rising power of the state. America's most vibrant political force at the moment is the anti-tax tea-party movement. Even in leftish Massachusetts people are worried that Mr. Obama's spending splurge, notably his still-unpassed health-care bill, will send the deficit soaring."[5]

In retrospect, it seems inevitable that the policies Obama and the Democrats pursued would spark an intense reaction on the right, but few saw ahead of time what form these reactions would take. The rise of right-wing populism has been one of the most important political stories of our time. The election of Obama only fed the fire.

The key point to remember about Obama's effect on right-wing populism is this: whereas for eight years under President Bush, the right was often in the position of playing defense, under President Obama conservative populists have found a rallying point for going back on the offensive. To some extent, any Democratic president would have given an impetus to the populist right. But it's hard to imagine anyone doing more to fire up a movement than President Obama. Almost his every move has generated outrage and sparked determined opposition, both in the conservative media and in Washington.

OBAMA'S ERODING POPULARITY

Obama's move leftward has cost him dearly in political support: his poll numbers are suffering from a combination of his leftist initiatives, right-wing attacks, and continued hard times in the United States, as economic recovery has been slow to take hold. His image as a nonpartisan, conciliatory figure has eroded substantially.

In fact, as of April 2009, a Pew Research report revealed that a majority of Americans (53 percent) believed that partisanship had increased. Another Pew report concluded that the partisan gap between the Democratic and Republican parties was wider than ever. This supports the findings of a survey conducted in late March and early April 2009, in which 61 percent of respondents indicated that the country was more politically divided than in the past—an astonishing statement when you consider how polarizing the Bush years were. In fact, in 2001, Bush's first year in office, 34 percent of Americans expressed their belief that the two parties were working together; in 2009, Obama's first year, only 25 percent of Americans said the same.

By March 2010, a poll conducted by Scott Rasmussen found that only 25 percent of Americans believed that the United States is heading in the right direction, an all-time low since Obama took office.

Doug's 2009 Aspen Survey found that despite the electoral support Obama received from independents and moderates during the presidential campaign, and his promises to bring change to Washington, as of June 2009, just 20 percent of Americans said that bipartisanship in Washington had improved since he took office. Forty-one percent said that it had gotten worse; 31 percent said it was about the same.

Obama's approval rating began to slide seriously just six months into his presidency, in July 2009, triggered by a bad unemployment report. He soon saw his approval rating among likely voters fall to the low fifties in most polls, and eventually below fifty—a relatively low rating for a new president still in his first year, though no different really than Ronald Reagan's numbers during his first year in office during the last recession with high unemployment.

Some of the blame is certainly due to the messaging around the administration's proposed healthcare plan. Whether or not the plan was good for the nation aside, it was unclear to most Americans what the plan was designed to do and why.

According to a poll conducted by Rasmussen Reports from early October 2009, 61 percent of likely voters wanted Congress to act on health care right away, but only 45 percent favored the current plan. Deficit reduction and reining in spending were critically important priorities for the vast majority of the electorate. Indeed, according to a Rasmussen Reports Poll conducted at the end of October 2009, voters said that deficit reduction was far more important than healthcare reform. Yet the nation saw its president putting most of his domestic energies into healthcare reform, even as they continually told pollsters that they believed the economy was the top issue facing the country by a wide margin compared to health care: by 47 percent to 17 percent, according to one measure in November 2009.

Moreover, the president's efforts in the healthcare area have not met with approval: a Rasmussen Reports poll taken after the House of Representatives passed healthcare reform by the narrowest of margins showed that 54 percent of likely voters said they were opposed to the plan, with only 45 percent in favor. Furthermore, in the all-important category of unaffiliated voters, 58 percent opposed the bill. That's one of the reasons why so many moderate Democratic House members opposed it.

By December 2009, a Rasmussen survey revealed that a majority of Americans (51 percent) opposed the healthcare reform plan outright. Overall support had fallen to 38 percent, the lowest yet, and at a time when the House and Senate were working to finalize a bill that the president could sign. While most Americans agreed that our healthcare system needs reform, most opposed what the president and Congress wanted to do about it. Two-thirds of respondents (66 percent) believed that market competition would do more than government regulation to reduce healthcare costs.

Polls also showed that a majority of Americans disapproved of Obama's handling of the economy, Afghanistan, Iraq, unemployment, illegal immigration, and the federal budget deficit. Put simply, there wasn't a critical problem facing the country on which the president had positive ratings. Majorities felt they were worse off economically; that the stimulus had not helped them; that the healthcare initiative was wrong-headed; and that they expected politics in Washington to become even more partisan in coming years. The president has also lost his image for honesty and the confidence of Americans that he would make the right decisions for the country.

WHERE TO GO FROM HERE?

No fair-minded political observer, from either side of the political spectrum, would begrudge President Obama some sympathy for taking office at a time of rare crisis in the nation's history. He assumed the presidency with lots of public goodwill and a general acceptance among most Americans that he would need to take serious actions in a number of areas to address deep-seated problems. What few Americans expected, though, was how aggressively left-populist most of the president's solutions would be. As they've come to understand this better, they have become much more critical of the president.

The future of Obama's presidency is imperiled by the state of the nation's economy and by the policy choices he has made. His policies have furthered the partisan divide in the country and made politics in Washington even more corrosive. The left-populist tilt of the Obama administration has exacerbated the fraying of the two-party system, which was already under way before he came on the scene.

What should Obama do? Put simply, he must begin to moderate his approach—a step he began to take in his 2010 State of the Union address to Congress.

For example, a clear, bipartisan majority favored a less costly healthcare bill that incrementally increased coverage, provided insurance reform involving pre-existing conditions, and experimented with tort reform and competition across state lines. Voters wanted to see compromises on key elements of health care to reduce costs, while the Democrats' plan appeared to focus largely on expanding coverage.

This same kind of moderate approach could have worked more effectively for Obama in a number of other areas, from financial reform to auto bailouts to cap-and-trade. Voters consistently agreed that these were areas with genuine problems that needed addressing, but they just as consistently felt that Obama and the Democrats were overreaching in their proposed solutions; in effect, they were playing too devotedly to the demands of the party's base. And they have good reason to feel this way.

By focusing exclusively on his left-wing base—and thereby forcing the hands of the Republican right to become more strident and uncompromising in response—Obama could create lasting political problems that plague the remainder of his term. Unless he changes his approach and starts governing in a more fiscally conservative, bipartisan manner, the Independents that provided his margin of victory in 2008 and gave the Democrats control of Congress will likely swing back to the Republicans, putting Democratic control of Congress in real jeopardy.

Right now, neither party is winning as a result of this. In fact, the Republican Party has consistently had a higher negative rating than the Democratic Party. In the *New York Times*/CBS News poll, in February 2010, the Democratic Party's unfavorability reached its peak since the Republican Revolution of 1994 and 51 percent said they viewed the Democratic Party unfavorably. Yet, the Republican Party's unfavorability was even higher at 57 percent.

And, more important, for the nation's well being, our politics will only continue their descent into super-charged partisanship, populist extremism of left and right, and ideological paralysis.

REGAINING THE CONSENT OF THE GOVERNED

In January 2010, during his first State of the Union Address, President Barack Obama acknowledged that the nation faces two massive deficits that need to be addressed. One is an unprecedented and structural federal budget deficit. The other is what the president described as a deficit of trust.

In fact, the president's speech that night highlighted just how big that deficit of trust has become:

- The president asserted that two million jobs had been created by the stimulus program he pushed through the year before. Only 35 percent of voters nationwide believed him.

- Obama stated that he had cut taxes for 95 percent of Americans, yet just 6 percent believed that their taxes would go down during the Obama years while nearly half believed they would face a tax hike.

This deficit of trust, combined with and a result of the historic forces we have catalogued in this book, is what makes the nation mad as hell. Unfortunately, while President Obama has acknowledged the problem, he has failed, according to the electorate, to offer any serious means of addressing it. In that, he shares common ground with his pre-decessor, George W. Bush, to name but one of several other presidents who faced similar predicaments going back several decades.

Analysts on the left and on the right can debate, ad nauseum, the merits of what President Bush and President Obama have tried to do in terms of bailouts, economic policy, and foreign policy. But what is in-disputable is that both have systematically caused trust and confidence in the American political system and institutions to decline, and decline substantially.

The truth is that this deficit of trust is much bigger than anybody in Washington wants to admit. It will not simply go away after an elec-tion or two, or disappear when the economy gets better. The American people recognize that something is fundamentally broken and needs to be fixed. That's why they voted against the party in power in 2006 and 2008. And even when the party in power changed, the voters continued to vote against the party in power in 2009 and 2010. This trend is likely to continue for the foreseeable future, because neither party seems ready, able, or willing to address the root dynamics that have and will increasingly incense American voters.

At a time when only 21 percent of voters believe that the govern-ment has the consent of the governed, nothing can be more important than for the government to regain its legitimate authority.

Enter the new populists—the disillusioned Obama voters. The frustrated Independents. And a loose collection of organizations and interests comprised of on the right, spanning from Dick Armey's FreedomWorks, with its conventional organizational structure and communication vehicles, to the hundreds, possibly thousands, of inde-pendent groups across the country made up of ordinary citizens, a large percentage of whom have never been in politics before, many of whom had vowed that they would never be in politics.

In this environment of instability, the broad-based Tea Party move-ment is graphic and demonstrative evidence of the pervasive instability of which we have spoken.

Put another way, the fact that millions of people now support a movement that did not exist at the start of the Obama administration is fundamentally earth-shattering in importance, with clear implications for the upcoming congressional elections as well as the presidential election in 2012. Astonishingly, what we've observed is that the Tea Party movement in its various forms is at least as popular as the Republican Party, if not more so, and commands support of up to 25 percent of the electorate.

The pundits, the prognosticators, the politicians in Washington, and certainly the political class have all tried to denigrate, minimize, and marginalize the importance of the Tea Party movement. But the victory of Scott Brown, the near miss in the New York 23rd Congressional District special election of Conservative Party candidate Doug Hoffman, the success of protests in cities across the nation in April and August of 2009, and the huge turnout at the capital on September 12 in response to Glenn Beck's rallying cry, as well as the noisy and vociferous protest outside of Congress during the passage of the healthcare bill demonstrate quite clearly the potency, size, and influence of the Tea Party movement. Electoral success aside, one must acknowledge the continued existence and growing momentum of the movement as a marker of accomplishment in and of itself.

The new populist movement, the implications of which have neither been fully realized nor appreciated, demands our attention regardless of where we as individuals fall along the political spectrum. This new wave of anti-establishment sentiment continues to rise—it has not yet crested in the turbulent sea of social and economic upheaval. It is tempting when writing a book like this to describe social phenomena as "unprecedented." But in this instance, to look at a now burgeoning movement that was at best nascent a year ago, we feel that characterization is fair, justified, and clear.

That such a movement has been able to attract such a large following in such a short period underscores the depth and dimensions of uncertainty and unpredictability in the American political system. If on election day in 2008 or even on inauguration day in 2009, we had said that there would be a force of millions of people equaling approximately a quarter of the electorate, a dedicated group of individuals willing to take up arms politically to speak out against the establishment, most people would have dismissed the notion entirely if they gave it any consideration at all.

It is important to note that the sentiments underlying this movement are not new. Indeed, new populism is merely the latest proxy for the anti-Washington, anti-systemic sentiment that we have seen running through American politics for generations. With this is mind, and in many respects, Barack Obama owes his election in 2008 to his ability to speak to these notions and capture key votes among center-right independents. Indeed, some of the most startling data in this book show that he captures 20 to 25 percent of the vote of Tea Party supporters, and a full third of his 2008 voters are favorable to the Tea Party movement.

Obama's honeymoon with the populists, however, was short-lived. The disaffected populists have drifted away from Obama and his party and are now more vocal than ever about their desire for widespread change in government—change that Democrats and the president have failed, in the view of most independents, to deliver.

Indeed, to the extent that the electorate is realigning itself politically, it is precisely against the two major parties. While the new populists malign Democrats for what they perceive as extravagant spending and government intervention, they have laid equally heavy criticism on Republicans for being ideologically weak and not fighting back aggressively enough. Independents have gotten stronger, more numerous, and more conservative.

Though one might be inclined to point to polling data showing increased support for conservative candidates and Scott Brown's upset victory in the Massachusetts Senate special election as evidence of a Republican realignment, the truth is that neither party has been winning anybody over recently.

To be sure, the new populists of the Tea Party movement are certainly much closer ideologically to the Republicans, but it would be a profound mistake to say that they are an adjunct of the GOP. Indeed, as Joe Trippi, Howard Dean's 2004 campaign manager said: "The mistake people are making is reading into this Tea Party as some kind of pro Republican thing," when the truth is that "it's anti-establishment and anti-elite."

Indeed, as protest organizer Eric Odom, cofounder of the conservative activist group DontGo, has noted, their aim is "not to promote Republicans at all." In fact, Odom turned down an invitation from Republican National Committee Chairman Michael Steele to speak at their Chicago event in April 2009. Odom has also commented that his organization's goal is to affect "the birth of a completely new base" of supporters.

We're already seeing the effects the Tea Party protests are having on the American political landscape. President Obama has employed rhetoric Democrats hope the supporters of the movement will respond to, epitomized in his recent State of the Union address by calls for a spending freeze, new limits on the size of large banks, and restrictions on banks' ability to make high-risk investments. The movement has also played a significant role in moving the Republican Party to the right. Many GOP politicians and candidates have tried to deal with Tea Party supporters by appealing to their commitment to ideological purity on a variety of social and fiscal issues. But the movement has accomplished much more than this.

While it's true that the Tea Party movement has caused the Democrats to reevaluate their stances on several key issues and has made impressive inroads into the Republican Party, it would be a mistake not to recognize it as the kind of force that could fundamentally alter American politics in its own right. The meeting of a charismatic leader with the Tea Party movement could prove to be a very powerful force in the Republican primaries or in an Independent candidacy movement in 2012.

Indeed, the ideas that the Tea Party stands for are close to the national consensus.

In light of these developments, we don't believe we're at all being hyperbolic in our observation that Americans' collective dissatisfaction with their government and mainstream political parties has reached its highest level ever. And while people have distanced themselves from the Congressional Democrats and President Obama, there has not been an accompanying movement toward the Republican Party.

Specifically, when the issue has turned to the question of support for the Tea Parties, some polling done by Rasmussen and other organizations has shown the Tea Parties in second place ahead of the Republicans, while other polls have shown them in a close third.

But it is clear that the Tea Parties, appealing primarily but not exclusively to Republican and Independent voters, have broad national support.

And the issues that the Tea Party stands for are arguably even more popular than the movement itself. According to a February 2010 Washington Post/ABC News poll, 45 percent of Americans agree with the Tea Party movement positions on the issues, and somewhere around a quarter of the electorate now call themselves active Tea Party supporters.

Take healthcare reform. From the beginning, for better or for worse, the Tea Party movement has been the lifeblood and the poster child of the anti-healthcare reform movement. But while media coverage has used talk of "death panels" and random isolated acts of racism and bigotry to delegitimize the Tea Party movement, it does not take away from the fact that the majority of Americans harbor similar views.

The movement's credibility stems from the fact that substantial numbers of Americans believe that the bill represents big government, more expensive health care, and a possible diminution of the quality of their own care.

As a CNN/Opinion Research Corporation Poll completed right before the healthcare vote, only 39 percent of respondents said that they favored the healthcare legislation while 59 percent opposed it, tracking with other polls that have consistently showed a solid majority against the healthcare bill, and only around 40 percent supporting it. The passage of the bill, albeit impressive, does obscure the basic fact that this bill is not popular with the American people, for reasons that the Democrats, by in large, failed to acknowledge and address.

Tea Party activists are well aware of this, and will use it to their advantage come November.

"We want to make this election a referendum on the bill," said Brendan Steinhauser, director of federal and state campaigns for Freedom-Works, the conservative organization that's closely aligned with Tea Party groups across the country.[1]

And as Fox News reported on March 22nd, 2010—despite lofty predictions that a broad-based Democratic constituency would be activated by the passage of the bill, the only group that was energized was the Tea Party:

"I am deluged with phone calls this morning (from) people wanting to join the Tea Party," said Gina Loudon, a founder of the St. Louis Tea Party, which campaigned against the bill during Obama's stop there two weeks ago. "I literally cannot even return the phone calls quickly enough. . . . This has absolutely awoken a giant."

Loudon said she and other activists, who met up at a pub in downtown St. Louis Sunday night to mourn the passage of the bill, are already drafting a game plan for the months ahead. This is simply extraordinary. It means that they have the capacity and the ability to influence every election in every jurisdiction in America, depending on the circumstances.

And voters are extremely receptive to an anti-systemic, anti-Washington, Independent political movement. Fifty-five percent of respondents in a February 2010 Rasmussen/Schoen Poll said that an independent movement like the Tea Party movement is positive for America.

Tea Party support transcends traditional demographic, ideological,

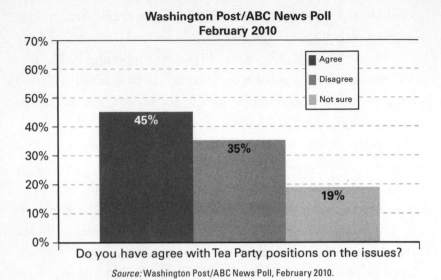

**Washington Post/ABC News Poll
February 2010**

Do you have agree with Tea Party positions on the issues?

Source: Washington Post/ABC News Poll, February 2010.

and partisan divisions. While 77 percent of Republicans and 67 percent of Independents say that an independent movement like the Tea Party is positive, so too do 30 percent of Democrats, and 31 percent of Obama voters.

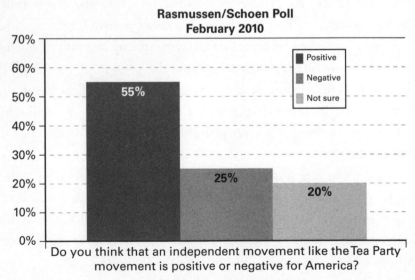

**Rasmussen/Schoen Poll
February 2010**

Do you think that an independent movement like the Tea Party movement is positive or negative for America?

Source: Rasmussen/Schoen Poll, February 2010.

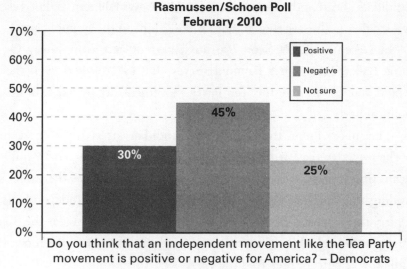

**Rasmussen/Schoen Poll
February 2010**

Do you think that an independent movement like the Tea Party movement is positive or negative for America? – Democrats

Source: Rasmussen/Schoen Poll, February 2010.

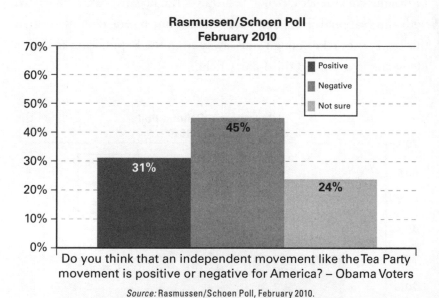

**Rasmussen/Schoen Poll
February 2010**

Do you think that an independent movement like the Tea Party movement is positive or negative for America? – Obama Voters

Source: Rasmussen/Schoen Poll, February 2010.

Specifically, when the issue has turned to the question of support for the Tea Party movement as a third party, some polling done by Scott Rasmussen and other polling organizations has shown a Tea Party candidate ahead of the Republicans in a three-way Generic Ballot Test, while other polls have shown them a close third to the Republicans.

In December 2009, Scott Rasmussen conducted a three-way Generic Ballot Test with a national survey that asked voters who they would vote for in case the Tea Party movement organized as a new political party.

The survey found the Democratic candidate attracting 36 percent of the vote, the Tea Party candidate picking up 23 percent, and Republicans finishing third at 18 percent. Even more telling was the survey's finding that the Tea Party is the frontrunner among Independents. Thirty-three percent of unaffiliated voters said that they favor the Tea Party candidate, while 25 percent said they would vote for a Democrat, and only 12 percent preferred the GOP.

By February 2010, the GOP overtook the Tea Party for second place in Rasmussen's Generic Ballot Test due to the negative press associated with the National Tea Party Convention, but recent polls show that the Tea Parties take enough votes away from the Republicans to elect a Democrat in a divided third-party field.

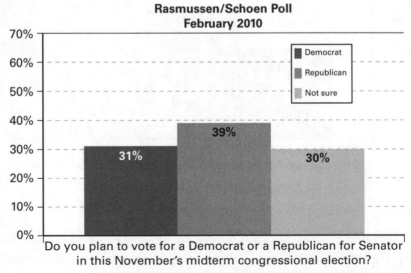

**Rasmussen/Schoen Poll
February 2010**

Do you plan to vote for a Democrat or a Republican for Senator in this November's midterm congressional election?

Source: Rasmussen/Schoen Poll, February 2010.

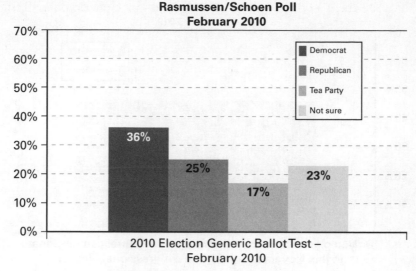

**Rasmussen/Schoen Poll
February 2010**

Democrat
Republican
Tea Party
Not sure

36%

25%

17%

23%

2010 Election Generic Ballot Test –
February 2010

Source: Rasmussen/Schoen Poll, February 2010.

If the Tea Party were to run a third-party candidate in the November 2010 Congressional election, it could pose a significant threat for the Republicans.

When respondents were given a choice between a Democrat or Republican candidate for U.S. Senator in our February 2010 poll, the Republican candidate leads 39 percent to 31 percent. Yet, when the option of a Tea Party candidate was thrown into the mix, we found that the Tea Party candidate would take away enough votes from the Republicans to elect a Democrat in a divided three-party field.

The Generic Ballot Test in a February 2010 CNN survey shows that in a two-way horserace the Democratic and Republican Parties are tied with 46 percent.

In a three-way horserace with a Tea Party endorsed candidate, however, the Republican Party's candidate trails the Democratic candidate 46 percent to 32 percent, with 16 percent voting for the Tea Party candidate.

Similarly, a March 24, 2010, Quinnipiac University National Poll found that the "Tea Party Could Hurt the GOP In Congressional

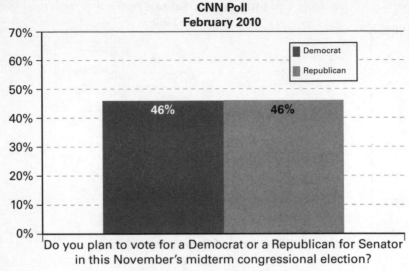

CNN Poll
February 2010

Do you plan to vote for a Democrat or a Republican for Senator
in this November's midterm congressional election?

Source: CNN Poll, February 2010.

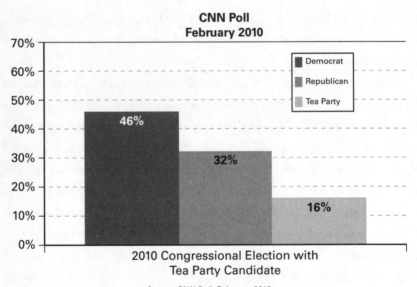

CNN Poll
February 2010

2010 Congressional Election with
Tea Party Candidate

Source: CNN Poll, February 2010.

Races; Dems Trail 2-Way Races, But Win If Tea Party Runs." "While
voters say 44 to 39 percent that they will vote for a Republican over a
Democratic candidate in this November's Congressional elections, if

there is a Tea Party candidate on the ballot, the Democrat would get 36 percent to the Republican's 25 percent, with 15 percent for the Tea Party candidate."

Thus, a Tea Party candidate running as an Independent could spell doom for Republicans in November. "The Tea Party movement is mostly made up of people who consider themselves Republicans. . . . They are less educated but more interested in politics than the average Joe and Jane Six-Pack and are not in a traditional sense swing voters. . . . The Tea Party could be a Republican dream—or a GOP nightmare. Members could be a boon to the GOP if they are energized to support Republican candidates. But if the Tea Party were to run its own candidates for office, any votes its candidate received would to a very great extent be coming from the GOP column," said Peter A. Brown, assistant director of the Quinnipiac University Polling Institute.

Brown has it exactly right. And, as of this writing, it seems more likely that the Tea Party will be a shot in the arm for the Republicans, rather than the divisive force some people fear.

And if it can maintain or perhaps even build upon the momentum it has established thus far, we expect the Tea Party movement to influence the 2012 presidential election both in terms of how Republican candidates fare in the primaries and caucuses and in the potential for an independent candidacy.

There is little, if any energy left in the Republican Party. In his Sunday column in late February 2010, *New York Times* columnist Frank Rich reiterated this point, writing: "The distinction between the Tea Party movement and the official G.O.P. is real, and we ignore it at our peril. While Washington is fixated on the natterings of Mitch McConnell, John Boehner, Michael Steele and the presumed 2012 Republican presidential front-runner, Mitt Romney, these and the other leaders of the Party of No are anathema or irrelevant to most Tea Partiers. Indeed, McConnell, Romney and company may prove largely irrelevant to the overall political dynamic taking hold in America right now. The old G.O.P. guard has no discernible national constituency beyond the

scattered, often impotent remnants of aging country club Republicanism. The passion on the right has migrated almost entirely to the Tea
Party's counterconservatism."[2]

In a March 7, 2010, piece titled "Tea party candidates falling short,"
Politico's Alex Isenstadt asked: "Can an organic and fledgling movement that lacks the institutional grounding and top-down organizational strength of either major political party transfer protest-oriented
grass-roots energy into tangible success at the polls?"[3]

The answer, he concludes is no, citing the case of Texas gubernatorial candidate Debra Medina, who only received 19 percent of the
vote in the Republican primary, despite going through great lengths to
brand herself as the Tea Party candidate.

Isenstadt fundamentally misread what happened in Texas, which we
believe ratifies our argument that the Tea Party movement is the most
potent force driving ideology, and pushing candidates in their direction.

What Isenstadt failed to address was that Texas Governor Rick
Perry was effectively already the Tea Party candidate, in fact all three
Republican primary candidates pledged to have Tea Party ties.

Governor Perry aligned himself with the Tea Party movement from
the beginning. While Medina resorted to legitimizing her candidacy
with the Tea Party name, Perry pointed to his track record of standing for Tea Party values. He has been anti-Washington long before
the birth of the Tea Party movement, or even the election of President
Obama. As governor, he promoted small government, fiscal conservatism, and individual liberty—even alluding to secession while addressing the crowd at an April 15, 2009, National Tax Day Tea Party.

It worked.

That Medina was able to garner 19 percent of the vote suggests how
powerful the Tea Party brand alone is, particularly in the aftermath of
an appearance on Fox News, where she went as far as to suggest there
may be some legitimacy to the 9/11 "truther." This is an outrageous and
irresponsible position, scorned by every single Fox News commentator,
which did irrevocable damage to Medina's campaign. Yet, the power of

the Tea Party label was such that she still managed to get 19 percent in an underfunded, largely discredited campaign—only because of her message.

Indeed, virtually every Republican candidate running for office this year has tried to proclaim in some way Tea Party credentials—tenuous or not, real or imagined. Put another way, being the Tea Party candidate has proven to be the clear, unambiguous source of validity for Republicans. And while individual Tea Party candidates may have been underfunded or unsuccessful in primary elections, it is the case that the Party itself has adopted the worldview of the Tea Party movement, both because it lacks a philosophy of its own and because the Tea Party movement represents the only activist, new ideas in the Party.

We've already seen in our polling data that Sarah Palin, Scott Brown, or Mike Huckabee is considered as a third-party candidate for president; they each garner in excess of 20 percent of the vote in a race with Mitt Romney and Barack Obama. We don't believe these findings reflect pure interest in these individual candidates. Rather, they demonstrate an expression of anger and outrage with the system, and reveal a desire at a time of record deficits and spending to cut back the size of government, the role of government, and the expenditures of government.

The primary results, as of late June 2010, certainly ratify our conclusion that the Tea Party movement is among the most potent forces in American politics—arguably as potent as the two major parties. And indeed, given the negative rating that the two parties garner, it is certainly the case that in terms of electoral potency, the Tea Party movement has proven itself in a way that the major parties themselves have not been able to demonstrate recently.

With the anti-Washington, anti-incumbent sentiment as apparent as it is, there is an argument—and it is a compelling one—that the Tea Party endorsement, particularly in the Republican primaries, is the most coveted support a candidate can achieve—even more so than mainstream endorsements.

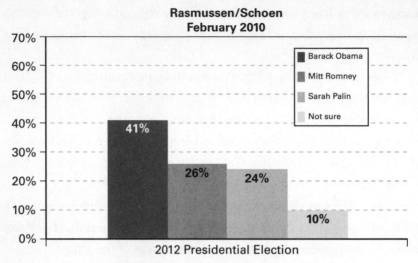

Source: Rasmussen/Schoen Poll, February 2010.

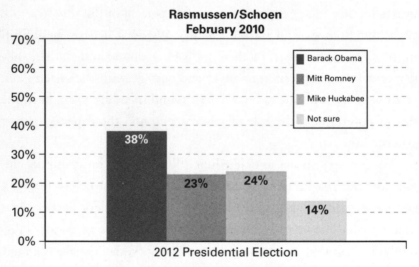

Source: Rasmussen/Schoen Poll, February 2010.

The fact that Republican Senator Robert Bennett in Utah was dispatched from his seat after three terms—not even making the primary ballot—is one indication of the power of the Tea Parties.

Moreover, Rand Paul's near-twenty-point victory in the Kentucky Primary, and the high level of interest in that contest, demonstrates the potency of the Tea Party appeal. Paul, after all, cruised to victory running against Trey Grayson, Kentucky's Secretary of State, who had the support of the GOP establishment and endorsements from the likes of Senate Minority Leader Mitch McConnell and former Vice President Dick Cheney.

In fact, Paul was able to hold on to a lead in the polls over Democratic nominee Jack Conway even after the very controversial and provocative comments he made about the 1964 Civil Rights Act came to dominate the media shortly after the Primary.

In Nevada, the Tea Party Express endorsement of Sharron Angle proved to be decisive in her overwhelming victory over two seemingly stronger and better-funded challengers—Danny Tarkanian, the son of Jerry Tarkanian, a former UNLV basketball coach, and a UNLV basketball star in his own right—and Sue Lowden, the former chairwoman of the Nevada Republican Party, who served one-term in the Nevada State Senate in the mid-1990s. And while Angle has taken positions arguably even more extreme than Paul, as of this writing she is currently running neck-in-neck in the polls with Senate Majority Leader, Harry Reid (D-NV).

And in South Carolina, notwithstanding allegations of infidelity, a vicious smear campaign about both her religious beliefs and Indian heritage, as well as the all out opposition of the GOP establishment, Nikki Haley won a landslide victory in the GOP's run-off election for Governor on June 22nd.

Haley, a self-described Tea Party candidate with little, if any, mainstream support, ultimately got close to two-thirds of the vote, and dominated both the initial primary and the run-off.

Moreover, a black conservative, Tim Scott, defeated the son of Strom Thurmond by thirty-six points in the "FT. Sumter" First congressional district, whose population is three-quarters white. Scott is virtually certain to be elected to Congress in November

These developments have not gone unnoticed in South Carolina and elsewhere.

"So much for the Tea Parties being a bunch of bigoted racists as portrayed by the mainstream media," observed Fox News contributor and former pollster to Jimmy Carter, Pat Caddell, who also lives in the state.

Moreover, the most important story from the June 8 primary elections—one that has gone largely unrecognized—is that for the first time in recent memory, inexperience has become a virtual badge of honor, as opposed to an impediment for winning both local and, indeed, even high national office.

Put simply, political experience of any type is now a negative, not a positive—that's how angry the electorate is today. Voters are less and less inclined than ever before to support incumbent members of the Senate and the House for reelection. And the unprecedented 2,300 new candidates running for Congress in 2010 are a clear indication that when voters are given the choice between an incumbent and someone new—whether well funded or not—they are leaning heavily in favor of the latter.

To be sure, the anti-incumbent tide only continued to swell in the weeks following the June 8th primary elections. For example, Rep. Bob Ingliss (R-SC), who supported the original TARP legislation, lost his bid for renomination in South Carolina's Fourth congressional district to Tea Party candidate Trey Gowdy by an astounding 70 percent–30 percent.

In the June Washington Post/ABC News Survey, only 29 percent of Americans said that they are inclined to support their House representative in November, even lower than in 1994, when voters swept the Democrats out of power in the that chamber after forty years in the majority.[4] Even more striking were the findings of a recent early June Gallup poll, where by a margin of nearly two to one, voters said they would rather vote for a candidate for Congress with no experience whatsoever than for a candidate who has been in Congress (60 percent to 32 percent).[5]

And come November, these candidates with little or no experience in either government or politics, who in past years would not be given much realistic chance of success, have the potential to fundamentally alter the political landscape inside-the-beltway and around the country.

To be sure, if elected, this band of outsiders has made it clear, both individually and collectively, that they have absolutely no intention of kowtowing to Party leaders, and indeed if anything, will resist the blandishments of the political establishment.

As *Politico's* Jonathan Martin noted in a June 23, 2010 piece:

> "They [the Tea Party candidates] owe little to the establishment—party leaders largely opposed their candidacies—and much to the fear-for-my-country movement from which they emerge. Many of them haven't followed the timeworn paths to elected office.
>
> Perhaps most important, they aren't expecting to come to the capital to go along so they can get along. They are non-conformists who tend to chafe at authority, with both Rand Paul in Kentucky and Sharron Angle in Nevada making names for themselves by bucking the established order."[6]

To be sure, not all of these candidates have broad popular appeal. Indeed, their greatest strength may be that they are running against a set of political arrangements that they and much of the electorate regard as illegitimate.

That is why a large percentage of Tea Party candidates—even if they are little known or under-financed, and take what some people perceive to be extreme positions—have the potential to fundamentally change American politics by scoring a series of upset wins.

Indeed, given the general climate of disaffection and mistrust with Democrats and Republicans alike—it's clear that the Republican Party's greatest asset overall right now is that elections are binary choices, and that disaffected voters tend to turn against incumbents. At this point, Democratic support has been so depleted that the only option the voters have is to support a largely, but not entirely discredited, GOP, which is running candidates, many of whom are less than ideal, but have the virtue of having no ties to the current political establishment.

Put simply, the Republicans are winning support because they are not Democrats. Nearly two-thirds (64 percent) of those who favored Republican control of Congress in the May Wall Street Journal/NBC News poll said they were motivated by opposition to Mr. Obama and Democratic policies, while less than one-third (31 percent) of those who favored Republican control said that was because they support the GOP and its candidates.[7]

Indeed, voters are no more confident with the Republican leadership's agenda than with the Democrats, and disapproval and disaffection with the GOP is just as high, if not higher. Consider the results of the June 8 Washington Post/ABC News poll, in which six-in-ten poll respondents said they have a negative view of the policies put forward by the Republican minority in Congress, and only one-third said they trust Republicans over Democrats to handle the nation's main problems.[8]

Given these problems, it should not be a surprise that candidates with no ties to either major party could well have more credibility in the fall than those with a more conventional skill set, as well as background and experience.

Looking ahead to the 2012 Presidential election, Mike Huckabee and Sarah Palin are effectively even with Mitt Romney, potentially electing Obama with close to or under 40 percent of the vote.

The bottom-line conclusion is clear. Despite efforts by many in the media and political class to downplay the notability of the Tea Party movement, they could and will demonstratively influence the 2010 congressional elections, which we expect will provide a substantial victory for the Republican Party.

Many misread the election results in 2008 as an expression of the American electorate for a desire to shift toward greater government involvement in the economy, as in the days of Roosevelt's New Deal.

In fact, we can see plainly now that precisely the opposite is true: more and more individuals are supporting anti-Washington, anti-Big Government policies, and indeed they were supporting these very same anti-big government and anti-Washington policies during the 2008 election, as Scott Rasmussen persuasively argued in his own piece for the *Wall Street Journal* immediately following the 2008 election about how Obama won the White House by campaigning like Ronald Reagan when he won the presidency in 1980. And there is certainly much more validity in this analysis than the one that sees Obama's victory as some sort of left-wing mandate. It wasn't.

In the eyes of the new populists, what happened was that Barack Obama went to the White House and became part of the establishment. Now, in 2010, the Tea Party movement has taken up the mantle of change.

One of the things the Tea Party supporters have said is that their movement is as strong as the movement to elect Obama was in 2008. And while this may be a bit of an overstatement, it's not an overstatement by much.

The key difference is that the Obama campaign was highly disciplined with a sophisticated communications strategy. They propagated their message via emails, text messages, signs, podcasts, and television spots. On the other hand, it is still to be seen whether the Tea Party supporters will be able to organize themselves in any tactically meaningful way from the perspective of a national election. State and local elections are one thing. A national campaign is another animal altogether.

What is now missing from Obama's governing initiative is a theme, a strategy and an approach—leading different people to draw different conclusions about who Obama is and what he is doing—virtually all negative. To the extreme left, Obama is not a true populist. To the center, he is seen as just offering a litany of policies. And to the right, his presidency is perceived to be a systematic, overarching attempt to expand the role of government, requiring significant resistance.

What the Tea Party movement undeniably has is a vast number

of supporters responding to an infectious message. We well remember some of the town halls of August 2009—when tens of thousands of people came out spontaneously to events around the country. We remember speaking to one activist—who agreed to talk to us on the grounds of confidentiality—who said: "We were trying to stimulate this to be sure. But where we expected 50 people, 500 would come. This went way beyond our organizational efforts and is truly a spontaneous movement. We'd like to take credit . . . but frankly, we couldn't and wouldn't because the numbers vastly exceeded any rational expectation."

Despite the Obama administration's attempts to placate the new populists, most still view the president through skeptical, untrusting eyes, as we noted above. Their reaction to the perceived growth of government and the expansiveness of President Obama's approach has provided additional fuel for the Tea Party movement.

But the truth, whether the political elites like it or not, is that the Tea Party movement represents a broad swath of the American electorate, and neither they nor the populist forces that have fueled their movement are going anywhere anytime soon.

There has been a reaction on the left as well, which has been less significant but nonetheless important to document. There have been a series of challenges to incumbent senators on the left, most notably challengers to Michael Bennett in Colorado and Arlen Specter in Pennsylvania, prospective challenges to Kirsten Gillibrand in New York, and, most recent, to Blanche Lincoln in Arkansas, from candidates who are mostly left, running on avowedly anti-Washington-change themes, reflecting the core of the left-wing populist argument.

Take for example remarks made by New York labor activist Jonathan Tasini, who plans to challenge New York's appointed Senator Kirsten Gillibrand in the New York Democratic Primary. There is a significant anti-systemic, anti-Washington undercurrent to his candidacy, and like his Tea Party counterparts, Tasini is framing himself as an outside reformer.

In an interview with *New York Magazine*, he explained: "In some ways, Kirsten Gillibrand is not the point. It really is a question of the insiders versus the outsiders. . . . I got into the race because of the moment in time, because of the crisis in the country, and the firm belief I had that people are fed up with, frankly, both parties, and the dysfunction in politics."[9]

Underfinanced and under-promoted, Tasini is not a serious threat, but his message is symptomatic of what the Tea Party movement and left-wing populists stand for.

This underscores one of our central conclusions, which is that there is strong anti-Washington, anti-incumbent on both sides of the aisle, although it is much stronger and more powerful on the center right.

A question thus arises: How does the Tea Party movement transition from popular faction to political powerhouse? In other words, what must the Tea Partiers do in order to convert themselves into a political force whose candidates could potentially challenge Republicans and Democrats in local, state, and national elections?

The first thing Tea Party supporters must do is address the fringe element within their movement. It is true that the vast majority of Tea Partiers are hardworking, decent, middle-class people who are fiscally conservative, worried about their position in the world, and looking for alternatives. However, there are people taking part in the movement who are outside the mainstream, people who have placed themselves at the periphery with ideas that may very well be outlandish, extreme, and sometimes even abhorrent. Indeed, several white supremacist and neo-Nazi groups, including the Council of Conservative Citizens and StormFront, have attempted to turn the Tea Party rallies into recruiting grounds for new members.

The leaders of the movement must find a way to silence this small but highly visible minority. If the Tea Partiers continue to tolerate the racist and anti-Semitic voices among their supporters, if they continue to permit those attending their rallies to wave signs emblazoned with references to white slavery and Nazi gas chambers, their movement will never garner the credibility it needs to realize its full political potential.

Additionally, as we mentioned above, the jury is still out as to whether the Tea Partiers will be able to integrate the disparate pieces of their movement to form a cohesive coalition. This piece is especially crucial. The Tea Party supporters must find a way to harness the collective energy of the various protest groups across the nation in order to make the changes they demand. They must establish a clear, well-articulated, and feasible set of goals that everyone in the movement can rally around. Only once they are well organized and they have developed a coherent agenda will they be able to become something more advanced than disjointed groups of angered citizens trying to have their voices heard.

Finally, the Tea Party movement must find a way to engage charismatic leaders with widespread appeal. It is essential for supporters to woo charismatic politicians in whom they have established trust. This task should not be too difficult, for as we've discussed, our numbers show that the Tea Party movement has more support than either of the major political parties. It would certainly require a leap of faith for a candidate to leave his or her party and jump ship to guide this fledgling movement. However, with support for the Tea Partiers growing on a daily basis, this scenario is becoming increasingly plausible.

Thanks to its millions of fervent supporters, the Tea Party movement has now moved beyond the control of either major party. Its leaders essentially control its fate. Will it develop into a potent political force or, hampered by its inability to organize and recruit effective leaders, or rid itself of its prejudiced elements, simply fall by the wayside?

It is true that several instances in the history of our nation where grass-roots populist movements developed in opposition to the actions of the government. But to be in a situation where elections in even the bluest of blue states can be swung in the matter of a week based on the demonstrations of local activists shows the extent to which the nation has fundamentally changed.

More general, what this shows is that American politics is in a state of uncertainty. As of this writing, the Tea Party movement is probably the strongest independent force in American politics, and is increasingly been recognized as such by a media that was, at the very least, late to the party.

That being said, the most notable thing about American politics is its unpredictability. We simply do not know what is going to happen next week, much less next year. We live in a time of uncertainty and instability and it is impossible to make firm judgments about the future. But what the Tea Party movement does suggest, and suggest compellingly, is the possibility for anti-systemic third parties to emerge.

Both of us, in different ways, have written about the possibility of third-party candidates emerging at different points in the recent past. And we both believe, coming from somewhat different perspectives, that this possibility exists in the future—be it from the Tea Party movement or some other force.

The Tea Party movement does underscore the degree to which anti-systemic, anti-Washington, pro-Constitution, fiscally conservative voters now are mobilized, organized, and able to make their voice heard in ways that are unprecedented and of potentially fundamental importance to the American political system.

To underestimate the importance of a movement that has fundamentally altered American politics and will almost certainly affect both the 2010 congressional elections and the 2012 presidential election would be the most profound mistake of all.

That said, it is not too late for the Democratic or Republican parties to recapture the trust of the nation, and in so doing obviate the need for the Tea Party movement and recapture the millions of disaffected voters, particularly on the right, who are currently in the Tea Party column.

The problem for Democratic and Republican politicians is that solving their current predicament and repairing the breach of trust will require doing something that they hate above all else: letting the American people back in the process. To that end, there is a simple, bold, three-step proposal that any president or presidential candidate could promise to enact. But doing so would make that candidate a pariah among career politicians.

The first step would be to level with the American people about the nature of the structural problems in Washington. At a most basic level this means letting people know that the vast majority of federal spending is consumed in just four areas: Social Security, Medicare, National Defense, and interest on the federal debt. Long-term trends are at work so that nothing done on a short-term basis will solve the problem. Moreover, the American people need to hear from the politicians what they already know. Washington is broken, and both parties are equally to blame.

The next step is to acknowledge that voters don't trust the nation's politicians to deal with these issues. By a two-to-one margin, voters believe that no matter how bad things are, Congress could always make it worse. The only way to address that problem is to give the voters final say over any fundamental proposal. A presidential candidate could pledge never to raise taxes without the specific approval of the American people. A similar pledge could be made on Social Security and Medicare: that no changes would be made without the voters giving their approval. Letting the people decide would break the back of a broken legislative system that protects politicians and prevents the voice of the people from being heard.

The final step would be to present a plan for addressing the long-term problems—both legislative and fiscal—and let the American people vote on it. If the voters approve the plan, that's great. If not, the politicians would do what schoolchildren do when their assignments don't measure up: try again. The legislators would have to go back to the drawing board and come up with another plan to present two years later.

This three-step approach recognizes two truths about American politics today. The first is that the American people need to be treated with respect and can be counted on to make the hard choices politicians are unwilling to make. The second is that letting the people vote on the solution is the *only* way that our government's fundamental commitments can regain the consent of the governed.

This approach has several other virtues in the early 21st century. The first is accountability. A president can implement most of it on his own by promising to veto any tax hike or benefit cut that is not approved by the voters. Because it is so clear-cut, a candidate could run on this issue and build support for it along the way.

Second, it would generate cleaner legislation rather than the horse-trading garbage that typically results from Congressional action. Why? Because the proposal would have to withstand months of scrutiny during any election campaign, and voters will not tolerate special deals for favored constituents.

Third, letting the people have the final say should make it easier to move proposals through Congress. It is likely that the president's proposed healthcare plan could have been cleared for submission to voters. After all, many in the GOP would have been happy to have it on the ballot in the fall of 2010. Presumably, members of Congress would figure out how to let people know they are against the plan but think the voters should have the final say.

Finally, letting voters have the last word will tremendously increase confidence in the process. In the current climate, even popular legislation is tainted by the fact that hardly anybody trusts Congress. When tougher issues are presented, the lack of trust almost guarantees legislative failure.

And, indeed, as we have discussed in previous chapters, the Tea Party movement has been developing its own "Contract From America," constructed under the three fundamental principles of economic freedom, individual liberty, and limited government with an agenda that includes:

- No More Bailouts
- Audit the Fed
- Reject Cap & Trade
- End Runaway Government Spending

- Pass Market-Based Health Care and Health Insurance Reform
- Stop the Tax Hikes

And some politicians, such as New Jersey Governor Chris Christie, have been taking tentative steps to take on spending and taxing issues; although, in reality, it is still a work in progress.

Think, for example, about a proposal for a temporary tax increase that might be proposed. If Congress passed that, voters would rightfully be skeptical about Congress ever ending the "temporary" nature of the revenue fix.

But if voters knew that they could read the fine print before voting and that they would have to approve any extension of the tax hike, support might be more forthcoming. Of course, voters would also have to be convinced that the spending problems would be addressed before even a temporary tax hike could be considered.

What kind of plan could win voter approval?

Any number of approaches might work, and the prospect of an election campaign would refine the best thinking of budget gurus. But the successful approach would help voters understand the choices before them. Bluntly, it would come down to a choice between significantly higher taxes to maintain the current level of commitments, or scaling back on spending commitments to keep taxes at a less offensive level.

But the specifics are a topic for another time.

For purposes of this book, we leave you with a final observation, analysis, and observation, rolled into one: quelling the voter anger will require substantive efforts to welcome voters back into the decision-making process. If the political class is unwilling to put the people back in charge, the public anger will not go away. On the other hand, by trusting, engaging, and empowering voters, Washington can solve the deficit of trust crippling our nation's ability to come to terms with problems of epic proportions. Whichever party does this first, and does it right—Republicans, Democrats, or Tea Partiers—will lead the charge to a new era of responsive and responsible government.

INTRODUCTION

1. Brian Beutler, "Pelosi: This Is Astroturf, Not Grassroots Protest," *Talkingpoints memo.com*, April 15, 2009. http://tpmdc.talkingpointsmemo.com/2009/04/pelosi -this-is-astroturf-not-grassroots-protest.php
2. Joseph Curl, "Study: Networks Snub, Malign Tea Party Movement," April 14, 2010. http://newsmax.com/InsideCover/tea-party-movement-ignored/2010/04/14/ id/355658?s=al&promo_code=9C03-1
3. "Big Government: Stop!" *The Economist*, January 21, 2010. www.economist.com/ opinion/displaystory.cfm?story_id=15330481
4. Andy Barr, "Poll: 28% support tea party," April 5, 2010. www.politico.com/news/ stories/0410/35395.html
5. James Taranto, "Strange New Respect," *Wall Street Journal*, April 5, 2010. http:// online.wsj.com/article/SB10001424052702304017404575165793481404002.html #printMode
6. Joseph Curl, "Study: Networks Snub, Malign Tea Party Movement," April 14, 2010. "http://newsmax.com/InsideCover/tea-party-movement-ignored/2010/04/14/ id/355658?s=al&promo_code=9C03-1
7. Sean J. Miller, "Survey: Four in 10 Tea Party members are Democrats or independents," *The Hill*, April 4, 2010. http://thehill.com/blogs/ballot-box/polls/90541 -survey-four-in-10-tea-party-members-dem-or-indie
8. Craig Crawford, "'Tea Party' Thoughts," CQ.com, April 8, 2010. http://blogs .cqpolitics.com/trailmix/2010/04/tea-party-thoughts.html
9. Shannon Travis, "Disgruntled Democrats Join the Tea Party," CNN.com, April 2, 2010. www.cnn.com/2010/POLITICS/04/02/democrats.tea.party/

CHAPTER 1

1. Michael Kazin, "The Outrage Factor," *Newsweek*, March 21, 2009, March 30, 2009.

CHAPTER 2

1. Steven Sark, "Right-Wing Populism," *The Atlantic Monthly*, February 1996. www .theatlantic.com/doc/199602/buchanan

2. Michael P. Federici, "The Challenge of Populism: The Rise of Right-Wing Democratism in Postwar America" (New York: Praeger, 1991), 28.

3. David Brooks, "The Tea Party Teens," *New York Times,* January 4, 2010, http://www.nytimes.com/2010/01/05/opinion/05brooks.html.

4. Paul Taggart, *Populism* (Philadelphia: Open University Press, 2000), 44.

5. Ibid., 44.

6. Thomas Jefferson, *The Writings of Thomas Jefferson*, vol. 15, ed. Andrew A. Lipscomb (Washington, DC: Thomas Jefferson Memorial Association, 1903), 20–21, 22.

7. Thomas Jefferson to James Madison, Paris, December 20, 1787.

8. Matthew Continetti, "The Palin Persuasion: A Case for the New Populism," *Weekly Standard*, November 16, 2009, Vol. 15, No. 9. http://weeklystandard.com/Content/Public/Articles/000/000/017/180xvziz.asp?pg=1

9. Michael Barone, "A short History of American Populism," *Wall Street Journal*, February 4, 2010. http://online.wsj.com/article/SB20001424052748703389004575033281965244048.html

10. David Oshinsky, "The Last Refuge of Everybody," *New York Times*, February 12, 1995. www.nytimes.com/1995/02/12/books/the-last-refuge-of-everybody.html

11. Jeffrey B. Gayner, "The Contract with America: Implementing New Ideas in the U.S.," October 12, 1995, Heritage Foundation. www.heritage.org/research/politicalphilosophy/hl549.cfm

12. Jeffrey B. Gayner, "The Contract with America: Implementing New Ideas in the U.S.," October 12, 1995, Heritage Foundation. www.heritage.org/research/politicalphilosophy/hl549.cfm

13. Kate Zernike, "Tea Party Avoids Divisive Social Issues," *New York Times*, March 12, 2010. www.nytimes.com/2010/03/13/us/politics/13tea.html

14. Ibid.

15. Ibid.

16. Patrik Jonsson, "In energetic 'tea party,' is there room for social conservatives?" *Christian Science Monitor*, March 13, 2010. http://www.csmonitor.com/USA/Politics/2010/0313/In-energetic-tea-party-is-there-room-for-social-conservatives

CHAPTER 3

1. Doug Schoen and Michael Berland, "How the Economic Crisis Changed Us," *Parade*, November 1, 2009. www.parade.com/news/ . . . /01-how-the-economic-crisis-changed-us.html

2. David Brooks, "The Tea Party Teens," *New York Times*, January 4, 2010. www.nytimes.com/2010/01/05/ . . . /05brooks.html

3. David Brooks "The Tea Party Teens," *New York Times*, January 4, 2010. www.nytimes.com/2010/01/05/ . . . /05brooks.html

4. Frank Rich, "Hollywood's Brilliant Coda to America's Dark Year," *New York Times*, December 12, 2009. http://www.nytimes.com/2009/12/13/opinion/13rich.html?pagewanted=all

5. Emmanuel Saez, "Striking it Richer: The Evolution of Top Incomes in the United States" *UC Berkeley* August 5, 2009

6. Thomas Kochran, "Waking Up to the Jobs Crisis," *Huffington Post*, March 4, 2010. www.huffingtonpost.com/thomas-kochan/wakng-up-to-the-jobs-cris_b_485249 .html

7. "Pulling Apart: A State-by-State Analysis of Income Trends," Center on Budget and Policy Priorities, April 9, 2008. www.cbpp.org/cms/?fa=view&id=255

8. "February Market Review," Seeking Alpha.com, March 10, 2010. http://seeking alpha.com/article/192899-february-market-review

9. Christopher Chantrill, "US Federal Deficit As Percent Of GDP," http://www .usgovernmentspending.com/federal_deficit_chart.html

10. Thomas Kochran, "Waking Up to the Jobs Crisis."

11. Ibid.

12. Barbara Hagenbaugh and Barbara Hansen, "Jobs: Map shows states hit hardest; forecasts for rebound," *USA Today*, February 10, 2009.

13. Alan Feuer, "A Study in Why Major Law Firms Are Shrinking," *New York Times*, June 5, 2009. www.nytimes.com/2009/06/07/nyregion/07law.html?pagewanted=all

14. Ibid.

15. Jane Porter, "The New Resume: Dumb and Dumber," *Wall Street Journal*, May 26, 2009. http://online.wsj.com/article/SB124328878436252195.html#mod=loomia ?loomia_si=t0:a16:g2:r1:c0.100303:b24795818

16. Thomas Kochran, "Waking Up to the Jobs Crisis."

17. Sara Murray, "The Curse of the Class of 2009," *Wall Street Journal*, May 9, 2009. http://online.wsj.com/article/SB124181970915002009.html

18. Ibid.

19. Jennifer Reingold, "The new jobless," CNN.com, February 3, 2009. http://money .cnn.com/2009/02/02/news/economy/jobless_complete.fortune/index.htm ?postversion=2009020412

20. Mimi Hall, "Obama visits job-starved Elkhardt, Indiana," *USA Today*, February 8, 2009. www.usatoday.com/money/economy/2009-02-08-elkhart_N.htm

21. Frank Newport, "Americans' Satisfaction at All-Time Low of 9%," *Gallup*, October 7, 2008. www.gallup.com/poll/110983/americans-satisfaction-alltime-low.aspx

22. Tom Smith and Kim Jibum, "Trust in People and Institutions: A 30-Year Trend from the GSS," Paper presented at the annual meeting of the American Association for Public Opinion Research, Sheraton Music City, Nashville, TN, August 16, 2003 (Not Available.) May 26, 2009. www.allacademic.com/meta/p116169_index.html

23. Adam Liptak, "Tea-ing Up the Constitution," *New York Times*, March 12, 2010. www.nytimes.com/2010/03/14/weekinreview/14liptak.html

24. Susan Page, "Analysis by Jim Norman of USA TODAY/Gallup Poll of 1,007 adults taken March 27–29," *USA TODAY*, April 14, 2009. www.usatoday.com/ news/washington/2009-04-14-biggovernment_N.htm#table

25. "Virtually No Change in Annual Harris Poll Confidence Index from Last Year," *Harris Interactive*, March 9, 2010. http://finance.yahoo.com/news/Virtually-No -Change-in-Annual-bw-169487445.html?x=0&.v=1&.pf=family-home&mod= pf-family-home

26. Lydia Saad, "Congressional Approval Hits Record-Low 14%," Gallup, July 16, 2008. www.gallup.com/poll/108856/congressional-approval-hits-recordlow-14.aspx

27. Gerald F. Seib, "Lawmakers Seek Middle Ground at Their Own Risk," *Wall Street*

Journal, March 12, 2010. http://online.wsj.com/article/SB1000142405274870434930
4575115583850338638.html

28. Ibid.
29. Ibid.
30. Eugene Robinson, "A Middle Ground Gone Missing," *Washington Post*, September 8, 2009. www.washingtonpost.com/wp-dyn/content/article/2009/09/07/AR200
9090702068.html
31. Gerald F. Seib,"Lawmakers Seek Middle Ground at their Own Risk." *The Wall Street Journal* March 12, 2010. http://online.wsj.com/article/SB200014240527487043
49304575115583850338638.html?mod=djemITP_h
32. Gerald F. Seib,"Lawmakers Seek Middle Ground at their Own Risk."
33. Ibid.
34. Ibid.

CHAPTER 4

1. Frank Rich, "Hollywood's Brilliant Coda to America's Dark Year," *New York Times*, December 12, 2009. www.nytimes.com/2009/12/13/opinion/13rich.html
2. Ibid.
3. David Brooks, "The Tea Party Teens," *New York Times*, January 4, 2010. www
.nytimes.com/2010/01/05/opinion/05brooks.html
4. Michael Lind, "To Have and to Have Not," *Harper's Magazine*, June 1995. www
.hartford-hwp.com/archives/45/006.html
5. David Brooks, *BOBOS in Paradise* (New York: Simon & Schuster, 2002), 14.
6. John Rosenberg, "Liberal Misunderstanding," *Discriminations*, October 6, 2005.
www.discriminations.us/2005/10/liberal_misunderstanding.html
7. Jo Becker and Gretchen Morgenson, "Geithner, Member and Overseer of Finance Club," *New York Times*, April 26, 2009. www.nytimes.com/2009/04/27/business/
27geithner.html?_r=1
8. Matt Apuzzo and Daniel Wagner, "Wall Street Speed Dial Gets Tim Geithner Directly," Associated Press, October 8, 2009. www.newsday.com/news/new-york/
wall-street-speed-dial-gets-tim-geithner-directly-1.1509253?qr=1
9. Glenn Greenwald, "Larry Summers, Tim Geithner and Wall Street's ownership of government," Salon.com, April 4, 2009. www.salon.com/opinion/greenwald/
2009/04/04/summers/index.html
10. "Henry M Paulson Jr." *Forbes* http://www.forbes.com/lists/2006/12/VY36.html
11. "Kenneth M. Duberstein, LL.D. '65. Alumni Citation Award Recipient—2009,"
Franklin & Marshall College. www.fandm.edu/x23066
12. Ross Douthat, "The Ghosts of 1994," *New York Times*, September 13, 2009. www
.nytimes.com/2009/09/14/opinion/14douthat.html?hp
13. Glenn Greenwald, "Who are the undeserving 'others' benefiting from expanded government actions?" Salon.com, September 14, 2009. www.salon.com/news/
opinion/glenn_greenwald/2009/09/14/resentment/index.html
14. Simon Johnson, "The Quiet Coup," *The Atlantic Monthly*, May 2009. www.the
atlantic.com/magazine/archive/2009/05/the-quiet-coup/7364/2/
15. "Glenn Greenwald on Bill Moyers Journal," PBS, February 6, 2009. www.pbs.org/
moyers/journal/02062009/transcript1.html

16. Ruy A. Teixeira and Joel Rogers, "America's Forgotten Majority," *The Atlantic Online*, June 2000. www.theatlantic.com/past/docs/issues/2000/06/rogers.htm

17. Paul Begala, "Sarah Palin Turns Pro," *Huffington Post*, July 3, 2009. www.huffing tonpost.com/paul-begala/sarah-palin-turns-pro_b_225633.html

18. Simon Johnson, "The Quiet Coup."

19. Simon Johnson, "The Quiet Coup."

CHAPTER 5

1. Full Transcript: President Barack Obama's Inaugural Address, *ABC News*, January 20, 2009. http://abcnews.go.com/Politics/Inauguration/president-obama -inauguration-speech-transcript/story?id=6689022

2. James F. Smith, "Ron Paul's Tea Party for Dollars," *Boston Globe*, December 16, 2007. www.boston.com/news/politics/politicalintelligence/2007/12/ron_pauls_tea _p.html

3. Brian Riedl, "The Obama Budget: Spending, Taxes, and Doubling the National Debt," Heritage Foundation, March 16, 2009. www.heritage.org/Research/bud get/bg2249.cfm

4. David Boaz, "We Miss You, Bubba," *Washington Times*, January 11, 2010.

5. Adam Liptak, "Tea-ing Up the Constitution," *New York Times*, March 12, 2010. www.nytimes.com/2010/03/14/weekinreview/14liptak.html

6. Richard Viguerie, "Why 'Leaderless' Tea Parties Are Beating the GOP," *American Thinker*, December 9, 2009. www.americanthinker.com/2009/12/why_leaderless _tea_parties_are.html

7. Kate Zernike, "Unlikely Activist Who Got to the Tea Party Early," *New York Times*, February 28, 2010. www.nytimes.com/2010/02/28/us/politics/28keli.html

8. John V. Last, "A Growing 'Tea Party' Movement?" *Weekly Standard*, March 4, 2009. www.cbsnews.com/stories/2009/03/04/opinion/main4843055.shtml

9. Ibid.

10. Ibid.

11. Ibid.

12. Alex Isenstadt, "Town Halls Gone Wild," Politico.com, July 31, 2009. www.polit ico.com/news/stories/0709/25646.html

13. Chris Good, "Lawmakers Will Face Tea Parties, And More, In August," *The Atlantic*, September 2007. www.theatlantic.com/politics/archive/2009/07/lawmakers -will-face-tea-parties-and-more-in-august/22470/

14. Lee Fang, "Right-Wing Harassment Strategy Against Dems Detailed In Memo: 'Yell,' 'Stand Up And Shout Out,' 'Rattle Him,'" *Think Progress*, July 31, 2009. http://thinkprogress.org/2009/07/31/recess-harassment-memo/

15. Jeremy W. Peters, "Conservative Loses Upstate House Race in Blow to Right," *New York Times*, November 3, 2009. www.nytimes.com/2009/11/04/nyregion/ 04district.html

16. Gabriel Sherman, "New Jersey Nasty," *New York Magazine*, October 11, 2009. http://nymag.com/news/politics/59895/

17. Brian Beutler, "Pelosi: This Is Astroturf, Not Grassroots Protest," Talkingpoints memo.com, April 15, 2009. http://tpmdc.talkingpointsmemo.com/2009/04/pelosi -this-is-astroturf-not-grassroots-protest.php

18. Janie Lorber and Liz Robbins, "Tax Day Is Met With Tea Parties," *New York Times*, April 15, 2009. www.nytimes.com/2009/04/16/us/politics/16taxday.html ?_r=1&ref=your-money

19. Paul Krugman, "Tea Parties Forever," *New York Times*, April 12, 2009. www.ny times.com/2009/04/13/opinion/13krugman.html

20. Transcript: "On the Record," FoxNews, April 15, 2009. www.foxnews.com/ story/0,2933,516618,00.html

21. George J. Marlin, "Understanding the Tea Party," McLaughlin & Associates http:// www.mclaughlinonline.com/6?article=27

22. Gary Fields, "Tea-Party Drive Steeped in Political Novices," Wall Street Journal, February 20, 2010. http://online.wsj.com/article/SB1000142405274870451130457507 5331410704288.html?mod=WSJ_WSJ_US_News_5

23. Ibid.

24. David Barstow, "Tea Party Lights Fuse for Rebellion on Right," New York Times, February 15, 2010. www.nytimes.com/2010/02/16/us/politics/16teaparty.html

25. Julia A. Seymour, "NBC's Chuck Todd Dismisses Tea Party Protests," Business & Media Institute, April 15, 2009. http://businessandmedia.org/articles/2009/2009 0415085228.aspx

26. The Early Adopters: Reading the Tea Leaves, Sam Adams Alliance, March 1, 2010. www.samadamsalliance.org/media/7936/early_adopters_report_v2.pdf

27. David Brooks, "The Wizard of Beck," New York Times, October 2, 2009. www .nytimes.com/2009/10/02/opinion/02brooks.html

CHAPTER 6

1. Michael Sokolove, "Dick Armey Is Back on the Attack," New York Times, November 4, 2009. www.nytimes.com/2009/11/08/magazine/08Armey-t.html?page wanted=all

2. Our Country Deserves Better, PAC Online "Issues." www.ourcountrydeserves better.com/about-us/issues/

3. Ed Hornick, "'Tea Party Express' trucks on with tour aimed at health care," CNN.com, August 28, 2009. www.cnn.com/2009/POLITICS/08/28/tea.party .express/index.html

4. Our Country Deserves Better.

5. Kate Zernike "Unlikely Activist Who Got to the Tea Party Early" New York Times February 27, 2010. http://www.nytimes.com/2010/02/28/us/politics/28keli .html

6. Jim Spellman, "Tea Party Movement Has Anger, No Dominant Leaders" CNN .com September 12, 2009. http://www.cnn.com/2009/POLITICS/09/12/tea.party .express/index.html

7. "Don't We Deserve Better than More Attack Ads?" Center for Media and Democracy, September 26, 2008. http://www.prwatch.org/node/7805

8. Charles Hurt, "Sarah's Tea Talk Sounds Presidential," New York Post, February 8, 2010. www.nypost.com/p/news/national/sarah_tea_talk_sounds_presidential _w3U7DqYM18s7uhq6ydzDiL

9. Sarah Palin, "Statement on the Current Health Care Debate," Facebook, Friday, August 7, 2009. www.facebook.com/note.php?note_id=113851103434

10. Dave Itzkoff, " 'Going Rogue' Goes to Top of Book Sales Chart," *New York Times*, November 25, 2009. http://artsbeat.blogs.nytimes.com/2009/11/25/going-rogue -goes-to-top-of-book-sales-chart/

11. Kevin Diaz, "Bachmann Cancels Tea Party Appearance" *Star Tribune*, January 28, 2010. http://www.startribune.com/blogs/82941292.html

12. "Who are the Tea Party activists?" CNN Polling Center, February 18, 2010. www .cnn.com/2010/POLITICS/02/17/tea.party.poll/index.html

13. "FOX News Exit Poll Summary," FOXnews.com, November 6, 2008. www .foxnews.com/story/0,2933,447844,00.html

14. Ibid.

15. Ibid.

16. Gary Langer et al., "Much-Diminished GOP Absorbs the Voters' Ire," *Washington Post*, November 8, 2006. http://abcnews.go.com/Politics/Vote2006/story?id=2637 650&page=1

17. Kenneth P. Vogel, "Weak Tea? Partiers Fear Fallout," *Politico*, March 22, 2010. www.politico.com/news/stories/0310/34790.html#ixzz0j82kvMHg

18. Jake Sherman, "Dick Armey: GOP must court grass roots," *Politico*, February 1, 2010. www.politico.com/news/stories/0110/32253.html

CHAPTER 7

1. "Party Affiliation: 2004–2009," Gallup. www.gallup.com/poll/15370/Party-Affili ation.aspx

2. Frank Rich, "The Axis of the Obsessed and Deranged" *New York Times*, February 27, 2010. http://www.nytimes.com/2010/02/28/opinion/28rich.html

3. Kate Zerninke, "Republicans Strain to Ride Tea Parrt Tiger," *New York Times*, January 23, 2010. www.nytimes.com/2010/01/23/us/politics/23teaparty.html?page wanted=print

4. Valerie Richardson, "Moderate Republicans Crash Tea Party," *Washington Times*, February 11, 2010. http://washingtontimes.com/news/2010/feb/11/moderate -republicans-crashing-the-tea-party/?page=2

5. Hillary Chabot, "Would-be Governors Seek Tea Party Invite," *Boston Herald*, February 11, 2010. http://news.bostonherald.com/news/politics/view/20100211would -be_governors_seek_tea_party_invite_scott_brown_win_puts_spotlight_on _disenchanted_voters/srvc=home&position=also

6. David Weigl, "A GOP-Tea Party Merger," *Washington Independent*, February 9, 2010. http://washingtonindependent.com/76142/a-gop-tea-party-merger

7. Larrey Anderson, "American Thinker: Populist Constitutionalism and the Tea Party" *American Thinker*, February 7, 2010. www.americanthinker.com/2010/02/ populist_constitutionalism_and.htm

8. Phillip Rucker, "Tea party leaders will meet with Steele and other Republican operatives," Washington Post, February 6, 2010. www.washingtonpost.com/wp -dyn/content/article/2010/02/15/AR2010021502211.html

9. David A. Patten, "Tea Party Patriots Say GOP's Steele 'Hijacking' Movement," *Newsmax*, February 16, 2010. www.newsmax.com/InsideCover/gop-tea-party -patriots/2010/02/16/id/350040

10. Jon Cohen and Philip Rucker, "Poll Finds Most Americans are Unhappy with

Government" *Washington Post*, February 11, 2010. http://www.washingtonpost.com/wp-dyn/content/article/2010/02/10/AR2010021004708.html

11. Anthony G. Martin, "Report: Tea Party candidates at risk from 'moderate' Republicans," Washington Examiner, February 11, 2010. www.examiner.com/x-376 20-Conservative-Examiner~y2010m2d11-Report-Tea-Party-candidates-at-risk -from-moderate-Republicans

12. Michael Muskal, "Scott Brown: Move over, Huck and Newt," Swamp, February 11, 2010. www.swamppolitics.com/news/politics/blog/2010/02/scott_brown_move _over_huck_and.html

13. "Marco 101," Marco Rubio For Senate, www.marcorubio.com/marco-101/

14. Peter Hamby, "Kasich: 'I was in the Tea Party before there was a Tea Party,'" CNN, January 14, 2010. http://politicalticker.blogs.cnn.com/2010/01/14/kasich-i -was-in-the-tea-party-before-there-was-a-tea-party/?fbid=-sLbmj5oHvz

15. Ibid.

16. "A Roadmap for America's Future," House Budget Committee. www.roadmap .republicans.budget.house.gov/

17. Ross Douthat, "Paul Ryan's Moment," *New York Times*, February 3, 2010. http://douthat.blogs.nytimes.com/2010/02/03/paul-ryans-moment/

18. Douglas W. Elmendorf, Congressional Budget Office. January 27, 2010. www.cbo .gov/ftpdocs/108xx/doc10851/01-27-Ryan-Roadmap-Letter.pdf

19. Paul D. Ryan, "A GOP Road Map for America's Future," *Wall Street Journal*, January 26, 2010. http://online.wsj.com/article/SB10001424052748703808904575025080 017959478.html

20. Paul Ryan, "Down With Big Business" Forbes.com December 11, 2009. http://www.forbes.com/2009/12/11/business-government-politics-reform-opinions -contributors-paul-ryan.html

21. http://blogs.abcnews.com/thenote/2010/02/palin-favorite-paul-ryan-rules-out -2012-run-for-president.html

22. Bill Steiden, "Is a New Revolution Brewing?" *Atlanta Journal-Constitution*, 14A, January 31, 2010.

23. Jackie Calmes, "Lawmakers Join Protest Over Bill," *New York Times*, November 7, 2009. http://prescriptions.blogs.nytimes.com/2009/11/07/lawmakers-join-protest -over-bill/

24. Kenneth P. Vogel, "Conservatives Target Their Own Fringe," *Politico*, February 27, 2010. http://dyn.politico.com/printstory.cfm?uuid=0D1D0BCC-18FE-70B2-A8 AAAE2A129A1676

25. Richard Viguerie, "Why Leaderless Tea Parties Are Beating the GOP," *American Thinker*, December 10, 2009. www.americanthinker.com/2009/12/why_leaderless _tea_parties_are.html

CHAPTER 8

1. "The Cigna 7 Speak" Chicago Single Payer Action Network http://chispan.org/ cigna.html

2. Michael P. Federici, *The Challenge of Populism* (New York: Praeger, 1991), 32.

3. Michael Kazin, "The Outrage Factor," *Newsweek*, March 21, 2009. www.news week.com/id/190341

4. Alan Brinkley, "Railing Against the Rich: A Great American Tradition," *Wall Street Journal*, February 7 2009.

5. Damian Paletta, "Consumer Protection Agency in Doubt," *Wall Street Journal*, January 15, 2010. http://online.wsj.com/article/SB10001424052748704363504575003 360632239020.html

6. Jennifer Liberto, "Sweeping bank reform bill clears House," CNN.com. December 11, 2009. http://money.cnn.com/2009/12/11/news/economy/financial_regula tory_reform/

7. Jonathan Cohn "Is Harry Reid Being Helpful?" *The New Republic*, July 8, 2009. http://www.tnr.com/blog/the-treatment/harry-reid-being-helpful

8. Bill Kristol "Will Obama Save Liberalism?" *New York Times*, January 26, 2009. www.nytimes.com/2009/01/26/ . . . /26kristol.html

CHAPTER 9

1. John V. Last, "A Growing 'Tea Party' Movement?" *Weekly Standard*, March 4, 2009. www.cbsnews.com/stories/2009/03/04/opinion/main4843055.shtml

2. Ibid.

3. Michael Calderone, "How to Fix CNN," *Politico*, March 31, 2010. www.politico .com/news/stories/0310/35257.html

4. "2010 Edelman Trust Barometer: Executive Summary," Edelman, 2010. www .edelman.com/trust/2010/docs/2010_Trust_Barometer_Executive_Summary.pdf

5. John Zogby "Why Do People Trust The Internet More?" Forbes.com July 18, 2009. www.forbes.com/ . . . /17/media-newspapers-radio-television-opinions-colum nists-john-zogby-internet.html

6. "Zogby Poll: Voters Believe Media Bias Is Very Real," March 14, 2007. www.zogby .com/templates/printnews.cfm?id=1262

7. Dean Baker, "It's the Housing Bubble, Not the ***** Credit Crunch!" The American Prospect, November 8, 2008. www.prospect.org/csnc/blogs/beat_the_press _archive?month=11&year=2008&base_name=its_the_housing_bubble_not_the

8. Julia A. Seymour, "Media Endorse $700 Billion Economic 'Rescue'" Business & Media Institute, October 8, 2008.

9. Liz Robbins, "Tax Day Is Met With Tea Parties," *New York Times*, April 15, 2009. www.nytimes.com/2009/04/16/us/politics/16taxday.html

10. Paul Krugman, "Tea Parties Forever," *New York Times*, April 12, 2009. www .nytimes.com/2009/04/13/opinion/13krugman.html

11. James Taranto, "Taking On the 'Democrat-Media Complex.'" *Wall Street Journal*, October 16, 2009. http://online.wsj.com/article/SB10001424052748704471504574451703003340362.html

12. Lachlan Markay, "Breitbart Unveils 'Big Journalism' to Combat 'Democrat-Media Complex,'" NewsBusters.org, December 10, 2009. http://newsbusters.org/blogs/ lachlan-markay/2009/12/10/breitbart-unveils-big-journalism-combat-democrat -media-complex

13. Colby Hall, "Exclusive Interview: Andrew Breitbart Announces Launch of New 'Big' Sites." Mediaite.com, December 10, 2009. www.mediaite.com/online/ andrew-breitbart-launching-new-sites/3/

14. Frances Martel, "Red State's Erick Erickson Relocating To John King,

USA," Mediaite.com, March 16, 2010. www.mediaite.com/online/red-states-erick
-erickson-relocating-to-john-king-usa/

15. Ibid.

16. Adam Smith, "The man behind RedState.com shakes up the Republican Party,"
St. Petersburg Times, January 4, 2010. www.tampabay.com/news/politics/state
roundup/the-man-behind-redstatecom-shakes-up-the-republican-party/1062928

17. Ibid.

18. Rem Rieder "Talking to Themselves" American Journalism Review, August/
September 2008. www.ajr.org/article.asp?id=4598

19. Steve Krakauer, "Still Surging: Fox News Has Best Quarter In Network History,"
Mediaite.com, March 30, 2010. www.mediaite.com/tv/still-surging-fox-news-has
-best-quarter-in-network-history/

CHAPTER 10

1. "The Economic Crisis and Populist Revolt at a Boiling Point," Democracy Corps,
January 26, 2010. www.democracycorps.com/strategy/2010/01/the-economic-crisis
-and-populist-revolt-at-a-boiling-point/?section=Analysis_

2. John Avlon, "Obama's Independent Edge," New York Post, April 29, 2008. www
.realclearpolitics.com/articles/2008/04/obamas_independent_edge.html

3. Jonathan McClory, "Obama's heavyweight cabinet," Guardian, December 9, 2008.
www.guardian.co.uk/commentisfree/2008/dec/09/obama-clinton-cabinet
-appointment

4. Fred Barnes "Why Obama Isn't Changing Washington" The Wall Street Journal,
November 26, 2009. http://online.wsj.com/article/SB10001424052748704779704574
555471947300090.html

5. "Big Government. Stop!" The Economist, January 21, 2010. www.economist.com/
opinion/displaystory.cfm?story_id=15330481

CONCLUSION

1. "Tea Partiers to Congressional Democrats: You'll Pay in November," FOXNews
.com, March 22, 2010. www.foxnews.com/politics/2010/03/22/tea-partiers-congres
sional-democrats-payback-time/

2. Frank Rich, "The Axis of the Obsessed and Deranged," New York Times, February 27, 2010. www.nytimes.com/2010/02/28/opinion/28rich.html

3. Alex Isenstadt, "Tea party candidates falling short" Politico.com, March 7, 2010.
www.politico.com/news/stories/0310/34041.html

4. Dan Balz and Jon Cohen, "Voters' support for members of Congress is at an all-
time low, poll finds" Washington Post, June 8, 2010 http://www.washingtonpost
.com/wp-dyn/content/article/2010/06/08/AR2010060800016.html

5. Jeffrey M. Jones, "U.S. Voters Favor Congressional Newcomers Over Incumbents"
Gallup, June 8, 2010 http://www.gallup.com/poll/139409/voters-favor-congres
sional-newcomers-incumbents.aspx

6. Jonathan Martin, "Gauging the Senate scenario in 2011" Politico, June 23, 2010

7. Peter Wallstein, Naftali Bendavid and Jean Spencer, "Voters Shifting to GOP, Poll

Finds" *Wall Street Journal*, May 13, 2010 http://online.wsj.com/article/SB100014240
52748704247904575240812672173820.html

8. Dan Balz and Jon Cohen, "Voters' support for members of Congress is at an all-
time low, poll finds" *Washington Post*, June 8, 2010 http://www.washingtonpost
.com/wp-dyn/content/article/2010/06/08/AR2010060800016.html

9. "Chatting With Kirsten Gillibrand's Primary Opponent, Who Exists," The Daily
Intel, *New York Magazine*, March 3, 2010. http://nymag.com/daily/intel/2010/03/
unbeknownst_to_most_people_kir.html#ixzz0ho0sDW46

PRESIDENT'S CLUB DINNER

THURSDAY, DECEMBER 9, 2010

Washington Marriott Wardman Park
WASHINGTON, DC

Menu

Baby Wedge Iceberg with Tomato Wedge,
Maytag Blue Cheese, with a
Watercress Champagne Vinaigrette

Tenderloin of Beef
Served with Mushroom Jus,
Sweet and Yukon Smashed Potatoes,
Sauteed Mushrooms with Caramelized Shallots, and Pearl Onions

Chocolate Caramel Truffle Dome,
Lemon Brittle Sauce,
Garnished with Sea Salt

Clos du Bois, Cabernet Sauvignon, Sonoma County

Clos du Bois, Chardonnay, Sonoma County

Program

Master of Ceremonies
Edwin J. Feulner, Ph.D.
President, The Heritage Foundation

National Anthem
Andrew Indorf
Georgetown University

Pledge of Allegiance
Carolyn Ritchie
The Woodlands, Texas
President's Club Member

Invocation
Pat Gavaghan
Raleigh, North Carolina
Associate and Member, North Carolina Committee for Heritage

Presentation of Clare Boothe Luce Award
to The Honorable James L. Buckley
Former United States Senator, Former Under Secretary of State,
Former Federal Appellate Judge, and Author, Freedom at Risk

Dinner

Introduction of Speaker
Kay Coles James
Midlothian, Virginia
Trustee, The Heritage Foundation

Keynote Address
The Honorable Newt Gingrich
Former Speaker of the United States House of Representatives

Closing Remarks
Edwin J. Feulner, Ph.D.

The Heritage Foundation
LEADERSHIP FOR AMERICA

214 Massachusetts Avenue, NE | Washington, DC 20002 | (202) 546-4400 | heritage.org